AAT

Management Accounting: Costing

Level 3

Advanced Diploma in Accounting

Course Book

For assessments from September 2017

Second edition 2017

ISBN 9781 5097 1204 5
ISBN (for internal use only) 9781 5097 1223 6

British Library Cataloguing-in-Publication Data
A catalogue record for this book is available from the British Library

Published by

BPP Learning Media Ltd
BPP House, Aldine Place
142-144 Uxbridge Road
London W12 8AA

www.bpp.com/learningmedia

Printed in the United Kingdom

Your learning materials, published by BPP Learning Media Ltd, are printed on paper obtained from traceable sustainable sources.

Contents

Introduction to the course

Syllabus overview

This unit teaches students the knowledge and skills needed to understand the role of cost and management accounting. Students will be able to gather, analyse and report cost and revenue information to support managerial planning, control and decision making. They will also develop a further understanding of the fundamental principles that underpin management accounting methodology and techniques, how costs are handled in organisations, and why different organisations treat costs in different ways.

Students will learn techniques for dealing with direct costs and revenues, the treatment of short-term overhead costs, as well as techniques required for decision making using both short-term and long-term estimates of costs and revenues.

Test specification for this unit assessment

Assessment method	Marking type	Duration of assessment
Computer based assessment	Computer marked	2.5 hours

Learning outcomes		Weighting
1	Understand the purpose and use of management accounting within an organisation	15%
2	Apply techniques required for dealing with costs	35%
3	Apportion costs according to organisational requirements	19%
4	Analyse and review deviations from budget and report these to management	10%
5	Apply management accounting techniques to support decision making	21%
Total		**100%**

Assessment structure

2½ hours duration

Competency is 70%

*Note that this is only a guideline as to what might come up. The format and content of each task may vary from what we have listed below.

Your assessment will consist of 10 tasks

Task	Expected content	Max marks	Chapter ref	Study complete
Task 1	**Inventory valuation** Calculation of inventory issues from stores and closing balance valuations using FIFO, LIFO or AVCO.	16	Materials costs and inventory valuation	
Task 2	**Cost journal entries** For example, calculation of labour costs including percentage bonuses and associated payroll journal entries.	16	Cost bookkeeping	
Task 3	**Labour costs** Calculation of basic pay, overtime and bonus based on number of units produced. Calculation of labour cost per unit and labour cost per employee and bonus cost per employee.	12	Labour costs	
Task 4	**Overheads** Identifying suitable bases of apportionment, reapportioning costs. Calculation of fixed and variable elements of cost using ratios.	18	Allocation and apportionment	
Task 5	**Absorption costing** OAR calculations, calculations of overheads absorbed, under/over absorption calculation.	15	Absorption costing	

Task	Expected content	Max marks	Chapter ref	Study complete
Task 6	**Absorption costing, marginal costing, reporting costs** Calculations including prime cost, marginal cost per batch, absorption cost per batch, marginal cost per unit, absorption cost per unit. Multiple choice questions on period costs, ethical behaviour, segmental reporting, responsibility centres.	25	Introduction to management accounting, Absorption costing, Marginal costing	
Task 7	**Breakeven analysis** Choosing correct descriptions of breakeven terms. Calculations such as: Breakeven volume Breakeven sales revenue Margin of safety Target profit sales volume	16	Short-term decision making	
Task 8	**Cost behaviour** This task requires students to choose the correct description for: Fixed cost Variable cost Semi-variable cost Stepped cost	16	Cost classification and cost behaviour	
Task 9	**Variance analysis** Flexing a budget and calculating the resulting variance, identifying variance which had the greatest impact on profit, identifying possible reason for variances	16	Budgeting: fixed and flexed budgets Variance analysis	
Task 10	**Investment appraisal** Identifying correct recommendation based on results of payback, IRR and NPV calculations versus company policy.	20	Long-term decision making	

Skills bank

Our experience of preparing students for this type of assessment suggests that to obtain competency, you will need to develop a number of key skills.

What do I need to know to do well in the assessment?

This unit is one of the mandatory Level 3 units. It takes you from Level 2 costing principles and prepares you for the Level 4 units *Management Accounting: Budgeting* and *Management Accounting: Decision and Control*.

To be successful in the assessment you need to:

- Understand cost and management accounting principles.

- Apply relevant techniques. This will often be tested in numerical questions, but you will also have to demonstrate your understanding of key data (such as reasons for variances) via a narrative multiple choice questions.

Assumed knowledge

Management Accounting: Costing is a **mandatory** unit and builds on the fundamental concepts and techniques introduced in Level 2 *Elements of Costing*. The following topics were introduced there and are also relevant to this assessment:

- Cost behaviour
- Absorption costing and marginal costing
- Coding
- Variance calculation
- Inventory and labour costs

Assessment style

In the assessment you will complete tasks by:

1   Entering narrative by selecting from drop down menus of narrative options known as **picklists**

2   Using **drag and drop** menus to enter narrative

3   Typing in numbers, known as **gapfill** entry

4   Entering **ticks**

5   Entering **dates** by selecting from a calendar

You must familiarise yourself with the style of the online questions and the AAT software before taking the assessment. As part of your revision, login to the **AAT website** and attempt their **online practice assessments**.

Introduction to the assessment

The question practice you do will prepare you for the format of tasks you will see in the *Management Accounting: Costing* assessment. It is also useful to familiarise yourself with the introductory information you **may** be given at the start of the assessment. For example:

You have **2 hours and 30 minutes** to compete this sample assessment.

This assessment contains **10 tasks** and you should attempt to complete every task. Each task is independent. You will not need to refer to your answers to previous tasks. Read every task carefully to make sure you understand what is required.

Where the date is relevant, it is given in the task data.
Both minus signs and brackets can be used to indicate negative numbers **unless** task instructions say otherwise.

You must use a full stop to indicate a decimal point. For example, write 1005.57 not 100,57 or 100 57
You may use a comma to indicate a number in the thousands, but you don't have to. For example 10000 and 10,000 are both acceptable.

---

1   As you revise, use the **BPP Passcards** to consolidate your knowledge. They are a pocket-sized revision tool, perfect for packing in that last-minute revision.

2   Attempt as many tasks as possible in the **Question Bank**. There are plenty of assessment-style tasks which are excellent preparation for the real assessment.

3   Always **check** through your own answers as you will in the real assessment, before looking at the solutions in the back of the Question Bank.

Key to icons

 Key term

A key definition which is important to be aware of for the assessment

Key term
 Formula to learn

A formula you will need to learn as it will not be provided in the assessment

 Formula provided

A formula which is provided within the assessment and generally available as a pop-up on screen

 Activity

An example which allows you to apply your knowledge to the technique covered in the Course Book. The solution is provided at the end of the chapter

 Illustration

A worked example which can be used to review and see how an assessment question could be answered

 Assessment focus point

A high priority point for the assessment

 Open book reference

Where use of an open book will be allowed for the assessment

Real life examples

A practical real life scenario

AAT qualifications

The material in this book may support the following AAT qualifications:

AAT Advanced Diploma in Accounting Level 3, AAT Advanced Diploma in Accounting at SCQF Level 6 and Further Education and Training Certificate: Accounting Technician (Level 4 AATSA)

Supplements

From time to time we may need to publish supplementary materials to one of our titles. This can be for a variety of reasons, from a small change in the AAT unit guidance to new legislation coming into effect between editions.

You should check our supplements page regularly for anything that may affect your learning materials. All supplements are available free of charge on our supplements page on our website at:

www.bpp.com/learning-media/about/students

Improving material and removing errors

There is a constant need to update and enhance our study materials in line with both regulatory changes and new insights into the assessments.

From our team of authors BPP appoints a subject expert to update and improve these materials for each new edition.

Their updated draft is subsequently technically checked by another author and from time to time, non-technically checked by a proof reader.

We are very keen to remove as many numerical errors and narrative typos as we can but given the volume of detailed information being changed in a short space of time we know that a few errors will sometimes get through our net.

We apologise in advance for any inconvenience that an error might cause. We continue to look for new ways to improve these study materials and would welcome your suggestions. Please feel free to contact our AAT Head of Programme at nisarahmed@bpp.com if you have any suggestions for us.

Introduction to management accounting

Learning outcomes

1	Understand the purpose and use of management accounting within an organisation

1.1	**Demonstrate an understanding of internal reporting**
	
	• The purpose of internal reporting and providing accurate information to management
	• How to calculate:
	  – Costs, contribution and reported profits for an organisation
	  – Segmented costs, contribution and reported profits by product

1.2	**Demonstrate an understanding of ethical principles in management accounting** • The need for integrity in preparing management accounts • That third parties (such as banks) may also be users of management accounts

1.3	**Critically compare different types of responsibility centres**
	
	• The differences in cost and revenue reporting between responsibility centres which are:
	  – Cost centres
	  – Profit centres
	  – Investment centres
	  – Revenue centres

5.1	**Estimate and use short-term future income and costs** • The importance of professional competence in estimating income and costs

Assessment context

The contents of this chapter mainly serve as an introduction to AAT's *Management Accounting: Costing* paper. However, it is examinable and you can expect questions on this chapter.

Qualification context

This chapter includes terminology that will be used throughout this paper and in Level 4 *Management Accounting* papers.

Business context

Every business needs to understand and control its costs. This can be done by producing good internal information and by assigning responsibility for costs to individuals using responsibility accounting.

Chapter overview

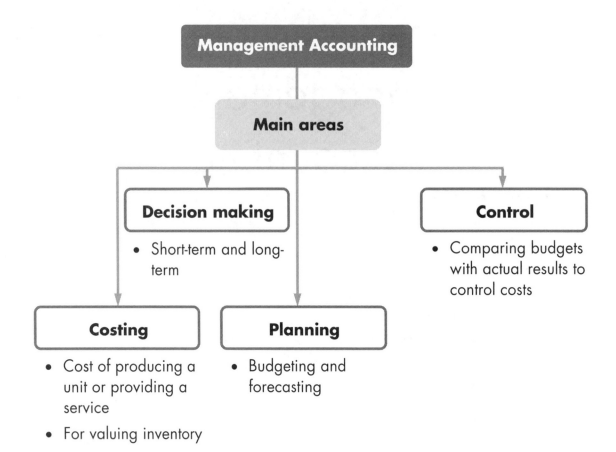

- **Management Accounting**
  - **Main areas**
    - **Decision making**
      - Short-term and long-term
    - **Control**
      - Comparing budgets with actual results to control costs
    - **Costing**
      - Cost of producing a unit or providing a service
      - For valuing inventory
    - **Planning**
      - Budgeting and forecasting

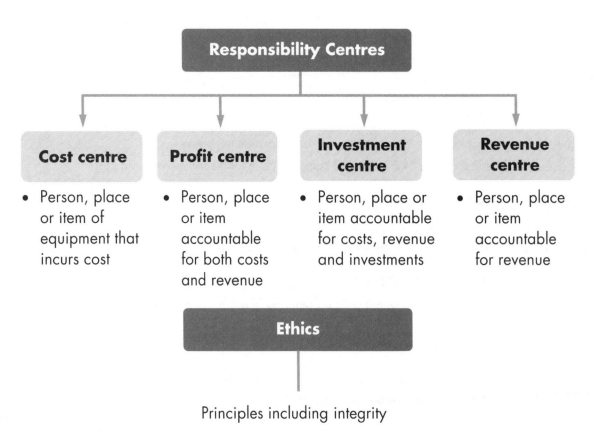

- **Responsibility Centres**
  - **Cost centre**
    - Person, place or item of equipment that incurs cost
  - **Profit centre**
    - Person, place or item accountable for both costs and revenue
  - **Investment centre**
    - Person, place or item accountable for costs, revenue and investments
  - **Revenue centre**
    - Person, place or item accountable for revenue

- **Ethics**

Principles including integrity

Introduction

In this opening chapter we will consider the overall purposes of cost or **management accounting** together with an introduction to the key concepts and terms that will be used throughout this book.

1 Internal reporting information

The accounting function of a business deals with providing information for both management accounting purposes and **financial accounting** purposes. However, the type of information required, the timing of the information and the format of the information will be different for each.

Financial accounting is mainly concerned with the collection and classification of historic data in order to prepare the financial statements of the business. These financial statements are prepared for users outside of the business such as shareholders and prospective investors.

Management accounting, by contrast, is all about providing the management of an organisation with the information that it needs to carry out its functions properly. Although management accounts are mainly used by internal management, sometimes third parties such as banks may wish to view management accounts.

1.1 Management accounting

The purpose of **management accounting** is to assist management in running the business to achieve an overall objective. (For a profit-seeking business, this is to maximise shareholder wealth by maximising profits.) Management accounting can be broken down into three main areas:

- Planning
- Control
- Decision making

Therefore the purpose of management accounting information is to be relevant to these functions.

This will require the provision of both historic information and estimates of future figures in a format that is useful to the relevant members of the management team. Most importantly, the information must be provided regularly and on a timely basis, particularly for the purposes of control, and can be one-off reports or information for decision-making purposes.

1.1.1 Planning

Planning involves defining objectives and assessing future costs and revenues to set up a budget.

Planning is essential to help assess the purchasing/production requirements of the business.

1.1.2 Control

Once plans have been made, the company must ensure they are being followed and assess any inefficiencies in the business.

1.1.3 Decision making

There are many decisions managers may have to make such as:

- What should we produce?
- How should we finance the business?
- Is a project worthwhile?

Activity 1: Information for management

Management accountants may provide information for management on which of the following?

	✓
Cost of goods and services	
Actual costs compared to expected costs	
Expected profits and production plans	

1.2 Calculating costs and segmented costs

One of the key concerns that management will have will be how much the products that it produces, or the services that it provides, cost.

Management need to know this for the statement of profit or loss, to help set prices and to value inventory in the statement of financial position.

Costs can be presented in different ways in order to give management different types of information.

Costs in both manufacturing industries and service industries are traditionally split between:

- Material costs
- Labour costs
- Overheads (or expenses)

There are a few important terms that you need to understand.

- Cost unit
- Cost card
- Segmented cost

1.2.1 Cost unit and cost card

Key term

A **cost unit** is a unit of product or service to which costs can be attached.

A **cost card** is a document which groups the costs of a product or service in order to arrive at a total cost.

A cost unit could be a single item such as a table, or a batch of items such as 200 loaves of bread. A batch is a more useful cost unit if the items are made in a batch and/or the individual cost of an item is very small: fractions of a penny, for example. For a restaurant, a cost unit could be a meal served.

The cost of a cost unit is an important piece of costing information that will be used in many different ways. The total cost is built up on a **cost card**, which groups the costs using the categories of materials, labour and overheads.

Cost card	£
Direct materials	X
Direct labour	X
Direct expenses	X
Prime cost	X
Production overheads	X
Production cost	X
Non-production overheads	
Selling and distribution	X
Administration	X
Finance	X
Total cost	X

A **direct cost** is a cost that can be directly attributed to a cost unit. **Indirect costs** cannot be attributed directly to a cost unit. The **prime cost** is the total of the direct costs. The production cost is the total of the manufacturing costs.

At this stage, don't worry too much about what each of the lines in the cost card mean. We will explain these in further detail in the next chapter.

1.2.2 Segmented cost

Presenting information using a segmental approach means showing how particular components or sections of a business generate sales revenue, costs and profits.

Illustration 1: Segmented cost

HF Co manufactures two products, product CT1 and product CT2. The profit for the business last year was as follows:

			£	£
Sales revenue		CT1		150,000
		CT2		120,000
				270,000
Less costs:	Materials	CT1	60,000	
		CT2	50,000	
	Labour	CT1	30,000	
		CT2	35,000	
	Overheads	CT1	40,000	
		CT2	45,000	
				260,000
Profit				10,000

This shows that the business made a profit of £10,000 for the year. It doesn't show which of the two products made the biggest profit. For this, we need a segmental approach as follows:

		CT1 £	CT2 £	Total £
Sales revenue		150,000	120,000	270,000
Less costs:	Materials	60,000	50,000	110,000
	Labour	30,000	35,000	65,000
	Overheads	40,000	45,000	85,000
		130,000	130,000	260,000
Profit/(loss)		20,000	(10,000)	10,000

Now we can see that product CT2 actually made a loss. This information is useful to management. They may now decide to discontinue making CT2. However, there may be other factors to consider when making this decision. For example, sales of CT1 may be linked to sales of CT2.

Assessment focus point

Assessment questions may present information to you using a segmented approach. Alternatively, questions may ask you to fill in a segmented table to show the individual segments and the company's total profit or loss.

2 Ethical principles

2.1 What do we mean by ethics?

Ethics is a set of moral principles to guide behaviour.

A professional accountant has a responsibility to act in the public interest, not just to satisfy the needs of a particular client or employer. Third parties, for example investors, governments and employees, rely on accountants and their expertise. Although management accounts are generally prepared for internal use, occasionally they are used by third parties, such as banks. Ethics are therefore important for all areas of accounting.

Professional accountants must be qualified but they also have an additional obligation to act ethically by following an ethical code. An ethical code helps maintain the reputation of the accounting profession.

Ethics and ethical codes are constantly changing to adapt with changes in business and society. High-profile cases of fraud in the US resulted in the perceived **integrity** of accountants becoming increasingly important.

2.2 Fundamental principles

The AAT publish the *AAT Code of Professional Ethics* (2014) which sets out a code of fundamental ethical principles with which students and members should comply. The code aims to:

- Give the required standards of professional behaviour
- Help protect the public interest
- Help maintain the AAT's reputation (AAT, 2014: p.4)

The five fundamental principles are summarised in the table.

Fundamental principles	
Professional behaviour	A professional accountant should 'comply with relevant laws and regulations' (AAT, 2014: p.9) and should avoid any action that discredits the profession.
Integrity	A professional accountant should be 'straightforward and honest in all professional and business relationships' (AAT, 2014: p.9).
Professional competence and due care	A professional accountant has a continuing duty 'to maintain professional knowledge and skill at the level required to ensure that a client or employer receives competent professional service based on current developments in practice, legislation and techniques ... [A professional accountant should] act diligently and in accordance with applicable technical and professional standards when providing professional services' (AAT, 2014: p.9).
Confidentiality	A professional accountant should 'respect the confidentiality of information acquired as a result of professional and business relationships and [should] not disclose any such information to third parties without proper and specific authority unless there is a legal or professional right or duty to disclose. Confidential information acquired as a result of professional and business relationships should not be used for the personal advantage of the professional accountant or third parties' (AAT, 2014: p.9).
Objectivity	A professional accountant should 'not allow bias, conflict of interest or undue influence of others to override professional or business judgements' (AAT, 2014: p.9).

Assessment focus point

Sample assessment 1 Task 6(g) requires you to understand that profits should be calculated objectively rather than subjectively. **Objectively** means considering the facts and not being influenced by personal feelings. **Subjectively** means based on personal opinions.

2.2.1 Integrity

Integrity is the important principle of honesty and requires accountants to be straightforward in all professional and business relationships. Particular care must be taken when reporting figures and statements. Leaving out key information, obscuring the facts or making calculations and decisions without due care could result in false or misleading information being produced and integrity being breached.

Integrity goes further than the work an accountant produces. It also requires the accountant to act in a professional, consistent manner. The accountant must treat everyone the same rather than being friendly to some colleagues but cold to others. It also means that they should not back down over their personal or professional values just to avoid a difficult situation.

3 Responsibility centres

3.1 Cost, revenue, profit and investment centres

Responsibility centres are areas of the business for which costs or revenues are gathered and compared to budgets for control purposes. There are different types of responsibility centre (cost, revenue, profit and investment centre) depending on the type of cost and/or revenue that the centre deals with.

The name 'responsibility centre' comes from the fact that each area of the business (each responsibility centre) has a manager who is responsible for the activities of that area.

3.2 Cost centres

Key term

A **cost centre** is a location, function or item of equipment in respect of which costs may be ascertained and related to cost units for control purposes.

Each cost centre acts as a 'collecting place' for certain costs before they are analysed further.

Note.

- Cost centres may be set up in any way the business thinks appropriate.
- Usually, only manufacturing costs are considered and hence we will focus on factory cost centres.

3.2.1 Service and production cost centres

- **Production cost centres**. These are factory cost centres through which units of production actually flow.
- **Service cost centres**. These support or service the production cost centres.

Activity 2: Production and service cost centres

Required

Classify each of the following cost centres as either a production cost centre or a service cost centre, by placing them into the correct column.

Production cost centres	Service cost centres

Picklist:

Assembly
Canteen
Finishing
Maintenance
Packing
Stores

3.3 Revenue centres

Some organisations work on a **revenue centre** basis. A revenue centre is similar to a cost centre but is accountable for revenue only.

3.4 Profit centres

Some organisations work on a **profit centre** basis. A profit centre is similar to a cost centre but is accountable for both costs and revenue. Commonly, several cost centres will together make up one profit centre.

3.5 Investment centres

Divisions in an organisation may be **investment centres**. An investment centre is accountable for costs, revenues and investments in assets. So it incorporates the features of a cost and a profit centre.

Chapter summary

- Financial accounting is concerned with providing historic information to parties external to the organisation in the form of annual financial statements.

- Management accounting is concerned with providing relevant, useful and timely information to management based upon actual costs and revenues and forecast figures in order that management can carry out its main functions of planning, control and decision making. Presenting information using a segmental approach means showing how particular components or sections of a business generate sales revenue, costs and profits

- Ethics is a set of moral principles to guide behaviour.

- Preparing management accounts requires integrity, the principle of honesty.

- Responsibility centres are used to compare actual costs and revenues to budgets. The main responsibility centres are cost, profit and investment centres.

Keywords

- **Cost card:** A document which groups the costs of a product or service in order to arrive at a total cost

- **Cost centre:** An area of the business for which costs are gathered

- **Cost unit:** The individual product or service for which costs are ascertained

- **Financial accounting:** The provision of financial statements for parties external to the organisation based upon historical data

- **Integrity:** The quality of being honest and fair

- **Investment centre:** Is similar to a profit centre, the difference being that the manager of an investment centre is responsible not only for the profit that is earned by the area of the business but also the net assets of the area of the business

- **Management (cost) accounting:** The provision of both actual figures and forecast figures to enable management to carry out their prime functions of planning, control and decision making

- **Profit centre:** An area of the business for which both revenues and costs can be ascertained and therefore a profit or loss for a period can be determined

- **Responsibility centres:** Areas of the business for which costs or revenues are gathered and compared to budgets for control purposes

Test your learning

1 **Which of the following is the correct definition of a cost unit?**

☐ The cost per hour of operating a machine

☐ The cost per unit of electricity consumed

☐ A unit of product or service in relation to which costs are ascertained

☐ A measure of work output in a standard hour

2 **A cost centre is**

☐ A unit of product or service in relation to which costs are ascertained

☐ An amount of expenditure attributable to an activity

☐ A production or service location, function, activity or item of equipment for which costs are accumulated

☐ A centre for which an individual budget is drawn up

3 **Which of the following items might be a suitable cost unit within the accounts payable department of a company?**

☐ Postage cost

☐ Invoice processed

☐ Supplier account

4 **Which of the following principles relates to honesty?**

☐ Professional competence

☐ Objectivity

☐ Integrity

☐ Confidentiality

5 **A manager has control of the costs, revenues and assets of their division. What type of responsibility centre is this?**

☐ Cost centre

☐ Profit centre

☐ Investment centre

Cost classification and cost behaviour

2

2	Apply techniques required for dealing with costs
2.4	Differentiate between cost classifications for different purposes
	The implications of different cost classifications for cost analysis, decision making and reporting. These are:
	• Fixed costs
	• Variable costs
	• Semi-variable costs
	• Stepped costs
5.2	Assess and estimate the effects of changing activity levels
	• The effect of changing activity levels on units costs and profits
	• Calculate changes in forecast unit costs and profits
	• Explain such effects

Assessment context

Assessment questions will test your understanding of cost classification and cost behaviour, including calculations that require the use of the high–low method. You need to understand cost behaviour to answer questions on budgets and variance analysis.

Qualification context

This chapter introduces concepts and terms that are fundamental to understanding *Management Accounting* at Level 3 and Level 4.

Business context

Grouping costs together is essential for a business to be able to analyse costs, prepare budgets and plan effectively.

Chapter overview

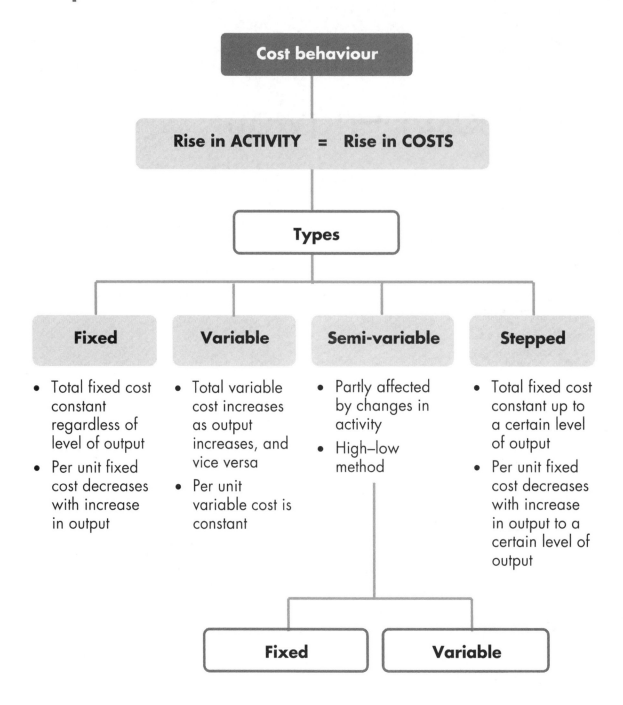

Cost behaviour

Rise in ACTIVITY = Rise in COSTS

Types

Fixed	**Variable**	**Semi-variable**	**Stepped**
• Total fixed cost constant regardless of level of output • Per unit fixed cost decreases with increase in output	• Total variable cost increases as output increases, and vice versa • Per unit variable cost is constant	• Partly affected by changes in activity • High–low method	• Total fixed cost constant up to a certain level of output • Per unit fixed cost decreases with increase in output to a certain level of output

Fixed   **Variable**

Cost classification by function

Arrange costs into logical groups for analysis

Production costs

- Associated with the production of goods and services

Non-production costs

- All other costs in a business eg
  selling and distribution
  administration
  financing

Materials

- Cost of material used in production

Labour

- Cost of workforce used in production

Overheads

- Cost of overhead required to support production

Direct cost

- Directly traced to product

Indirect cost

- Incurred as a result of making a product but not directly traceable

Introduction

A business will incur many different types of cost from day to day. For cost accounting purposes it is useful to group or classify these costs. There are, however, a number of different ways of doing this.

1 Classification

Cost classification is the arrangement of cost items into logical groups, for example by their **function** (such as administration or production) or by their **nature** (such as materials or wages).

The eventual aim of costing is to determine the cost of producing a product/providing a service.

1.1 Capital and revenue expenditure

The expenses of a business can be categorised as either capital expenses or revenue expenses.

Capital expenditure includes:

- The purchase of non-current assets (for example, machinery)
- The improvement of the earning capability of non-current assets

Non-current assets are assets that are used in the business for more than one accounting period to provide benefits. These benefits are (we hope!) the profits earned from using the non-current assets in the business. Plant and machinery, land and buildings, office equipment and motor vehicles are all examples of non-current assets that play their part in earning profits by being used within the business rather than being bought to make profit on their resale.

Revenue expenditure includes:

- The purchase of goods for resale
- The maintenance of the existing earning capacity of non-current assets
- Expenditure incurred in conducting the business

Capital expenditure is shown as a non-current asset in the statement of financial position, while revenue expenditure is charged as a cost in the statement of profit or loss. In costing terms, capital expenditure is not included in the cost of a product, only revenue expenses are included. It is therefore important to distinguish correctly between capital and revenue items, as this could hit profit quite hard given the relatively large figures involved where non-current assets are concerned. It would also mean that the statement of financial position would not show the correct cost of assets used by the business. For costing purposes it would mean that the amounts included in the calculations of **product costs** (costs of a finished product built up from its cost elements) would be inaccurate.

Some tricky items you might come across when deciding between capital and revenue categories often involve changes to non-current assets:

	Capital	Revenue
Extension to a building	✓	
Repairs to a building or machine		✓
Legal costs of buying a new factory	✓	
Installation of new machinery	✓	
Redecorating offices		✓

1.2 Classification by function

Revenue expenditure can be classified according to the function that causes the cost. The main functions within a manufacturing business will give rise to the following cost categories:

- **Production costs.** Materials and labour used to make the products, maintenance costs of the machinery and supervision of the workforce are examples of costs caused by the production function of a business.

- **Non-production costs – selling and distribution costs.** Advertising, delivery costs and sales staff salaries would be caused by the selling and distribution function.

- **Non-production costs – administration costs.** The administration function gives rise to management, secretarial and accounting costs in coordinating the other functions of the business.

- **Non-production costs – financing costs.** The financing function gives rise to all the expenses associated with raising money to finance the business, such as a loan or overdraft.

The distinction between these categories is not always clear, particularly when we are talking about administration costs, as there are no rules or regulations to follow, just common sense. What's more, these are not the only possible functions within a business. Large companies often have a research and development function, or a training function. It depends on the type of business.

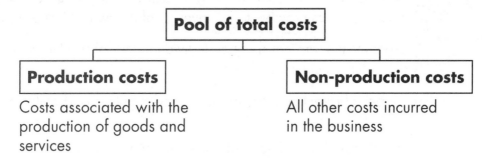

Pool of total costs

Production costs
Costs associated with the production of goods and services

Non-production costs
All other costs incurred in the business

1.3 Direct and indirect cost elements

A different way of classifying production costs looks at the three major cost elements.

- Materials
- Labour
- Expenses

Each category is then sub-divided into either:

- **Direct costs**; or
- **Indirect costs**.

Key term

> **Direct costs** are costs that can be directly identified with a particular unit of production or service provided.
>
> **Indirect costs** are costs that cannot be directly identified with a unit of production or service.

It is usually easy to identify the amount of a direct expense that is spent on one unit, but it is more difficult to do so with indirect costs as they are not spent directly on one unit. They are usually spent in relation to a number of units.

Here are some examples:

Direct materials	Materials that are incorporated into the finished product (eg wood used in the construction of a table).
Indirect materials	Materials that are used in the production process but not incorporated into the product (eg machine lubricants and spare parts). Insignificant costs that are attributable to each unit are sometimes included in indirect materials for convenience (eg nails and glue).
Direct labour	Wages paid to those workers who make products in a manufacturing business (eg machine operators) or perform the service in a service business (eg hairdressers in a hair salon).
Indirect labour	Wages and salaries of the other staff, such as supervisors, storekeepers and maintenance workers.
Direct expenses	Expenses that are identifiable with each unit of production, such as patent royalties payable to the inventor of a new product or process.
Indirect expenses	Expenses that are not spent on individual units of production (eg rent and rates, electricity and telephone).

In costing, the three types of direct cost are often lumped together and called **prime cost**.

Prime cost = Direct materials + Direct labour + Direct expenses

The three types of indirect cost are often lumped together and called **overheads**.

Overheads = Indirect materials + Indirect labour + Indirect expenses

2 Cost behaviour

Costs can also be classified by their behaviour, that is, how the total cost is affected by a change in output or activity level (ie the number of units produced). Costs behave in different ways when the levels of activity in the organisation change. The main classifications are:

- **Fixed costs**
- **Variable costs**
- **Semi-variable costs**
- **Stepped costs**

Key term

Fixed costs are total cost remains the same as output increases.

Variable costs are total cost increases as output increases.

Semi-variable costs are costs that contain elements of both fixed and variable costs. Also known as mixed costs.

Stepped costs are costs that remain the same up to a certain level of activity and then jump. Fixed costs often behave like this in practice.

These classifications only apply in the short term, as in the long term all costs are variable. Each of these will be illustrated in this chapter, and the concepts will then be used in later chapters in order to produce relevant management information.

2.1 Fixed costs

Fixed costs are not affected by changes in production level. They remain the same in total whether no units or many units are produced. They are incurred in relation to a period of time rather than production level, and are often referred to as **period costs**. This is the case with the salary of a supervisor, the rent of a factory or straight-line depreciation of plant and machinery.

A graph of fixed costs against output level would produce a horizontal line.

Graph of total fixed costs

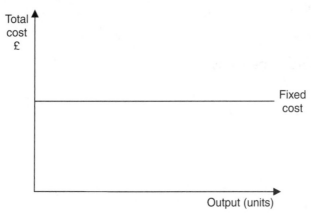

In practical terms fixed costs are only truly fixed over the **relevant range**. For example, the rent of the factory will only remain constant provided that the level of activity is within the production capacity of the factory. If production levels increase above the capacity of the current factory then more factory space must be rented thus increasing the rent cost for this level of production.

As the activity level increases the fixed cost remains fixed in total, but the fixed cost per unit will fall as the total cost is split over more units. This gives management an incentive to increase production as it will mean that each unit is cheaper to produce. This is demonstrated in the graph below.

Graph of fixed cost per unit

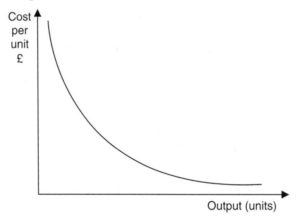

Activity 1: Fixed cost per unit

Sleet Ltd makes garden benches and incurs fixed costs of £20,000 per year.

Required

Calculate the fixed cost per garden bench at the following output levels:

(a) 1,000 units

(b) 10,000 units

(c) 20,000 units

(d) 100,000 units

The fixed cost per garden bench is:

(a) £ [   ]

(b) £ [   ]

(c) £ [   ]

(d) £ [   ]

2.2 Variable costs

Variable costs are costs that vary directly in line with changes in the level of activity. Direct materials are often viewed as variable costs. For example, if 1 kg of a material is needed for each cost unit then 100,000 kg will be required for 100,000 units of production and 500,000 kg for 500,000 units of production.

The total variable cost can be expressed as:

Total variable cost = Variable cost per unit × Number of units

A graph can be used to illustrate the total variable cost as activity levels change:

Graph of total variable costs

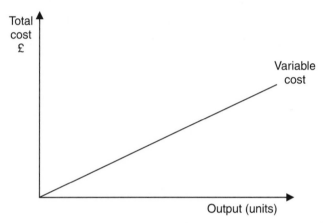

As a general rule, as the direct cost is spent directly on each unit of production, this will be the same amount for each unit, so a graph of unit cost against level of output will be horizontal.

Graph of variable cost per unit

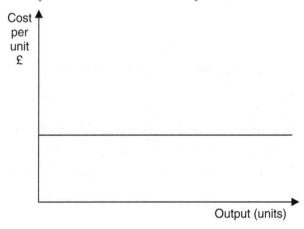

Assessment focus point

Assessment questions may ask you to calculate budgeted cost per unit using total budgeted costs and the number of units. You need to understand that

Total variable cost = Variable cost per unit × Number of units

and

Variable cost per unit = Total variable costs ÷ Number of units

2.3 Stepped costs (sometimes called step-fixed costs)

Stepped costs are costs that are fixed over a relatively small range of activity levels but then increase in steps when certain levels of activity are reached. For example, if one production supervisor is required for each 30,000 units of a product that is made then three supervisors are required for the production of 90,000 units, four for the production of 120,000 units, five for the production of up to 150,000 units and so on.

Stepped costs can be illustrated on a graph:

Graph of total stepped costs

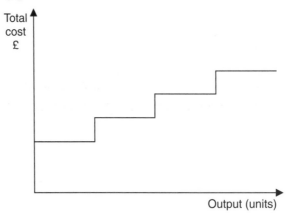

Stepped costs are really a fixed cost with a relatively short relevant range.

2.4 Semi-variable costs

Semi-variable costs are costs that have a fixed element and also a variable element. For example, the telephone bill includes a fixed element being the fixed line rental for the period and a variable element that will increase as the number of calls increases.

The total of a semi-variable cost can be expressed as:

Total cost = Fixed element + (Variable cost per unit × Number of units)

A semi-variable cost can be illustrated on a graph as follows:

Graph of total semi-variable costs

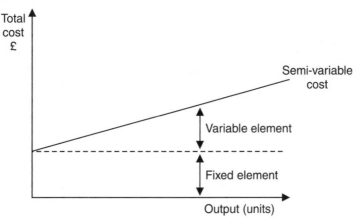

There are several ways of calculating the fixed and variable elements of a semi-variable cost. You could be given a percentage to use or you might have to use the **high–low method** (covered later in this chapter).

3 Calculating the fixed and variable elements of semi-variable costs

Assessment focus point

Assessment questions could ask you to calculate the fixed and variable elements of costs based on a particular percentage.

Activity 2: Fixed and variable elements of cost

An overhead cost of £580,000 is made up of a fixed and variable element. The fixed element is 55% of the total cost and the rest is variable.

The fixed element of the overhead cost is | £ | |

The variable element of the overhead cost is | £ | |

Another way of calculating the fixed and variable elements of a cost is to use the high–low method. The high–low method requires several observations of the costs incurred at different output levels. This data can then be used to predict costs that would be incurred at other output levels.

Illustration 1: High–low method

Over the last five years, Stormbreak Ltd has recorded the following costs:

Year	Output Units	Total cost £
20X1	32,000	505,000
20X2	37,000	580,000
20X3	48,000	745,000
20X4	53,000	820,000
20X5	51,000	790,000

Stormbreak Ltd wants to estimate the cost for 20X6, when they expect to produce 52,000 units.

This problem can be tackled by following four steps.

Step 1 Identify the high and low output and associated costs.

Look carefully at the information given and identify the highest and lowest output levels. Write these down, along with the total costs at those levels. (Don't be put off by any other information, such as the year, or the order in which the data is given, even if the cost column is given first – it is the highest and lowest outputs that matter.)

	Output Units	Total cost £
Highest	53,000	820,000
Lowest	32,000	505,000

Step 2 Deduct the lowest output/costs from the highest output/costs.

	Output Units	Total cost £
Highest	53,000	820,000
Lowest	32,000	505,000
Increase	21,000	315,000

This tells us that an increase of 21,000 units has led to an increase in costs of £315,000. This is due to the variable costs only, and gives us the figures we need for the next step.

Step 3 Calculate the variable cost per unit.

$$\text{Variable cost per unit} = \frac{\text{High cost} - \text{Low cost}}{\text{High output} - \text{Low output}}$$

$$= \frac{£315,000}{21,000}$$

$$= £15$$

Step 4 Find the fixed costs at one of the output levels used in the above calculations.

Choose either the highest or the lowest output level. Both will give the same result. Calculate the variable cost by taking the cost per unit from Step 3 multiplied by the number of units of output. Deduct this from the total cost at the same level of output and you will be left with the fixed cost.

At 53,000 units:

	£
Total cost	820,000
Less: variable cost (53,000 × £15)	795,000
= fixed cost	25,000

At 32,000 units (as a check):

	£
Total cost	505,000
Less: variable cost (32,000 × £15)	480,000
= fixed cost	25,000

Now we are in a position to answer the actual question asked, which is 'What are the expected costs when output is 52,000 units?' All we need to do is build up the total cost from the fixed and variable elements at this level of output.

	£
Fixed cost	25,000
Add: variable cost (52,000 × £15)	780,000
= total cost	805,000

Activity 3: High-low method - manufacturing business

S and N recorded the following costs for the last four months.

Month	Cost £	Production volume Units
1	106,000	7,000
2	115,000	8,000
3	112,300	7,700
4	97,000	6,000

Required

Calculate the costs that should be expected in month 5 when output is expected to be 7,500 units.

The total cost in month 5 when output is expected to be 7,500 units is

£ [   ] .

Activity 4: High-low method - service business

P and Q recorded the following information over the last five months.

Month	Cost £	Electricity consumed Units
January	204	2,600
February	212	2,800
March	200	2,500
April	220	3,000
May	184	2,100

Required

Using the high-low method, determine the cost of electricity in June if 2,750 units of electricity are consumed.

The cost of electricity in June if 2,750 units are consumed is £ [   ] .

Tutor's note

It is important to note that when we talk about different types of **cost behaviour**, we are usually referring to the short term. Over longer periods of time, however, say a number of years, all costs will tend to vary in response to large changes in activity level. Costs traditionally classified as fixed will become step costs as no cost can remain unchanged forever. And so as the time span increases, step costs become variable costs, varying with the passing of time. For example, when considered over many years, rent will appear as a variable cost, varying in the long term with large changes in the level of activity. So, in the long run, all costs are variable.

Chapter summary

- Costs are either capital or revenue in nature. Revenue expenditure is included in the cost of a product, but capital expenditure is not.

- Costs can be classified by several methods:

  - By function: production, selling and distribution, administration and finance

  - By element

	Materials
Direct	Labour
	Expenses
	Materials
Indirect	Labour
	Expenses

  - By nature or cost behaviour: fixed, variable, stepped, semi-variable

  But in the long run, all costs are variable.

- Direct costs are costs that can be related directly to a cost unit whereas indirect costs are initially allocated or apportioned to a cost centre.

- At different production levels:

  - Variable costs will change in line with the quantity produced, but fixed costs will remain the same.

  - The variable cost per unit will be the same, but the fixed cost per unit will fall as the quantity produced increases.

- The high–low technique can be used to find the variable and fixed elements of a semi-variable cost by identifying the costs at the highest and lowest levels of output.

Keywords

- **Cost behaviour:** The way a cost changes as production quantity or activity level changes

- **Direct costs:** Can be directly identified with a unit of production or service

- **Fixed costs:** Costs that do not vary with changes in production level

- **High–low method:** A method for estimating the fixed and variable parts of a semi-variable cost

- **Indirect costs**: Cannot be directly identified with a unit of production or service

- **Overheads:** Indirect costs (ie indirect materials, labour and expenses)

- **Period costs:** Costs which relate to a time period rather than the output of products or services

- **Prime cost:** The total of direct costs

- **Product cost:** A cost of a finished product made up from its cost elements

- **Production cost:** The total of manufacturing costs

- **Relevant range:** The relevant range of a fixed cost is the range of activity within which the cost does not change

- **Semi-variable (or semi-fixed, or mixed) costs:** Costs that have both a fixed element and a variable element

- **Stepped costs:** Costs that are fixed over a certain range, but when output increases beyond a certain level, there will be a sudden jump in cost to a higher fixed amount

- **Variable costs:** Vary according to the level of production

1   **Study the list below and decide which items are capital and which are revenue. Tick the appropriate box.**

	Capital ✓	Revenue ✓
A new telephone system		
Depreciation of vehicles		
Salesperson's car		
Road fund licence for delivery van		
Telephone bill		
Computer software costing £10,000		
Repairs to the Managing Director's company car after an accident		

2   **Look at the following sketch graph and then decide which of the suggested costs could account for that shape of graph. (Tick the correct answers.)**

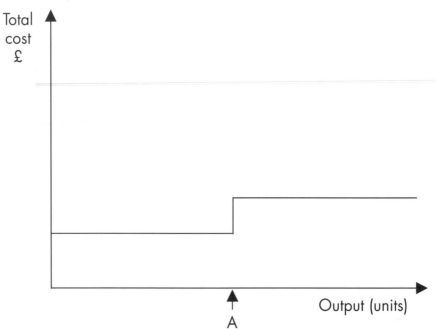

		Cost behaviour	
		Does fit the graph shape	Does NOT fit the graph shape
(a)	Plastic used in the manufacture of moulded plastic furniture. A bulk-buying discount is given at point A on the graph.		
(b)	Straight-line depreciation of a freehold factory. A new factory is bought at point A.		
(c)	Rent of a warehouse. A further warehouse is rented at point A.		
(d)	Electricity costs that have a standing charge and a cost per unit of power used. At point A the level of production reaches the point where a night shift is required, which uses electricity at a cheaper rate.		

3 **Use the high–low technique to predict the costs at a production level of 12,000 units, given the observed data in the table below.**

Year	Production level	Total cost
	Units	£
20X2	9,000	22,500
20X3	6,500	17,500
20X4	13,500	31,500
20X5	10,300	25,100
20X6	12,600	29,700

Total cost at 12,000 units   £ [ ]

4 **Draw up a cost card using the following information. All costs given are per cabinet.**

To make a filing cabinet, metal sheeting to the value of £3.80 is cut, formed, welded and painted by machine. A group of machines are monitored, the production overhead cost of which has been worked out at £0.30. Metal fixtures costing £1.80 are attached manually, and the cabinets are then assembled and packaged. The labour cost of assembly and packaging is £6.70, and the packaging materials cost £0.90. The power used by the factory gives a cost of £0.20, and delivery costs and advertising works out at £3.00.

Cost card: Filing cabinet	£
Direct materials	
Direct labour	
Prime cost	
Production overheads	
Production cost	
Non-production overheads	
Selling and distribution	
Total cost	

5 **Variable costs are conventionally deemed to:**

☐ Be constant per unit of output

☐ Vary per unit of output as production volume changes

☐ Be constant in total when production volume changes

☐ Vary, in total, from period to period when production is constant

6 The following is a graph of cost against level of activity:

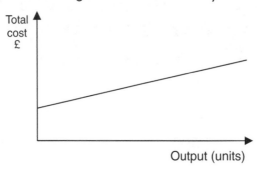

To which one of the following costs does the graph correspond?

☐ A Electricity bills made up of a standing charge and a variable charge

☐ B Bonus payment to employees when production reaches a certain level

☐ C Salesperson's commissions payable per unit up to a maximum amount of commission

☐ D Bulk discounts on purchases, the discount being given on all units purchased

The following information relates to questions 7, 8 and 9.

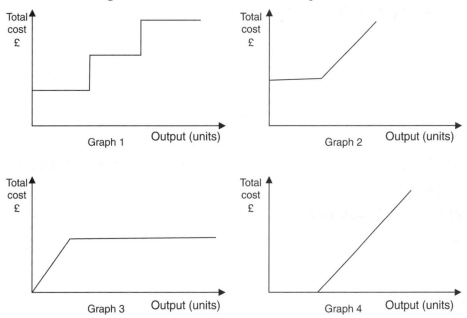

Which one of the graphs depicts the costs described in questions 7, 8 and 9?

7   Photocopier rental costs, where a fixed rental is payable up to a certain number of copies each period. If the number of copies exceeds this amount, a constant charge per copy is made for all subsequent copies during that period.

   ☐   Graph 1

   ☐   Graph 2

   ☐   Graph 3

   ☐   Graph 4

8   Supervisor salary costs, where one supervisor is needed for every five employees added to the staff.

   ☐   Graph 1

   ☐   Graph 2

   ☐   Graph 3

   ☐   Graph 4

9 Vehicle hire costs, where a constant rate is charged per mile travelled, up to a maximum monthly payment regardless of the miles travelled.

☐ Graph 1

☐ Graph 2

☐ Graph 3

☐ Graph 4

10 A production worker is paid a salary of £650 per month, plus an extra 5 pence for each unit produced during the month.

This labour cost is best described as:

☐ A variable cost

☐ A fixed cost

☐ A stepped cost

☐ A semi-variable cost

11 **Prime cost is**

☐ All costs incurred in manufacturing a product

☐ The total of direct costs

☐ The material cost of a product

☐ The cost of operating a department

12 **Which of the following costs are part of the prime cost for a manufacturing company?**

☐ Cost of transporting raw materials from the supplier's premises

☐ Wages of factory workers engaged in machine maintenance

☐ Depreciation of lorries used for deliveries to customers

☐ Cost of indirect production materials

13 **Which of the following are direct expenses?**

☐ The cost of special designs, drawing or layouts

☐ The hire of tools or equipment for a particular job

☐ Salesperson's wages

☐ Rent, rates and insurance of a factory

Materials costs and inventory valuation

3

Learning outcomes

2	Apply techniques required for dealing with costs
2.1	**Record and calculate materials, labour and overhead costs** • Prepare and interpret inventory records

2.3	**Apply inventory control methods**
	• Inventory control measures, including different valuation methods. These include:
	  – Inventory buffers, fixed quantity methods, lead times, just in time, minimum/maximum order quantities
	  – The concept of economic order quantity
	  – Compliance with inventory control policies
	  – The effect on reported profits of choice of method
	• Account for inventories using FIFO, LIFO (for internal reporting) and AVCO methods
	• Analyse closing inventory balances
	• Make calculations for the inventory control measures listed above

Assessment context

Materials cost is a key cost within a manufacturing environment. This is an important part of the syllabus and you need to be happy with all relevant calculations. Task 1 in the assessment could ask you to use first in, first out (FIFO) or last in, first out (LIFO) or average cost (AVCO) calculations.

Qualification context

This unit gives you a good grounding in the inventory control process and introduces some theoretical techniques to help with inventory ordering and valuation. Some of the basics were covered in Level 2 so may be familiar to you.

Business context

Many businesses use materials and hold inventory. Management accountants need to understand the costs involved with holding and ordering materials and inventory. In order to control the inventory that is held, businesses will regularly count their inventories and compare the physical quantity with the inventory records; any discrepancies should be investigated and corrected.

Chapter overview

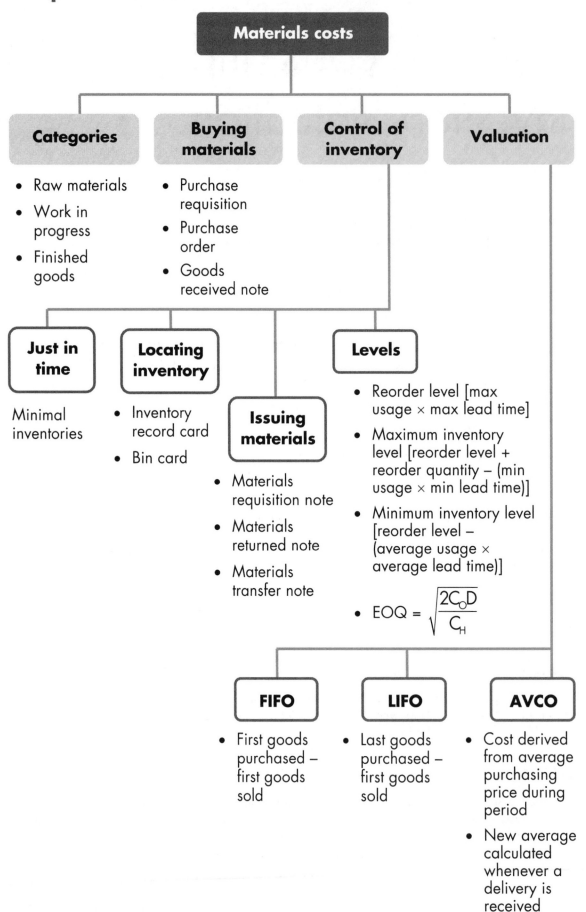

Materials costs

Categories
- Raw materials
- Work in progress
- Finished goods

Buying materials
- Purchase requisition
- Purchase order
- Goods received note

Control of inventory

Valuation

Just in time

Minimal inventories

Locating inventory
- Inventory record card
- Bin card

Issuing materials
- Materials requisition note
- Materials returned note
- Materials transfer note

Levels
- Reorder level [max usage × max lead time]
- Maximum inventory level [reorder level + reorder quantity − (min usage × min lead time)]
- Minimum inventory level [reorder level − (average usage × average lead time)]
- $EOQ = \sqrt{\dfrac{2C_oD}{C_H}}$

FIFO
- First goods purchased − first goods sold

LIFO
- Last goods purchased − first goods sold

AVCO
- Cost derived from average purchasing price during period
- New average calculated whenever a delivery is received

Introduction

Materials are an important component of any production process and often make up a significant proportion of the costs in manufacturing accounts. Having enough materials available for production when needed is crucial. However, storing materials is expensive. Businesses therefore need to strike a balance between holding enough materials and holding too many.

1 Types of material

Materials are broken down into three major categories for costing purposes:

Raw materials. Goods purchased for making into products for sale.

Work in progress (WIP). The stages in between raw materials and finished goods at which the purchased goods are being made ready for sale.

Finished goods. Manufactured goods ready for sale or despatch.

When these are stored before use or sale, materials are known as **inventory**.

Raw materials and components used by a manufacturer are classified as direct costs for costing purposes. Examples are fabric in a tailoring company, paper in a printing company and electrical components in a manufacturer of electrical goods.

A retailer, such as a shop, and a wholesaler, which acts as a 'middle man' between the manufacturer and the retailer, would buy the products of the manufacturing companies. So, the clothing, printed matter and electrical goods produced by the manufacturers would be the materials of the retailer and wholesaler.

All businesses will buy some sort of goods for consumption, which are generally classified as indirect materials and included in overheads. In a manufacturing business, machine spares and lubricants would be production overheads, while office stationery would be a non-production overhead.

2 Ordering and receiving raw materials

2.1 Purchase requisitions, purchase orders and goods received notes

Every movement of material should be documented in order that a proper physical record is kept and the correct entries can be entered in the 'books' of the company. Purchase requisitions are sometimes called materials requisitions.

Inventory control process:

Purchase requisition	Purchase requisition

Purchase requisition

- When the stores department need more materials they issue a purchase requisition, which is sent to the purchasing department.

Purchase requisition			
Job		No.	
Supplier		Date	
Requested by			
Quantity	Code	Description	Cost
Authorised:			

Purchase order (PO)

- The purchasing department raise a PO, which is sent to:
  - The supplier
  - The accounts department
  - Stores

Purchase order			No.	
To			Date	
Order ref				
Address				
Quantity	Code	Description		Cost
			Subtotal	
			VAT @ 20%	
			Total	

When the goods arrive at stores:

Delivery note/goods received note (GRN)

- Received with the goods into the stores department
- Signed off to confirm quantity and quality
- Sent to:
  - Purchasing department
  - Accounts department

Goods received note		
Date		No.
Time		
Out order no.		
Supplier no.		
Quantity	No./Code	Description
Received in good condition............................		

The accounts department should match the purchase order to the GRN and then to the invoice when it arrives from the supplier.

2.2 Cost bookkeeping for materials

The materials movements are recorded in the **materials control account** at their valuation from the inventory control account. We will start with the opening balance, a debit entry in the account, as it is an asset, the opening inventory.

Materials control account

		£			£
1 May	Opening balance	400			

Next, each of the purchases in the period are entered as debits in the materials control account with the credit entry being to payables or cash depending upon whether the purchase was on credit or not.

Materials control account

		£			£
1 May	Opening balance	400			
5 May	Bank/payables	840			
21 May	Bank/payables	1,350			

Then the issues to production should be recorded. They are entered as a credit entry in the materials control account and a debit entry in the **work in progress control account**. The work in progress control account is the account in which we are going to gather together all of the direct costs of production during the period, starting here with the materials cost.

Materials control account

		£			£
1 May	Opening balance	400	10 May	WIP	568
5 May	Bank/payables	840	15 May	WIP	420
21 May	Bank/payables	1,350	28 May	WIP	252

Work in progress control account

		£			£
10 May	Materials control	568			
15 May	Materials control	420			
28 May	Materials control	252			

Finally, the materials control account can be balanced to show the closing balance at 31 May.

Materials control account

		£			£
1 May	Opening balance	400	10 May	WIP	568
5 May	Bank/payables	840	15 May	WIP	420
21 May	Bank/payables	1,350	28 May	WIP	252
			31 May	Closing balance	1,350
		2,590			2,590

2.3 Direct and indirect costs

We saw earlier in this Course Book that materials, labour and expenses can be classified as either direct or indirect depending upon whether or not they relate to a specific unit of product or service. The importance of this distinction is that the direct materials are part of the cost of the units produced which is being gathered together in the work in progress control account, whereas the indirect materials are overheads which must be recorded separately in a **production overhead control account**.

Illustration 1: Cost bookkeeping for materials

During the month of June Gilchrist Chemicals made total purchases of materials of £71,400. Direct materials valued at £69,200 were issued to the factory for production and indirect materials for machine maintenance during the month were £3,600. At the beginning of June the total inventory valuation was £7,300.

The materials control account is initially debited with the opening inventory valuation and the purchases for the month.

Materials control account

		£			£
1 Jun	Opening balance	7,300			
30 Jun	Purchases	71,400			

The issues from stores must now be entered on the credit side of the materials control account. The direct materials are debited to the work in progress control account while the indirect materials are debited to the production overhead control account.

Materials control account

		£			£
1 June	Opening balance	7,300	30 June	Direct materials – WIP	69,200
30 June	Purchases	71,400	30 June	Indirect materials – Production o/h control	3,600

Work in progress control account

		£			£
30 June	Materials control	69,200			

Production overhead control

		£			£
30 June	Materials control	3,600			

Finally, the materials control account can be balanced to find the closing inventory value. However, we will not balance the other two accounts yet as there are more entries to be made to them in the next two chapters.

Materials control account

		£			£
1 June	Opening balance	7,300	30 June	Direct materials – WIP	69,200
30 June	Purchases	71,400	30 June	Indirect materials – Production o/h control	3,600
			30 June	Closing balance	5,900
		78,700			78,700

3 Inventory costs and control

There are many different costs that can occur if a business keeps inventory. These need to be controlled and kept to a minimum.

(a) **Holding costs**. For example, warehouse rent, insurance, security, obsolescence and deterioration.

(b) **Ordering costs**. For example, admin costs associated with placing an order, transport inwards costs.

Activity 1: Holding inventory

Required

Which of the following are reasons for holding inventory? Tick all those that are valid reasons.

	✓
To avoid production stoppages due to a shortage of materials	
To take advantage of quantity discounts	
To avoid the detrimental effect of price fluctuations	
To provide a buffer or fail-safe in times of general shortage or heavy demand	

There are two approaches to purchasing inventory – just-in-time and buffer inventory.

3.1 Just-in-time (JIT) inventory control techniques

Some organisations operate a **just-in-time (JIT)** inventory system. With a JIT system, supplies are ordered and delivered just as they are needed for production, and goods are manufactured just as they are needed for sales. **Inventory is therefore kept to a minimum**, and the system relies on **accurate forecasting** and **reliable suppliers**.

3.2 Minimum inventory level and buffer inventory

The minimum level is an inventory level below which inventory should not normally fall.

It acts as a warning sign to management that inventory is very low and that there is an increased risk of running out of inventory.

In practice, most organisations keep a certain amount of inventory in reserve. This is known as **buffer inventory**.

Lead time is the time between placing an order for inventory and receiving the inventory.

 Formula to learn

Minimum inventory level = Reorder level – (Average usage × Average lead time)

3.3 Reorder level

When the level of inventory falls to the '**reorder level**', more inventory should be ordered.

It is set so that, in theory, it is not possible to run out of inventory, based on the maximum usage of inventory and the maximum delivery days or lead time.

Formula to learn

Reorder level = (Max usage × Max lead time) + Buffer inventory

Note. There may not be a buffer inventory each time, in which case buffer inventory is zero.

3.4 Maximum inventory level

The maximum level is an inventory level above which inventory should not normally rise.

It acts as a warning sign to management that too much inventory is held, which may be uneconomical.

Formula to learn

Maximum inventory level = Reorder level + Reorder Quantity – (Min usage × Min lead time)

3.5 Additional terminology

Formula to learn

Average inventory = Minimum inventory + ½ Reorder quantity

The average inventory formula assumes that inventory levels fluctuate evenly between the minimum inventory level and the highest possible inventory level (the amount of inventory immediately after an order is **received**).

3.6 Reorder quantity

This is the quantity of inventory which is to be ordered when inventory reaches the reorder level. This is calculated as the **economic order quantity (EOQ)** (see later in this chapter).

Note that the EOQ minimises the annual costs of holding inventory and ordering inventory.

Activity 2: Inventory control levels

A large retailer with multiple outlets maintains a central warehouse from which the outlets are supplied.

The following information is available for part number CB 2005:

Average usage	350 parts per day
Minimum usage	180 parts per day
Maximum usage	420 parts per day
Lead time for replenishment	11 days–15 days
Reorder quantity	6,500 parts

Required

(a) What is the reorder level?

Reorder level is ☐ parts.

(b) What is the minimum inventory level?

Minimum inventory level is ☐ parts.

(c) What is the maximum inventory level?

Maximum inventory level is ☐ parts.

3.7 The economic order quantity (EOQ)

Key term

Economic order quantity (EOQ) is a mathematical tool to calculate the amount of inventory to order in each order and minimise the holding costs, ordering costs and purchase costs.

Formula to learn

Total inventory costs = Ordering costs + Purchase costs + Holding costs

The total cost is minimised when:

Formula to learn

$Q = EOQ = \sqrt{\dfrac{2C_oD}{C_H}}$ **(Formula will NOT be given in the assessment.)**

Terms

D = annual demand in units
Co = fixed cost per order
C_H = cost of holding one unit for one year
Q = number of units ordered

The EOQ formula assumes that:

(a) Demand is constant
(b) Delivery is instantaneous or lead time is constant
(c) Purchase costs are constant (no discounts)

Activity 3: EOQ

The demand for a product is 150 units per month.

It costs £25 per unit to purchase the product.

The fixed cost per order is £32.

The holding cost is 18% pa of the purchase price.

Required

What is the EOQ (in units)?

4 FIFO, LIFO, AVCO valuation

The **stores ledger accounts** or inventory record cards record the value of materials purchased, and this information can be obtained from the purchase order and invoice. When goods are issued to the production department from stores or a warehouse, a value will need to be recorded on the stores ledger accounts and on the costing details for the job or department that is going to bear that cost. The question is how do we value these issues if prices are changing regularly? How should the remaining inventories on hand be valued? This is not just a costing problem; it is also something that is needed for the preparation of the financial accounts.

Some items can be specifically priced from an invoice as they are individual items. However, most materials are bought in quantity and added to existing inventory where it is difficult to track the individual costs. Here, one of the following methods can be used to estimate the cost.

4.1 First in, first out (FIFO)

First in, first out (FIFO) assumes that the first items bought are the first items issued. So:

oldest prices cost.

- Items issued are costed at the earliest invoice prices related to the inventory held, working forwards through to the later prices; and

- Inventory on hand is valued at the latest prices, working back. *latest prices cost*

FIFO is most appropriate in businesses where the oldest items are actually issued first, which is the case with perishable goods such as food, but actually this is a very popular method in many types of business.

Note that in a time of rising prices generally, FIFO values inventory at the highest amounts. This leads to a high value of closing inventory at the end of an accounting period, which can make that period's profit look better.

Say, for example, ABC Ltd's inventory consisted of four deliveries of raw material in the last month:

	Units		
1 September	1,000	at	£2.00
8 September	500	at	£2.50
15 September	500	at	£3.00
22 September	1,000	at	£3.50

If on 23 September 1,500 units were issued to production, 1,000 of these units would be priced at £2.00 (the cost of the 1,000 oldest units in inventory) and 500 at £2.50 (the cost of the next oldest 500). 1,000 units of closing inventory would be valued at £3.50 (the cost of the 1,000 most recent units received) and 500 units at £3.00 (the cost of the next most recent 500).

Note that FIFO (and **LIFO** and **AVCO**) are just methods for **accounting** for inventory. They are not used for **physically issuing** inventory. For example, the inventory is not issued on a FIFO basis, it is just valued on a FIFO basis.

Advantages and disadvantages of the FIFO method

Advantages	Disadvantages
• It is a logical pricing method which probably represents what is physically happening: in practice the oldest inventory is likely to be used first	• FIFO can be cumbersome to operate because of the need to identify each batch of material separately
• It is easy to understand and explain to managers. FIFO also complies with the IAS 2 accounting standard so can be used for inventory valuation in financial accounting	• Managers may find it difficult to compare costs and make decisions when they are charged with continually varying prices for the same materials
• The closing inventory value will probably be similar to its replacement cost	

4.2 Last in, first out (LIFO)

Last in, first out (LIFO) is the opposite of FIFO. It assumes that the last items bought are the first items issued. So:

- Items issued are costed at the latest invoice prices, working backwards through to the earlier prices; and

- Inventory on hand is valued at the earliest prices related to the inventory held, working forward.

LIFO is appropriate if new deliveries are physically piled on top of existing inventories, and goods issued are picked from the top of the pile. In fact, from a financial accounting point of view, LIFO is not a permitted method of inventory valuation, so in practice it is rarely seen.

Note that in times of general price inflation, LIFO means a lower value of inventory at the end of a period than FIFO, so that period's profit tends to look worse.

In the example above it will be 1,000 units of issues which will be valued at £3.50, and the other 500 units issued will be valued at £3.00. 1,000 units of closing inventory will be valued at £2.00 and 500 at £2.50.

Advantages and disadvantages of the LIFO method

Advantages	Disadvantages
• Inventory is issued at a price which is close to current market value. This is not the case with FIFO when there is a high rate of inflation	• The method can be cumbersome to operate because it sometimes results in several batches being only part-used in the inventory records before another batch is received
• Managers are continually aware of recent costs when making decisions, because the costs being charged to their department or products will be close to current costs	• LIFO is often the opposite to what is physically happening and can therefore be difficult to explain to managers
	• Managers may find it difficult to compare costs and make decisions when they are charged with continually varying prices for the same materials

4.3 Average cost (AVCO)

With the **average cost (AVCO)** method, a weighted average cost is calculated each time a new delivery is received. The weighting is provided by the number of units at each price brought into the calculation. The general formula is

Formula to learn

$$\text{Average price per unit} = \frac{\text{Total value of opening inventory} + \text{Total value of units added to inventory}}{\text{Units of opening inventory} + \text{Units added to inventory}}$$

AVCO would be most appropriate if the inventories were to be mixed when they are stored, for example chemicals stored in a vat.

When prices are generally rising, AVCO distorts period profits less than FIFO or LIFO, since it uses an average of the prices at which the actual inventory was purchased.

Advantages and disadvantages of the AVCO method

Advantages	Disadvantages
• Fluctuations in prices are smoothed out, making it easier to use the data for decision making	• The resulting issue price is rarely an actual price that has been paid and can run to several decimal places
• It is easier to administer than FIFO and LIFO, because there is no need to identify each batch separately	• Prices tend to lag a little behind current market values when there is rapid inflation

Illustration 2: FIFO, LIFO and AVCO

ABC Ltd recorded the following transactions during May:

Transactions during May 20X3

	Quantity Units	Unit cost £	Total cost £	Sales price per unit on date of transaction £
Opening balance, 1 May	100	2.00	200	
Receipts, 3 May	400	2.10	840	2.11
Issues, 4 May	200			2.11
Receipts, 9 May	300	2.12	636	2.15
Issues, 11 May	400			2.20
Receipts, 18 May	100	2.40	240	2.35
Issues, 20 May	100			2.80
Closing balance, 31 May	200			2.83
			1,916	

FIFO

Using FIFO, the cost of issues and the closing inventory value in the example would be as follows.

Date of issue	Quantity issued Units	Value	£	£
4 May	200	100 o/s at £2.00	200	
		100 at £2.10	210	
				410
11 May	400	300 at £2.10	630	
		100 at £2.12	212	
				842
20 May	100	100 at £2.12		212
Cost of issues				1,464
Closing inventory value	200	100 at £2.12	212	
		100 at £2.40	240	
				452
				1,916

The cost of materials issued plus the value of closing inventory equals the cost of purchases plus the value of opening inventory (£1,916).

The value of closing inventory represents the latest items to be bought, 100 @ £2.12 + 100 @ £2.40.

The market price of purchased materials is rising dramatically. In a period of inflation, there is a tendency with FIFO for materials to be issued at a cost lower than the current market value, although closing inventories tend to be valued at a cost approximating to current market value.

The format for the FIFO Inventory record card is as follows:

	Purchases			Sales			Balance	
Date	**Quantity Units**	**Cost £**	**Total cost £**	**Quantity Units**	**Cost £**	**Total cost £**	**Quantity Units**	**Total cost £**
Balance at 1 May							100	200
3 May	400	2.10	840				500	1,040
4 May				100 100	2.00 2.10	200 210	300	630
9 May	300	2.12	636				600	1,266
11 May				300 100	2.10 2.12	630 212	200	424
18 May	100	2.40	240				300	664
20 May				100	2.12	212	200	452

LIFO

Using LIFO, the cost of issues and the closing inventory value in the example above would be as follows.

Date of issue	Quantity issued Units	Valuation	£	£
4 May	200	200 at £2.10		420
11 May	400	300 at £2.12	636	
		100 at £2.10	210	
				846
20 May	100	100 at £2.40		240
Cost of issues				1,506
Closing inventory value	200	100 at £2.10	210	
		100 at £2.00	200	
				410
				1,916

Notes

(a) The cost of materials issued plus the value of closing inventory equals the cost of purchases plus the value of opening inventory (£1,916).

(b) In a period of inflation there is a tendency with LIFO for the following to occur:

    (i) Materials are issued at a price which approximates to current market value.

    (ii) Closing inventories become undervalued when compared to market value.

The format of the LIFO inventory record card is as follows:

Inventory record card								
	Purchases			**Sales**			**Balance**	
Date	**Quantity Units**	**Cost £**	**Total cost £**	**Quantity Units**	**Cost £**	**Total cost £**	**Quantity Units**	**Total cost £**
Balance at 1 May							100	200
3 May	400	2.10	840				500	1,040
4 May				200	2.10	420	300	620
9 May	300	2.12	636				600	1,256
11 May				300	2.12	636	200	410
				100	2.10	210		
18 May	100	2.40	240				300	650
20 May				100	2.40	240	200	410

AVCO

The average costing method or cumulative weighted average pricing method calculates a **weighted average price** for all units in inventory. Issues are priced at this average cost, and the balance of inventory remaining would have the same unit valuation. The average price is determined by dividing the total cost by the total number of units.

A new weighted average price is calculated whenever a new delivery of materials into store is received. This is the key feature of cumulative weighted average pricing.

In our example, issue costs and closing inventory values would be as follows:

Date	Received Units	Issued Units	Balance Units	Total inventory value £	Unit cost £	£
Opening inventory			100	200	2.00	
3 May	400			840	2.10	
			* 500	1,040	2.08	
4 May		200		(416)	2.08	416
			300	624	2.08	
9 May	300			636	2.12	
			* 600	1,260	2.10	
11 May		400		(840)	2.10	840
			200	420	2.10	
18 May	100			240	2.40	
			* 300	660	2.20	
20 May		100		(220)	2.20	220
						1,476
Closing inventory value			200	440	2.20	440
						1,916

* A new inventory value per unit is calculated whenever a new receipt of materials occurs.

Notes

(a) The cost of materials issued plus the value of closing inventory equals the cost of purchases plus the value of opening inventory (£1,916).

(b) In a period of inflation, using the cumulative weighted average pricing system, the value of material issues will rise gradually, but will tend to lag a little behind the current market value at the date of issue. Closing inventory values will also be a little below current market value. The value of closing inventory is calculated using the latest average inventory value per unit.

The format of the AVCO Inventory record card is as follows:

	Purchases			Sales			Balance	
Date	**Quantity Units**	**Cost £**	**Total cost £**	**Quantity Units**	**Cost £**	**Total cost £**	**Quantity Units**	**Total cost £**
Balance at 1 May							100	200
3 May	400	2.10	840				500	1,040
4 May				200	2.08	416	300	624
9 May	300	2.12	636				600	1,260
11 May				400	2.10	840	200	420
18 May	100	2.40	240				300	660
20 May				100	2.20	220	200	440

Assessment focus point

Assessment questions may give you an inventory record card and ask you to identify which method is being used. Make sure you look at the basis on which the first **issue** has been made in the record.

Activity 4: CCS Ltd

The demand for a product is 150 units per month.

Charlotte's Country Soups Ltd (CCS) is a new business that has only been established since March 2009. The company makes a small range of specialist organic soups that it sells to supermarkets and independent retailers.

Prices of all the ingredients that the company has to buy are increasing. Bearing this in mind, CCS would like to use the inventory issue and valuation method that would give it the highest reported profit in its first year of trading.

Required

(a) Identify the method that would achieve this.

(b) Use the method identified in (a) to complete the inventory record card below.

Inventory record card for potatoes

Date	Receipts Quantity tonnes	Receipts Cost per tonne £	Receipts Total cost £	Issues Quantity tonnes	Issues Cost per tonne £	Issues Total cost £	Balance Quantity tonnes	Balance Total cost £
Balance as at: 1 June							72	10,512
2 June	70	150.00	10,500				142	21,012
3 June				90				
4 June	50	152.00						
5 June				70				

A business may choose to use FIFO, LIFO or AVCO but it is important that it uses a consistent inventory valuation policy and doesn't change it without good reason.

5 Inventory counting (stocktaking)

Another aspect of inventory control is the minimisation of inventory discrepancies. A major part of this is inventory counting: the counting of physical quantities of inventory. It is sometimes called an 'inventory count'. If the inventory count list does not match the stores ledger accounts then the differences should be investigated and the system tightened up where necessary.

Periodic inventory counting is usually carried out once per year with all inventory being counted on a particular day. Many businesses will use this method to actually establish an inventory figure for their annual accounts as they do not keep a perpetual (continuously updated) inventory.

Continuous inventory counting occurs on a year-round basis. A number of items are checked each week so that each inventory line will have been checked over the period of one year, while valuable or high-turnover items are checked more often. This method is run alongside a perpetual inventory system as updated inventory records are needed for checking. It also means that the inventory value shown in the records can be used in the financial accounts without the disruption that is often caused by a periodic inventory count.

Chapter summary

- Inventory movements are recorded in the materials control account.

- Direct materials issued to production are debited to the work in progress control account and indirect materials issued are debited to the production overhead control account.

- When a business holds inventories it will incur two main types of costs: the holding costs of that inventory and the ordering costs. The purpose of inventory control is to balance these two costs in order to minimise the overall cost of holding the inventory.

- With a JIT system, supplies are ordered and delivered just as they are needed for production, and goods are manufactured just as they are needed for sales.

- The reorder level for inventory is calculated to ensure that the inventory levels should never fall to zero during the lead time.

- The economic order quantity is the amount that should be ordered when each order is placed to ensure the minimisation of the overall cost of holding inventory.

- Often a business will set a minimum inventory level below which the inventory level should not be allowed to fall.

- The valuation of inventory normally requires an assumption to be made regarding the valuation method; this will be FIFO, LIFO or AVCO.

- In order to control the inventory that is held, businesses will regularly count their inventories and compare the physical quantity with the inventory records; any discrepancies should be investigated and corrected.

Keywords

- **AVCO (average cost):** A weighted average cost is calculated each time a delivery is received, subsequent issues and inventory on hand are valued at this cost

- **Economic order quantity (EOQ):** The amount to order each time in order to minimise inventory holding costs

- **FIFO (first in, first out):** Assumes that the earliest purchases or production are used first. Inventory on hand is valued at the latest prices, issues at earlier prices

- **Holding costs:** Costs of holding inventory, such as storage costs, cost of capital tied up, insurance, obsolescence and security

- **Inventory:** Goods held by the business as a current asset made up of raw materials, work in progress and finished goods

- **Inventory control:** The regulation of inventory levels so that the costs associated with inventory are kept to a minimum

- **Just-in-time (JIT):** A system where inventory is ordered only when it is needed for production, aiming for zero inventory levels

- **Lead time:** Time taken from an order being placed to the goods arriving

- **LIFO (last in, first out):** Assumes that the latest purchases are used first, inventory on hand is valued at earlier prices and issues are at the latest prices at the time of the issue

- **Materials control account:** Cost ledger account where inventory movements are recorded

- **Materials requisition:** A request for materials by the production department sent to the stores

- **Maximum inventory level:** The level above which inventory cannot be allowed to rise

- **Minimum inventory level:** The level below which inventory should not be allowed to fall as a general rule

- **Ordering costs:** Costs of ordering materials, such as administrative costs and transport inwards

- **Production overhead control account:** Cost ledger account for all production overheads

- **Reorder level:** The inventory level that triggers the placing of an order

- **Work in progress control account:** Cost ledger account where all the direct costs of production are gathered

Test your learning

1 **Using the:**

(a) **FIFO**

(b) **LIFO**

(c) **AVCO methods**

Calculate the cost of materials issues and the value of closing inventory using the information below. Enter your answer into the inventory record cards below. (For AVCO, work to the nearest penny.)

January 3	Balance	100 kg	Valued @ £8.80 per kg
January 16	GRN 423	400 kg	Invoiced @ £9.00 per kg
January 27	Materials requisition 577	250 kg	
February 5	Materials requisition 582	180 kg	
February 9	GRN 439	400 kg	Invoiced @ £9.30 per kg
February 17	Materials requisition 589	420 kg	
February 25	GRN 446	500 kg	Invoiced @ £9.35 per kg

(a) **FIFO**

	Inventory record card							
	Purchases			Requisitions			Balance	
Date	Quantity kg	Cost £	Total cost £	Quantity kg	Cost £	Total cost £	Quantity kg	Total cost £
3 Jan								
16 Jan								
27 Jan								
5 Feb								
9 Feb								
17 Feb								
25 Feb								

(b) **LIFO**

	Inventory Record Card							
	Purchases			Requisitions			Balance	
Date	Quantity kg	Cost £	Total cost £	Quantity kg	Cost £	Total cost £	Quantity kg	Total cost £
3 Jan								
16 Jan								
27 Jan								
5 Feb								
9 Feb								
17 Feb								
25 Feb								

(c) **AVCO**

	Inventory Record Card							
	Purchases			Requisitions			Balance	
Date	Quantity kg	Cost £	Total cost £	Quantity kg	Cost £	Total cost £	Quantity kg	Total cost £
3 Jan								
16 Jan								
27 Jan								
5 Feb								
9 Feb								
17 Feb								
25 Feb								

2 On 1 March a business has £12,400 of materials inventories. During March there were £167,200 of purchases and issues to production totalling £160,400. There were also £8,300 of indirect materials issued to the factory.

Write up the cost ledger accounts to reflect the month's transactions.

Materials control account

	Detail	£			£

Work in progress control account

		£			£

Production overhead control account

		£			£

3 Eagle Printing Company Limited print posters for which they buy paper on rolls. Each roll costs £12.00. Each week, 15 rolls are used; the company operates every week of the year. Each time an order for more rolls of paper is placed, it costs the company £50.00, and the estimated cost of storing one roll is £19.65 per annum.

You are required to calculate the EOQ.

☐ rolls

4 Kestrel Limited experiences a lead time of 4–8 days for orders of paint. Paint usage is between 150 and 200 litres per day.

What would be a suitable reorder level?

☐ litres

5   XYZ Co had an opening inventory value of £880 (275 units valued at £3.20 each) on 1 April.

The following receipts and issues were recorded during April.

8 April	Receipts	600 units @ £3.00 per unit
15 April	Receipts	400 units @ £3.40 per unit
30 April	Issues	900 units

Using the FIFO method, the total value of the issues on 30 April is

£ [ ]

6   2,400 units of component C, valued at a price of £6 each, were in inventory on 1 March. The following receipts and issues were recorded during March.

3 March	Received	4,000 units @ £6.20 per unit
12 March	Received	2,000 units @ £6.86 per unit
23 March	Issued	5,100 units

Using the weighted average price method of inventory valuation, the total value of the components remaining in inventory on 23 March was

£ [ ]

7   2,400 units of component C, valued at a price of £6 each, were in inventory on 1 March. The following receipts and issues were recorded during March.

3 March	Received	4,000 units @ £6.20 per unit
12 March	Received	2,000 units @ £6.86 per unit
23 March	Issued	5,100 units

Using the FIFO method of inventory valuation, the total value of the components issued on 23 March was £ [ ] (to the nearest £)

Labour costs

4

2	Apply techniques required for dealing with costs
2.1	Record and calculate materials, labour and overhead costs
	• Calculate direct labour costs per unit of production or service • Calculate overtime premiums and bonuses • Complete timesheets and pay calculations (including overtime and bonus) • Calculate direct labour cost per equivalent finished production

Assessment context

As with materials costs, the labour cost within a manufacturing or a service environment is a key area of the syllabus. You can expect to see questions on this topic in your computer based assessment.

Qualification context

This is an introductory chapter and includes basic control mechanisms that a company can use for labour costs and expenses.

Business context

Most businesses employ labour and labour can be a significant cost. It is therefore important for the management accountant to understand labour costs.

Chapter overview

Labour costs

Time based systems

- Hourly wage rate = direct cost
- Overtime premium for more than basic hour = an indirect cost

  Unless:
  - Specific requests for particular job
  - Regular/usual occurrence
- Paid absence = unproductive time = indirect cost
- Idle time/unproductive hours

Non-productive hours hourly rate = Cost of idle time = an indirect cost

Bonus/incentives for time based systems

- To promote efficiency and productivity
- Time saved bonus
- Discretionary bonus
- Group bonus
- Profit sharing scheme

Piecework systems

- Wages calculated on number of units/items produced
- Guaranteed minimum wage
- Rates of pay depending on levels of production: differential piecework

Introduction

The principle of recording and controlling costs incurred by a business, already demonstrated in respect of materials, also applies to labour costs. Businesses will normally require a system capable of analysing both labour times and costs. Labour costs include the gross pay of the employee, employer's national insurance, training costs and benefits such as company cars. All employees will give rise to labour costs. Office workers in administration departments, canteen staff, maintenance staff and supervisory staff are examples of **indirect labour**. **Direct labour** costs arise from the employees that work directly on the goods produced by a manufacturing business, or employees that provide the service in a service business.

1 Remuneration methods

1.1 Time based system using a time-rate

A **time-rate** means that a basic amount is paid per hour worked. So wages are determined by the number of hours worked.

Wages = Hours worked × Basic rate of pay per hour

If an employee works more than their basic hours they may be paid an **overtime premium**.

Attendance records usually take the form of **timesheets**. These can be completed by the employee or compiled from **clock cards** that record time in and out.

If employees are working on specific jobs then attendance is sometimes recorded directly on **job cards** rather than timesheets.

If a worker is directly involved in production, their basic hourly rate is always a direct cost when they are working on production.

1.2 Overtime

An overtime premium is the amount paid to an employee over and above the basic hourly wage. For example, if an employee is normally paid £7.50 per hour but is paid £10.00 per hour during **overtime,** the premium is £2.50.

An overtime premium is normally treated as an indirect cost (overhead).

The two exceptions are:

- The overtime is worked at the specific request of a customer for a particular job. In this case the overtime premium is treated as a direct cost of the job.

- The overtime is worked regularly by the production department. In this case the overtime premium may be treated as a usual occurrence and incorporated into an average hourly rate.

Note that in your assessment you may be told exactly how to treat overtime premiums so read the requirements carefully.

Activity 1: Overtime premium

Mark worked from 8am until 5pm with a one-hour lunch break. His normal hours are 9am–5pm with a one-hour lunch break. His basic wage is £15 per hour and overtime is paid at time and a half.

Required

Calculate the basic pay, overtime premium and Mark's total wage for the day.

Basic pay   £ [ ]

Overtime premium   £ [ ]

Mark's total wage   £ [ ]   for the day

Activity 2: Job 146

The following data relates to job 146:

Total direct labour hours worked	45,000
Basic hours	12,000
Basic wage rate	£7 per hour
Overtime premium	25%

Required

Calculate the direct labour cost of job 146, assuming that overtime is worked at the specific request of the customer.

Basic pay   £ [ ]

Overtime premium   £ [ ]

Direct labour cost of Job 146 is   £ [ ]

Activity 3: Component C

The following information relates to skilled direct labour costs incurred in producing 500,000 units of Component C during January 20X6:

Normal time hours worked = 5,000 hours

Overtime at time and a half worked = 2,000 hours

Overtime at double time worked = 1,000 hours

Normal time hourly rate = £10 per hour

Overtime premiums paid are included as part of direct labour cost.

Required

(a) Calculate the correct total cost of direct labour used to produce Component C in January 20X6.

(b) Calculate the direct labour cost per unit.

(a)	Total cost of direct labour	£	

(b)	Direct labour cost per unit	£	

1.3 Idle time

Idle time arises if employees are paid an hourly rate but some of the hours for which they are paid are non-productive. For example, if there is a machine breakdown the workers will still be paid but will be unable to work.

Idle time may be recorded separately on timesheets or separate idle time cards may be produced.

The cost of idle time is always treated as an indirect cost (overhead).

1.4 Piecework systems

Under a **piecework** system, wages are calculated on the number of units/items produced. It is usual for pieceworkers to be guaranteed a minimum wage.

Different rates of pay may apply to different levels of production. This is known as **differential piecework**.

The amount pieceworkers produce is recorded on a piecework ticket or an operation card. It may record total units produced and number of rejects.

Activity 4: Piecework system

Simon sews pockets in a tailoring factory. He is paid 10p for every pocket sewn up to a total of 4,000 in one week. Thereafter, he receives an extra 2p per pocket for every extra 500 he sews. So 4,500 pockets would include 4,000 pockets at 10p and 500 at 12p. 4,501 pockets would include 4,000 pockets at 10p, 500 at 12p and 1 at 14p. One week he sews 4,730 pockets.

Required

What will his gross pay be in that week?

Gross pay for the week   £ [   ]

Workings

Activity 5: Remuneration systems

For each of the statements in the table below, one of the highlighted words will relate to the **time rate** remuneration system and the other to the piecework rate remuneration system.

Required

Write the appropriate words in the appropriate boxes.

	Time rate	Piecework rate
Easy/complicated to calculate an employee's pay		
Can/can't be used for all direct labour employees		
More efficient workers are paid **more than/the same as** less efficient workers		
The quality of the goods produced **is/is not** affected by workers being tempted to rush a job so that they earn more		
The employees' pay **fluctuates/remains the same** if output fluctuates		
More supervisors/more inspectors may be needed for this system		
Production problems **can/cannot** lead to a cut in pay		
Systems **do/do not** need to be set up to check the amount of work produced by each employee		

1.5 Bonus and incentive schemes

These schemes were introduced to incentivise workers paid under a time based system who, unlike pieceworkers, could not increase their pay by being more efficient. The main aim of all these schemes is to increase productivity.

Examples of bonus schemes include:

- Time saved bonus
- Discretionary bonus
- Group bonus
- Profit sharing scheme

If a bonus is directly attributable to a particular cost unit then it should be treated as a direct cost. Otherwise it should be treated as an indirect cost.

A standard working week at Tristan Ltd is 37.5 hours. Any hours worked over and above the standard working week are paid at time and a half. All overtime is worked at the specific request of a customer.

The hourly wage rate is £8.50.

The expected production rate is 24 units per hour. In any one day if this target is exceeded the employee receives a bonus equal to half the hourly rate for the additional hours' worth of production. Bonuses cannot be directly attributed to a particular cost unit.

Required

Complete the following wages calculation sheet, calculating for each day the overtime payment, the bonus payable and the total wages for the day, and calculate the total wages payable for the week. Work to two decimal places.

Wages calculation sheet

Employee name: James Declan
Clock number: H63
Week beginning: 9 June 20X6

	Mon	Tues	Wed	Thurs	Fri	Total
Hours worked	7.5	8.0	9.0	8.5	9.5	
Standard pay						
Overtime hours						
Overtime payment						
Units produced	191	197	225	204	245	
Extra units						
Bonus payable						
Total payable for the day						

Total wages payable for the week:

	£
Direct wages	
Indirect wages	
Total wages	

1.6 Absence

If an employee is absent but still paid there is a cost relating to the unproductive time. Since it does not relate to the production of any specific units it should be treated as an indirect cost.

2 Recording labour costs

2.1 Timesheets

Assessment focus point

You may be asked to complete a timesheet in the assessment. This will normally take the form of a timesheet that has been filled in with hours worked, and you will be expected to complete it with calculations of pay and overtime or bonus payments. Let's look at an example here.

Illustration 1: Basic pay, overtime and bonus

There are six employees in department A who are paid a basic rate of £15 per hour. Overtime is paid as follows:

Overtime rate 1 – basic pay plus 50%

Overtime rate 2 – basic pay plus 100%

Department A employees receive a bonus of 10% of basic pay for every unit produced in excess of 2,000 units. During the period, they produced 2,500 units.

All employees work the same number of hours and all overtime and bonuses are included as part of the direct labour cost.

(a) Complete the gaps in the table below to calculate the total labour cost for department A.

Labour cost	Hours	£
Basic pay	600	
Overtime rate 1	50	
Overtime rate 2	40	
Total cost before bonus	690	
Bonus payment		
Total cost including bonus		

(b) **What is the total labour cost per unit for the period?**

£ _____

(c) **The basic pay and overtime for each employee of department A for the period was** £ _____ **and the bonus payable to to each employee was £**

(a) Basic pay: 600 × £15 = £9,000
Overtime rate 1: 50 × £15 × 150% = £1,125

Overtime rate 2: 40 × £15 × 200% = £1,200

Total cost before bonus: £9,000 + £1,125 + £1,200 = £11,325

Bonus payment: (2,500 – 2,000) × £15 × 10% = £750

Total cost including bonus: £11,325 + £750 = £12,075

(b) Total labour cost per unit = £12,075/2,500 units = £4.83

(c) The basic pay and overtime for each employee was £11,325/6 = £1,887.50

The bonus payable to each employee was £750/6 = £125.00

Illustration 2: Weekly time sheet

Rubble Industries pay their employees basic and overtime pay under the following arrangement:

For a basic seven-hour shift every day from Monday to Friday – basic pay.

For any overtime in excess of the basic seven hours, on any day from Monday to Friday – the extra hours are paid at time and a half (basic pay plus an overtime premium equal to half of basic pay).

For three contracted hours each Saturday morning – basic pay.

For any hours in excess of three hours on Saturday – the extra hours are paid at double time (basic pay plus an overtime premium equal to basic pay).

For any hours worked on Sunday – paid at double time (basic pay plus an overtime premium equal to basic pay).

Complete the columns headed Basic pay, Overtime premium and Total pay.

(**Note.** Zero figures should be entered in cells where appropriate; overtime pay is the premium amount paid for the extra hours worked.)

Employee's weekly timesheet for week ending 5 April

Employee: F. Flintstone   **Profit Centre**: Stone carving

Employee number: P450   **Basic pay per hour**: £12.00

	Hours spent on production	Hours worked on indirect work	Notes	Basic pay £	Overtime premium £	Total pay £
Monday	5	2	10am–12am Polishing rock drill			
Tuesday	3	4	9am–1pm HR awareness course			
Wednesday	8					
Thursday	7					
Friday	6	1	3pm–4pm health and safety training			
Saturday	4					
Sunday	1					
Total	**34**	**7**				

The hours recorded in the timesheet can be used to calculate F. Flintstone's pay for the week.

Employee's weekly timesheet for week ending 5 April

| **Employee:** F. Flintstone | | | | **Profit Centre:** Stone carving | | |
| **Employee number:** P450 | | | | **Basic pay per hour:** £12.00 | | |

	Hours spent on production	Hours worked on indirect work	Notes	Basic pay £	Overtime premium £	Total pay £
Monday	5	2	10am–12am Polishing rock drill	84	–	84
Tuesday	3	4	9am–1pm HR awareness course	84	–	84
Wednesday	8			96	6	102
Thursday	7			84	–	84
Friday	6	1	3pm–4pm health and safety training	84	–	84
Saturday	4			48	12	60
Sunday	1			12	12	24
Total	**34**	**7**		492	30	522

3 The wages control account

Payroll is a record showing each employee's gross pay, net pay and deductions such as PAYE, national insurance and pensions. There is also usually an analysis, which is used for cost accounting purposes. The payroll analysis can analyse gross pay by department, class of labour and product, and be broken down into various constituents such as direct, indirect and idle time.

A wages control account is used to record the payroll costs. Obviously, the amount debited as the wages expense will be the gross pay, as this will be the cost to the business and the cost that needs to be used for costing purposes. However, the constituents of gross pay will be posted separately to the wages control account.

- Net pay is posted from the cash book.
- Deductions are debited with the credit entries being recorded in payables accounts until the amounts are due to be paid to the HMRC/pension scheme.

The credits to the wages control account are:

- Direct labour (debited to WIP)
- Indirect production labour (debited to a production overheads account)
- Administration labour (debited to a non-production overheads account)

Illustration 3: Wages control account

Gilchrist Chemicals has on its payroll records the following details for the month of June.

	£
Net pay	100,000
PAYE and NIC deductions	25,000
Contributions to company welfare scheme	15,000
Gross pay	140,000

The payroll analysis shows that £110,000 relates to direct labour and £30,000 is for indirect labour.

These details are recorded in the wages control account as follows.

Wages control account

	£		£
Bank	100,000	WIP	110,000
HM Revenue & Customs	25,000	Production o/h	30,000
Welfare scheme contributions	15,000		
	140,000		140,000

The other sides of the entries are added to the materials entries in the work in progress control account and the production overheads control account.

Work in progress control account

		£		£
30 June	Materials control	69,200		
30 June	Wages control	110,000		

Production overhead control

		£		£
30 June	Materials control	3,600		
30 June	Wages control	30,000		

You will notice that the wages control account has no balance carried down as it simply shares out the total gross wage cost between direct and indirect labour costs. The other two accounts will not yet be balanced as there would be overhead expenses still to enter.

Chapter summary

- Remuneration methods generally fall into one of the following categories:

  - Time rate   - Bonus system

  - Piecework   - Salary

- Employees record their attendance times on attendance records, signing-in books or clock cards.

- Job costing requires more detailed records of time spent on each job, and this is recorded on a timesheet or a job card.

- Piecework is recorded on a piecework ticket (or operation card).

- The wages control account records payroll costs. These may also be charged to the work in progress control account and production overhead control account in a manufacturing business.

Keywords

- **Bonus system:** The payment of an amount in addition to the time rate or salary if a target is exceeded
- **Clock card:** A card for each employee that records the start and finish times of periods of work
- **Differential piecework:** The piecework rate increases for additional units over and above a pre-set quantity
- **Job card:** Details the task to be performed on a particular job, and follows the job round; each employee records the time spent on their operation on the job
- **Overtime:** A higher rate of pay if hours worked in a week exceed a pre-set limit
- **Overtime premium:** The additional cost of overtime hours above the basic rate
- **Payroll:** Record showing each employee's gross pay, net pay and deductions
- **Piecework:** An amount paid for each unit or task successfully completed
- **Salary:** The payment of a set amount at agreed intervals, usually weekly or monthly
- **Timesheet:** A form completed by an employee detailing the time spent on each client's work each day, or week
- **Time rate:** A basic amount paid per hour

Test your learning

1   Cockerel Breakfast Cereals Limited pays a time rate of £7 per hour for a 35-hour week. Overtime is paid at time and a half for time worked in excess of 7 hours on weekdays, and double time for any work done at the weekend.

Calculate the gross pay of the employees whose clock card information is summarised below.

Hours worked				
	J. Sparrow	**K. Finch**	**M. Swallow**	**B. Cuckoo**
Monday	7	7	7.25	7
Tuesday	7	8	7	7
Wednesday	7.5	7	7.5	7
Thursday	8	8	7.5	7.5
Friday	7	7.5	7.5	7
Saturday	3		2	2

	J. Sparrow	**K. Finch**	**M. Swallow**	**B. Cuckoo**
Total hours				
Total basic pay				
Time and a half				
Double time				
Total gross pay				

2   John Gosse is a direct worker who operates a lathe. During one week he works 40 hours, 35 of which are paid at a time rate of £10 per hour, the remainder being overtime which is paid at a premium of £4 per hour.

Calculate the direct and indirect labour cost.

Direct labour cost   £ [   ]

Indirect labour cost   £ [   ]

3   Alpha Industries pay their employees basic and overtime pay under the following arrangement:

For a basic six-hour shift every day from Monday to Friday – basic pay.

For any overtime in excess of the basic six hours, on any day from Monday to Friday – the extra hours are paid at time and a half (basic pay plus an overtime premium equal to half of basic pay).

For four contracted hours each Saturday morning – basic pay.

For any hours in excess of four hours on Saturday – the extra hours are paid at double time (basic pay plus an overtime premium equal to basic pay).

For any hours worked on Sunday – paid at double time (basic pay plus an overtime premium equal to basic pay).

Complete the columns headed Basic pay, Overtime premium and Total pay.

Note. Zero figures should be entered in cells where appropriate; overtime pay is the premium amount paid for the extra hours worked.

Employee's weekly timesheet for week ending 5 April

Employee: M. Rooney			**Profit centre:** Widget carving			
Employee number: A450			**Basic pay per hour:** £10.00			
	Hours spent on production	**Hours worked on indirect work**	**Notes**	**Basic pay £**	**Overtime premium £**	**Total pay £**
Monday	6	2	10am–12am Machine calibration			
Tuesday	2	4	9am–1pm HR awareness course			
Wednesday	8					
Thursday	6					
Friday	6	1	3pm–4pm Customer care training			
Saturday	6					
Sunday	3					
Total	**37**	**7**				

4   X Co has recorded the following wages costs for direct production workers for November.

Basic pay	£70,800
Overtime premium	£2,000
Gross wages	£72,800

The overtime was not worked for any specific job.

The accounting entries for these wages would be (tick the correct answer):

☐	DEBIT	Work in progress control account	£72,800	
	CREDIT	Wages control account		£72,800
☐	DEBIT	Wages control account	£72,800	
	CREDIT	Work in progress control account		£72,800
☐	DEBIT	Wages control account	£72,800	
	CREDIT	Overhead control account		£2,000
	CREDIT	Wages control account		£70,800
☐	DEBIT	Work in progress control account	£70,800	
	DEBIT	Overhead control account	£2,000	
	CREDIT	Wages control account		£72,800

5   Darren paints vases in a pottery. He is paid 50p for every vase painted up to a total of 400 in one week. Thereafter, he receives an extra 20p per additional vase up to 100 additional vases; his rate further increases by 20p for each 50 further vases. One week he paints 530 vases.

What will his gross pay be in that week?

£ [   ]

Allocation and apportionment

5

Learning outcomes

3	Apportion costs according to organisational requirements
3.1	Calculate and use overhead costs
	Different methods of indirect cost allocation, apportionment or absorption Attribute overhead costs to production and service cost centres: • Allocation versus apportionment • Direct method • Step down method

Assessment context

Absorption costing is a core topic and you should expect one or two tasks/questions on this area in the computer based test.

Qualification context

Overhead treatment is assumed knowledge for Level 4 *Management Accounting* units. Specific comparisons of absorption costing with activity based costing scenarios are a likely assessment question at the higher level.

Business context

Every business needs to understand and control its costs. Overhead costs can sometimes be a very large proportion of a business's total costs.

Chapter overview

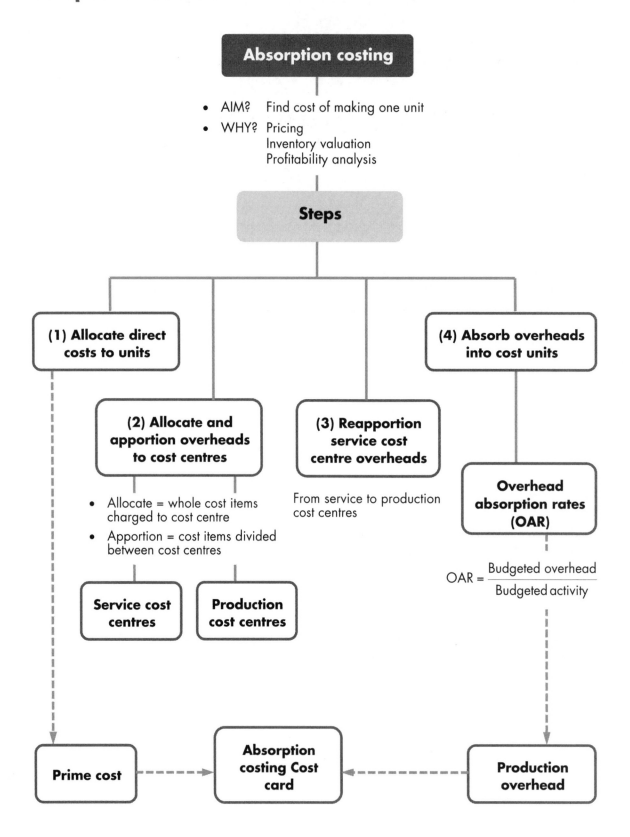

Absorption costing

- AIM? Find cost of making one unit
- WHY? Pricing
        Inventory valuation
        Profitability analysis

Steps

(1) Allocate direct costs to units

(2) Allocate and apportion overheads to cost centres

- Allocate = whole cost items charged to cost centre
- Apportion = cost items divided between cost centres

Service cost centres

Production cost centres

(3) Reapportion service cost centre overheads

From service to production cost centres

(4) Absorb overheads into cost units

Overhead absorption rates (OAR)

$$OAR = \frac{Budgeted\ overhead}{Budgeted\ activity}$$

Prime cost

Absorption costing Cost card

Production overhead

Overheads and absorption costing

- All production costs used to compute value of cost units

↓

Total production costs

Direct cost	+	Indirect cost

- Direct materials x kg of material at £y per kg
- Direct labour x hrs of labour at £y per hour

Cost centres

PRODUCTION CENTRES
(manufacture units)

SERVICE CENTRES
(support/service the production cost centres)

Reapportion
- Direct method
- Step-down method

COST UNIT

Introduction

One of the key functions of a management accountant is costing. This involves calculating the cost to produce one unit. There are different techniques which can be applied to calculate this information. Chapters 5 and 6 will consider one of the key techniques of absorption costing.

AIM?   To find the cost of making one unit

WHY?   Pricing
        Inventory valuation
        Profitability analysis

HOW?   **Absorption costing** (this chapter and the next chapter)
        OR
        Activity based costing (next chapter)
        OR
        Marginal costing (later chapters)

Under absorption costing, a 'full' production cost per unit is calculated by including both direct production costs and an element of indirect production costs (production overheads).

1 Absorption costing

1.1 Overheads

From previous chapters, we know that the three types of indirect cost are often considered in total and called overheads.

Overheads = Indirect materials + Indirect labour + Indirect expenses

Overheads tend to be grouped as to their function:

- **Production (or factory) overheads** include indirect materials, indirect factory wages, factory rent and rates, and power and light used in the factory

- Non-production overheads:

    - **Administration overheads** include office rent and rates, office salaries, indirect office materials and depreciation of office equipment that is used for administration (rather than the main activity of the business)

    - **Selling and distribution overheads** include delivery costs, salaries of sales staff and depreciation of delivery vehicles

    - **Finance overheads** are bank interest and charges

In most cost accounting systems the aim will be to find the full production cost of the cost units. This means that a method, such as absorption costing, has to be used to include the **production overheads only** in the cost of each cost unit.

Since production overheads are not identified with specific cost units, a process must be followed to charge a share of the total production overhead to each cost unit.

2 Absorption costing overview

Absorption costing uses several stages to attach overhead costs to units of activity. By the final stage, which is absorption, an overhead absorption rate (OAR) is calculated which is used to absorb overheads into cost units. In this way, all cost units have an additional overhead charged to them.

2.1 Method

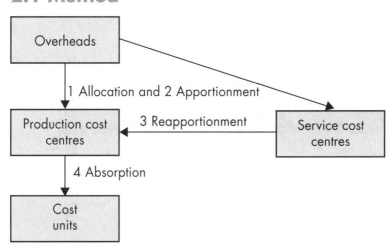

To calculate the overhead cost per unit there are four steps:

(1) **Allocation** – this is where total overheads are charged to the relevant cost centre in full.

(2) **Apportionment** – overheads are shared across each cost centre using a fair basis.

(3) **Reapportionment** – all service cost centre overheads are shared out between the production cost centres.

(4) **Absorption** – Production cost centre overheads are 'absorbed' into cost units using a suitable basis.

3 Allocation and apportionment

3.1 Allocation

Allocation of overheads is the charging of an overhead to a single responsibility centre that has incurred the whole of that overhead. For example, the cost of a supervisor could be allocated to the department supervised and the depreciation of the warehouse could be allocated to the warehouse directly.

Remember that a responsibility centre is a function or department of an organisation that is headed by a manager who has direct responsibility for its performance.

Responsibility centres include cost centres, profit centres and investment centres. The process of absorption costing usually focuses on cost centres.

Assessment focus point

Assessment questions may ask you to look at a list of costs for a business and decide whether they can be allocated to particular cost centres.

Activity 1: Allocation

Below are some overhead costs for a business for last month. This business includes a cost centre for department A and a cost centre for department B.

Required

Using the picklist, decide whether the indirect costs can be allocated or not, and which cost centre they should be allocated to.

Cost		
Wages of the supervisor of department A		▼
Wages of the supervisor of department B		▼
Indirect materials consumed in department A		▼
Rent of the factory shared by departments A and B		▼

Picklist

Allocate to department A
Allocate to department B
Cannot be allocated

3.2 Apportionment

As you saw in Activity 1, not all overheads can be allocated to a particular cost centre. For costs that cannot be allocated, we use apportionment.

Apportionment of overheads is the charging of a proportion of an overhead to each responsibility centre that incurs part of the overhead. For example, rent of a business premises might need to be shared between the various departments making up the business. When apportioning overheads the basis used should ensure that the share charged to a cost centre reflects its usage of that overhead. This means that each type of overhead needs to be considered separately to find a suitable basis.

Examples of commonly used methods are given in the table below.

Overhead	Suitable basis for apportionment
Buildings costs such as rent, rates, repairs, insurance, heating and lighting	Floor area or volume of space occupied by the cost centre
Canteen costs	Number of employees using the cost centre
Equipment costs such as insurance and depreciation	Cost or net book value of equipment (carrying amount of equipment)
Maintenance costs	Amount of usage of maintenance department

Assessment focus point

Assessment questions may ask you to look at a list of costs for a business and decide what the best basis of apportionment is.

Activity 2: Apportionment bases

Below are some overhead costs for a business for last month.

Required

Using the picklist, choose the most appropriate basis of apportionment for each cost.

Cost	Basis of apportionment
Rent, rates and insurance	▼
Light, heat and power	▼
Depreciation charge of machinery	▼
Canteen costs	▼

Picklist

Carrying amount
Floor space (square metres)
Number of employees

Illustration 1: Apportionment

McQueen Co has incurred the following overhead costs.

	£000
Depreciation of factory	100
Factory repairs and maintenance	60
Factory office costs (treat as production overhead)	150
Depreciation of equipment	80
Insurance of equipment	20
Heating	39
Lighting	10
Employee welfare	90
	549

Information relating to the production and service departments in the factory is as follows.

	Department				
	Production 1	Production 2	Service 100	Service 101	Totals
Floor space (square metres)	1,200	1,600	800	400	4,000
Volume (cubic metres)	3,000	6,000	2,400	1,600	13,000
Number of employees	30	30	15	15	90
Book value of equipment	£30,000	£20,000	£10,000	£20,000	£80,000

Required

Determine how the overhead costs should be apportioned between the four departments.

Solution

Costs are apportioned using the following general formula.

$$\frac{\text{Value of apportionment base of cost centre}}{\text{Total value of apportionment base}} \times \text{Total overhead cost}$$

For example, heating for department 1 = $\frac{3,000}{13,000} \times £39 = £9$

Item of cost	Basis of apportionment	Total cost	To department			
			1	2	100	101
		£000	£000	£000	£000	£000
Factory depreciation	(floor area)	100.0	30.0*	40.0	20.0	10.0
Factory repairs	(floor area)	60.0	18.0	24.0	12.0	6.0
Factory office costs	(number of employees)	150.0	50.0	50.0	25.0	25.0
Equipment depreciation	(book value)	80.0	30.0	20.0	10.0	20.0
Equipment insurance	(book value)	20.0	7.5	5.0	2.5	5.0
Heating	(volume)	39.0	9.0	18.0	7.2	4.8
Lighting	(floor area)	10.0	3.0	4.0	2.0	1.0
Employee welfare	(number of employees)	90.0	30.0	30.0	15.0	15.0
Total		549.0	177.5	191.0	93.7	86.8

$* \dfrac{\text{Value of apportionment base of cost centre}}{\text{Total value of apportionment base}} \times \text{Total overhead cost}$

$\dfrac{1,200}{4,000} \times 100 = £30 \qquad \dfrac{1,600}{4,000} \times 100 = £40 \qquad \dfrac{800}{4,000} \times 100 = £20 \qquad \dfrac{400}{4,000} \times 100 = £10$

Assessment focus point

Assessment questions may ask you to look at a list of costs for a business and decide whether they can be allocated to particular cost centres, or whether they need to be apportioned to cost centres.

Activity 3: Allocation and apportionment basis

Required

Match the overhead with an appropriate basis for allocation and/or apportionment.

Overhead	Basis of apportionment
Rent/rates	Number of employees
Depreciation	Volume of space occupied/floor area
Staff canteen costs	Floor area
Heat, light	Value of equipment insured
Insurance of equipment	Allocate to stores cost centre
Stores costs	NBV or cost of equipment

Activity 4: Overhead apportionment

A company has incurred the following overhead costs for a period:

	£
Factory rent	20,000
Factory heat	5,040
Processing department – supervisor	15,000
Packing department – supervisor	10,000
Depreciation of equipment	7,000
Factory canteen expenses	18,000
Welfare costs of factory employees	5,000
	80,040

Suitable cost centres in the company:

Processing department

Packing department

Canteen

	Processing dept £	Packing dept £	Canteen £
Cubic space	50,000 m³	25,000 m³	5,000 m³
NBV equipment	£300,000	£300,000	£100,000
Number of employees	50	40	10

Required

Allocate and apportion the overhead costs incurred to the three cost centres using the most suitable basis.

	Basis	Processing dept £	Packing dept £	Canteen £	Total £
Canteen					
Processing dept supervisor					
Packing dept supervisor					
Rent					
Heat					
Depreciation					
Welfare					
Total					

4 Reapportionment

The initial allocation or apportionment will be to production and service cost centres. However, only the production departments manufacture units, which means all the overheads must be charged to these departments only. Reapportionment is the process of removing all overheads from the service cost centres and splitting them on a suitable basis between the production cost centres.

Where there is more than one service cost centre, any work performed for one another (inter service department work) must be split appropriately.

There are two methods to approach this which are assessable in this unit:

(a) Apportion costs of each service department to production departments only. This ignores any work that the service department do for each other (**the direct method**).

(b) Apportion the costs of each service department to production but also allow one service department to allocate costs to the other service department (**the step-down method**).

Illustration 2: Reapportionment

Let's look at each method individually and see how the reapportionment is achieved.

A company has two production and two service departments (Stores and Maintenance). The following information about activity in the most recent costing period is available.

	Total £	Components shop £	Assembly dept £	Stores £	Maintenance £
Overheads	51,950	24,975	16,925	3,100	6,950

Direct reapportionment

Suppose the Maintenance and Stores departments do no work for each other. This enables us to use the direct method as all the service department costs are incurred in servicing the production departments. All we have to do is find a suitable basis for reapportioning each service cost centre's costs. For Stores, the number or value of materials requisitions could be used. For Maintenance, we could use the number of hours worked or the value of machinery.

Budgeted use of service cost centres:

	By the Components shop	By the Assembly department
Number of materials requisitions from Stores	750	200
Maintenance hours required	300	120

The final apportionment to production cost centres will be as follows.

	Total £	Components shop £	Assembly dept £	Stores £	Maintenance £
Overheads	51,950	24,975	16,925	3,100	6,950
Reapportion maintenance					
300:120 (W1)		**4,964**	**1,986**		**(6,950)**
(hours required as above)					
Reapportion stores					
750:200 (W2)		**2,447**	**653**	**(3,100)**	
(materials requisitions					
as above)	51,950	32,386	19,564	–	–

The total overheads of £51,950 have been apportioned to the two production cost centres, and the figures are now ready for the third stage of the process of finding the overhead cost per unit or absorption.

Workings

		£
1	£6,950 × 300/(300 + 120) =	4,964
	£6,950 × 120/(300 + 120) =	1,986
		6,950

		£
2	£3,100 × 750/(750 + 200) =	2,447
	£3,100 × 200/(750 + 200) =	653
		3,100

The step-down method

This time, let's assume that Maintenance makes use of Stores by requisitioning spare parts for machinery and other materials, but Stores does not use the services of Maintenance at all.

Budgeted use of service cost centres:

	By the Components shop	By the Assembly department	By Maintenance
Number of materials requisitions from Stores	750	200	50
Maintenance hours required	300	120	

The step-down method is appropriate in this case, which means that we must give some thought to which department is reapportioned first. If we empty Maintenance first, when we reapportion Stores costs we will put some costs back into Maintenance, as a charge for the services provided by Stores. Therefore it is more efficient to do Stores first, and then Maintenance, as no further reapportionment will be necessary.

	Total £	Components shop £	Assembly dept £	Stores £	Maintenance £
Overheads	51,950	24,975	16,925	3,100	6,950
Reapportion stores first					
750:200:50 (W1)		**2,325**	**620**	**(3,100)**	**155**
(materials requisitions)					7,105
Reapportion maintenance next					
300:120 (W2)		**5,075**	**2,030**		**(7,105)**
(maintenance hours)					
	51,950	32,375	19,575	–	–

Notes

1   Stores are reapportioned first as some costs will go to Maintenance too.
2   Maintenance costs are reapportioned **after** Stores costs are added in.

Workings

		£
1	£3,100 × 750/(750 + 200 + 50) =	2,325
	£3,100 × 200/(750 + 200 + 50) =	620
	£3,100 × 50/(750 + 200 + 50) =	155
		3,100
2	£7,105 × 300/(300 + 120) =	5,075
	£7,105 × 120/(300 + 120) =	2,030
		7,105

Assessment focus point

Assessment questions may ask you to reapportion service centre costs to production cost centres.

Activity 5: Overhead reapportionment – Direct method

Using the following data, reapportion the overheads of Stores and Maintenance and General administration overheads to production departments X and Y using the direct method.

	Production		Service centres		
	X £	Y £	Stores £	Maintenance £	General administration overheads £
Allocated & Apportioned overheads	70,000	30,000	20,000	15,000	6,000
Value of machinery	8,000	7,000			

- 62.5% of the stores department's time is spent on production department X. The remaining time is spent on production department Y.

- The maintenance costs are to be apportioned between the production departments on the basis of value of machinery.

- General administration overheads are to be apportioned equally between the two production departments.

Direct method

	Production depts			Service centres	
	X **£**	**Y** **£**	**Stores** **£**	**Maintenance** **£**	**General admin overheads** **£**
Overheads					
Reapportion Stores					
Reapportion Maintenance					
Reapportion general admin overheads					
Total					

Activity 6: Overhead reapportionment
– step down method

Using the following data, reapportion the overheads of Stores and Canteen to production departments X and Y using the step-down method starting with Stores

	Production		Service centre	
	X **£**	**Y** **£**	**Stores** **£**	**Canteen** **£**
Allocated & Apportioned overheads	70,000	30,000	20,000	15,000
Number of employees	45	50	5	–

- 50% of the stores department's time is spent on production department X. 30% of stores department's time is spent on production department Y. 20% is spent on canteen.

- The canteen costs are to be apportioned between the production departments on the basis of number of employees.

Step-down method

	Production depts		Service centre	
	X £	Y £	Stores £	Canteen £
Allocated overhead				
Apportion stores				
Apportion canteen				
Total				

We have now covered allocation, apportionment and reapportionment. We will look at absorption in the next chapter.

Chapter summary

- Absorption costing is a method used to charge an appropriate amount of production overheads to cost units.

- Some overheads can be allocated to a cost centre, others have to be apportioned or split between a number of cost centres.

- The first step in absorption costing is allocation. Allocation is the process by which whole cost items are charged direct to a cost unit or cost centre.

- The second step in absorption costing is overhead apportionment. This involves apportioning general overheads to cost centres

- The third step then reapportions the costs of service cost centres to production departments. Service cost centre overheads must be reapportioned to the production cost centres; reapportionment of service cost centre costs is achieved using an appropriate method depending upon whether one service cost centre provides services for another cost centre. There are several methods of reapportioning service department overheads to production departments.

  - Direct method (ignores inter-service department work)
  - Step-down method (recognises some inter-service department work)

Keywords

- **Absorption costing:** A way of finding an appropriate amount of overhead per cost unit so that the total cost of producing a product or job can be found

- **Allocation:** Where the whole of an overhead has been incurred by one cost centre, so it is charged in full to that cost centre

- **Apportionment:** Where overheads are shared, on a fair basis, among the cost centres that jointly incurred the cost

- **Overheads:** Indirect labour, indirect materials and indirect expenses

- **Production cost centres:** A cost centre that actually produces cost units

- **Reapportionment:** Apportionment of service cost centres costs to the production cost centres that use their service

- **Service cost centres:** A cost centre that is not directly involved with production, but with supporting production by providing a service, eg maintenance and stores

1 **Overhead apportionment is used to (tick the correct answer):**

☐ Charge whole items of costs to cost centres

☐ Charge cost units with an appropriate share of overheads

☐ Charge whole items of costs to cost units

☐ Spread common costs over cost centres

☐ Ensure budgeted overheads are not exceeded

2 Bramble Fabrications Limited has three production departments: the machine shop, assembly and painting. There is one service department which usually spends 40% of its time servicing the machine shop and the rest of the time equally in the other two production departments. Budgeted overheads to be apportioned between the departments are:

	£
Factory rent, rates and insurance	9,000
Depreciation of machinery	4,000
Supervisor's salary	8,000
Heat and light	2,000

Information for apportionment purposes:

	Machine shop	Assembly	Painting	Services
Floor area (m²)	500	200	300	200
Value of machinery	£12,000	£4,000	£3,000	£1,000
Number of employees	8	9	5	2

You are required to calculate the final apportionment of budgeted overheads to the three production departments by:

(a) Apportioning the budgeted overheads to the four departments

(b) Reapportioning the service department overheads

(a)

	Total £	Machine shop £	Assembly £	Painting £	Services £
Factory rent, rates and insurance	9,000				
Depreciation of machinery	4,000				
Supervisor's salary	8,000				
Heat and light	2,000				
Apportionment to all departments	23,000				

(b)

Reapportionment of services					
Total after reapportionment	23,000				Nil

3   Vine Limited has two production departments, V and W. There are two service departments, S1 and S2. The budgeted costs of each department, along with overheads which have yet to be allocated or apportioned, are listed below, along with details which can be used for allocation and apportionment.

	Total £	V £	W £	S1 £	S2 £
Indirect materials	310,000	160,000	120,000	10,000	20,000
Indirect labour	1,125,000	400,000	650,000	40,000	35,000
Buildings depreciation and insurance	100,000				
Cleaning	25,000				
Machinery depreciation and insurance	1,500,000				
Supervision of production	70,000				
Power	250,000				
Heat and light	20,000				

	Total	V	W	S1	S2
Volume occupied (m³)	10,000	6,000	3,000	800	200
% of power usage		25%	45%	20%	10%
Supervisor hours worked per week		15	20		
Value of machinery	£1,000,000	£380,000	£600,000		£20,000
% use of department S1		40%	60%		
% use of department S2		40%	50%	10%	
Direct labour hours worked		200,000	500,000		

You are required to calculate:

(a) The total overheads for each department after allocation and apportionment

(b) The overheads in departments V and W after reapportionment of the service departments using the step-down method

(a) **Basis of apportionment**

	Total £	V £	W £	S1 £	S2 £
Indirect materials					
Indirect labour					
Buildings depreciation and insurance					
Cleaning					
Machinery depreciation and insurance					
Supervision of production					
Power					
Heat & light					
Total					

(b) **Reapportionment**

	Total £	V £	W £	S1 £	S2 £
Step down S2 first					
S1 next 40:60					
Total after reapportionment					

Absorption costing

6

Learning outcomes

3.1	**Calculate and use overhead costs**
	• The concept of activity based costing, including appropriate cost drivers
3.2	**Calculate overhead recovery rates using traditional methods**
	Calculate overhead recovery rates in accordance with suitable bases of absorption.
	These are:
	• For a manufacturer: machine hours or direct labour hours
	• For a service business: suitable basis for the specific business
3.3	**Calculate overhead recovery rates using activity based costing**
	• Calculate overhead recovery rates using appropriate cost drivers
3.4	**Demonstrate understanding of the under or over recovery of overheads**
	• Account for under or over recovered overhead costs in accordance with established procedures. These include:
	– Making under or over absorption calculations
	– Interpreting the significance of under or over recoveries of overhead costs

Assessment context

There is likely to be a task asking you to calculate an overhead absorption rate and over- or under-absorption.

Qualification context

Once you have a good foundation of absorption costing you will be using the concept when studying standard costing and variance analysis at Level 4. Absorption costing will be assumed knowledge at Level 4.

Business context

Every business needs to understand and control its costs. Overhead costs can sometimes be a very large proportion of a business's total costs.

Chapter overview

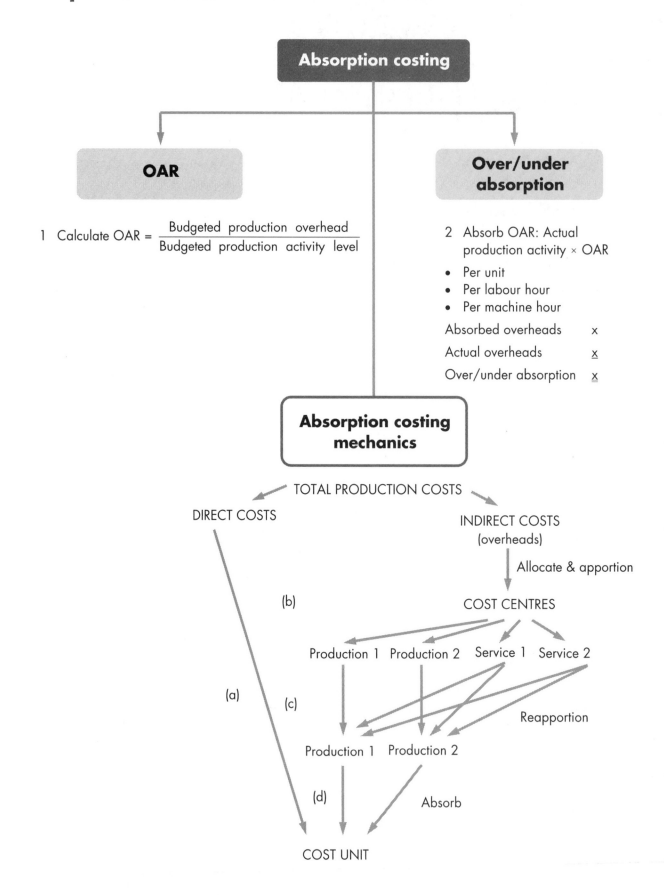

Activity based Absorption

What is it?

- Alternative to absorption costing
- Developed for modern businesses that have a higher proportion of overheads
- Based on cost drivers – factors that cause costs

Calculating product costs

Step 1
Identify an organisation's major activities.

Step 2
Identify the costs drivers which cause the costs of the activities.

Step 3
Collect the costs associated with each activity into **cost pools**.

Step 4
Charge the costs of activities to products on the basis of their usage of the activities.

Introduction

In the previous chapter we covered the first three steps involved in reaching the absorption cost of a unit of production.

To get the full (absorbed) production cost the four steps are:

(1) **Allocation** – charging whole cost items to responsibilty centres

(2) **Apportionment** – sharing production overheads among cost centres

(3) **Reapportionment** – sharing overheads in service cost centres to production cost centres

(4) **Absorption** – absorbing overheads into cost units

In this chapter we will cover step 4 and we will also look at an alternative to absorption costing, called **activity based costing (ABC)**.

1 Absorption

Overhead absorption is the way that overheads are charged to output (cost units). This is also known as **overhead recovery**. Once all of the production overhead costs have been apportioned to the production cost centres, we need to charge these to the cost units passing through the production cost centres. This is termed **absorption**. We are going to absorb an element of total production overhead into each cost unit.

$$\text{OAR (overhead absorption rate)} = \frac{\text{Production overhead}}{\text{Activity level}}$$

Activity can be expressed in a number of ways – hours worked, machine hours used, costs incurred or units produced – and any of these can be used to calculate the absorption rate.

Ideally, the basis chosen should be the one which most accurately reflects the way in which the overheads are in fact being incurred.

	Basis	Used when
(a)	Per labour hour	The production process is labour intensive
(b)	Per machine hour	The production process is machine intensive
(c)	Per unit	Units are identical (not used in your assessment)

Assessment focus point

Assessment questions may ask you to decide what the most appropriate basis for absorption is for a particular responsibility centre.

Activity 1: Overhead absorption bases

Mars Ltd has two production departments, mixing and stirring, in which it makes a variety of products.

	Mixing	Stirring
Direct labour hours	20,000	5,000
Direct machine hours	2,000	60,000

Required

Based on the above information, what are the most appropriate overhead absorption bases for the mixing and stirring departments?

Mixing department: OAR should be based on [   ]

Stirring department: OAR should be based on [   ]

Picklist

Budgeted direct labour hours

Budgeted direct machine hours

2 Predetermined overhead absorption rates

Businesses need to cost their production throughout the year, not at the end of an accounting period. Therefore they predetermine or estimate their absorption rates for the year in advance, based on the budgeted overheads and the budgeted level of activity.

Formula to learn

$$\text{OAR (overhead absorption rate)} = \frac{\text{Total budgeted production overhead}}{\text{Total budgeted activity level}}$$

Assessment focus point

Assessment questions may ask you to calculate a budgeted overhead absorption rate (OAR) for a manufacturing business, based on budgeted labour hours or budgeted machine hours.

For a service business, the basis for the budgeted overhead absorption rate will depend on the specific business.

Always remember that the OAR is calculated using **budgeted** figures (not actual figures).

Activity 2: Overhead absorption rates (OAR) 1

Budgeted information for department A is as follows:

	Department A
Budgeted overheads	40,000
Direct machine hours	2,000

Required

Calculate the budgeted overhead absorption rate per machine hour for department A?

Budgeted OAR =   £ [   ]   per machine hour

The amount absorbed into production is:

Formula to learn

Amount absorbed = Actual production activity × OAR

This occurs during the year or month as production takes place.

Illustration 1: Overhead absorption rates

Bluebell Electronics makes two products, the Videobooster and the Blastbox. It is trying to decide on an appropriate basis to absorb overheads. The following budgeted information is provided.

Production units	Videobooster 4,000		Blastbox 6,000	
	Components shop hours	Assembly hours	Components shop hours	Assembly hours
Direct labour				
Hours per unit	1.25	0.50	2.00	1.00
Total hours	5,000	2,000	12,000	6,000
Machine hours				
Hours per unit	2.00	1.00	0.30	0.20
Total hours	8,000	4,000	1,800	1,200

Calculate:

(a) **Separate departmental overhead absorption rates using first labour hours and then machine hours as the absorption basis**

(b) **The overhead absorbed by each product under each of the overhead absorption bases**

Note. The final apportionment of overheads to the two production cost centres was: Components shop, £32,375; and Assembly, £19,575.

(a) Departmental absorption rates

	Components	Assembly

Rate per direct labour hour

$$\frac{\text{Overheads}}{\text{Direct labour hours}} = \frac{£32,375}{5,000 + 12,000} \qquad \frac{£19,575}{2,000 + 6,000}$$

$$= \quad £1.90 \text{ per direct labour hour} \qquad £2.45 \text{ per direct labour hour}$$

Rate per machine hour

$$\frac{\text{Overheads}}{\text{Machine hours}} = \frac{£32,375}{8,000 + 1,800} \qquad \frac{£19,575}{4,000 + 1,200}$$

$$= \quad £3.30 \text{ per machine hour} \qquad £3.76 \text{ per machine hour}$$

(b) The overhead absorbed by each product

Rate per direct labour hour

	Videobooster	£	Blastbox	£
Components shop	£1.90×1.25hrs	2.38	£1.90×2.00hrs	3.80
Assembly	£2.45×0.50hrs	1.23	£2.45×1.00hr	2.45
Total absorbed per unit		3.61		6.25

Rate per machine hour

	Videobooster	£	Blastbox	£
Components shop	£3.30×2.00hrs	6.60	£3.30×0.30hrs	0.99
Assembly	£3.76×1.00hr	3.76	£3.76×0.20hrs	0.75
Total absorbed per unit		10.36		1.74

2.1 Which absorption rate should you use?

As you can see from the example above, the type of absorption rate used can have a huge effect on the cost of a product. The amount of overhead absorbed into the Blastbox varied from £1.74 to £6.25! It is therefore important to consider very carefully which rate is appropriate for each department. The way in which the cost is incurred can guide us towards the best method.

- A rate per direct labour hour would be appropriate if the department is labour intensive and most of the overheads relate to labour (this may apply to Bluebell's Assembly department).

- A rate per machine hour is a fair method if the department is largely mechanised, with relatively little labour input (perhaps Bluebell's Component shop).

Activity 3: Overhead absorption rates (OAR) 2

Mars Ltd has two production departments, mixing and stirring, in which it makes a variety of products. Budgeted overheads are £10,000 and £15,000 respectively, and the following budgeted information has also been collected.

	Mixing	Stirring
Direct labour hours	20,000	5,000
Direct machine hours	2,000	60,000
Number of units	10,000	10,000

Required

Calculate appropriate overhead absorption rates for both the Mixing department and the Stirring department.

Mixing department OAR is £ [   ] per [   ]

Stirring department OAR is £ [   ] per [   ]

2.2 Why do we bother with predetermined OARs?

Many overheads are not known until the end of a period. If we waited until the end of a period, this would cause delays in invoicing, inventory valuation and so on. This is why we calculate an OAR based on budgeted figures. It gives us a way of taking account of overheads before we actually know what they are.

2.3 What basis of absorption would be used in a service sector organisation?

A rate per machine hour or per direct labour hour is suitable for a manufacturing business, but may not be suitable for a service business. For a service business, a suitable basis will depend on the specific business. If you get a service sector organisation in your assessment, you will need to use an appropriate **volume** basis. For example, the number of miles travelled for a bus company.

Activity 4: Overhead absorption rates in the service sector

Bus route X11 has total budgeted overheads for the year of £130,000. The expected miles travelled for the year are 325,000.

Required

Calculate an appropriate overhead absorption rate.

OAR is £ [   ] per [   ]

3 Over- and under-absorption of overheads

3.1 What happens at the end of the year?

At the end of the year, actual overhead costs will be known.

However, using budgeted figures to calculate the overhead absorption rate means that the actual overhead cost is unlikely to be the same as the overheads absorbed into production. This is because we had to rely on two estimates:

- Overhead costs
- Activity levels

These will inevitably differ from the actual values that are experienced during the period. Consequently, at the end of the period when the statement of profit or loss is drawn up, the profit figure will be wrong as the overhead charge will be the absorbed amount (which was based on estimates) rather than the actual amount.

The error in the profit figure results from one of two possibilities.

(1) If more overheads are absorbed than have actually been incurred, this is known as **over-absorption**.

(2) If fewer overheads are absorbed than have actually been incurred, this is known as **under-absorption**.

The amount over- or under-absorbed is adjusted for in the statement of profit or loss after the production cost has been charged. Under-absorption means that too little overhead has been charged in the production cost, so a deduction is made from profit. Over-absorption means that too much overhead has been charged, so there is a compensating addition to profit.

The organisation needs to review the bases of calculation of the OAR as the activity changes over time. For instance, if an organisation becomes more automated and requires fewer workers, it would seem appropriate to change from calculating overheads based on labour hours to those based on machine hours.

Illustration 2: Over- and under-absorption

Cowslip Ltd budget to make and sell 10,000 units of their product in each of the next three months. They will be sold for £20 each and direct costs per unit are £6. Budgeted overheads are £15,000 per month, which is recovered using a rate per machine hour basis. Each unit requires three hours of machine time, the budgeted machine hours being 30,000. Actual overheads over the next three months are:

	£
February	15,000
March	14,000
April	16,000

All other actual costs, revenues and quantities are as budgeted (ie only the overheads incurred differ from budget).

The overhead absorption rate will be

$$= \frac{\text{Overheads}}{\text{Machine hours}}$$

$$= \frac{£15,000}{10,000 \text{ units} \times 3 \text{ hrs per unit}}$$

$$= £0.50 \text{ per machine hour}$$

First, **in February**, the actual and budgeted overheads are the same at £15,000.

Statement of profit or loss for February

	£
Sales (10,000 × £20)	200,000
Less: production cost of sales	
direct costs (10,000 × £6)	(60,000)
overheads (30,000 hrs × £0.50)	(15,000)
Profit	125,000

A comparison of actual overheads and absorbed overheads will show that the two are the same:

	£
Actual overheads	15,000
Absorbed overheads (10,000 units × 3 hrs × £0.50)	15,000
Under/over absorption	Nil

In March, however, actual overheads are lower than budget, at £14,000. The production cost charged in the statement of profit or loss will still be the same, as the same number of machine hours have been used. But we can't leave profit at the same level as before: the overheads are £1,000 less than were budgeted for, so we should have a profit of £1,000 more. By including 30,000 machine hours at a cost of £0.50 per hour in the statement of profit or loss, we have absorbed more overheads than were actually incurred, which is an over-absorption.

	£
Actual overheads	14,000
Absorbed overheads (30,000 hrs × £0.50)	15,000
Over-absorption	1,000

This is credited to the statement of profit or loss.

Statement of profit or loss for March

	£
Sales (10,000 × £20)	200,000
Less: production cost of sales	
direct costs	(60,000)
overheads	(15,000)
	125,000
Add: over-absorption of overheads	1,000
Profit	126,000

In April actual overheads are £16,000

	£
Actual overheads	16,000
Absorbed overheads (30,000 hrs × £0.50)	15,000
Under-absorption	1,000

The under-absorbed overheads will be debited to the statement of profit or loss. Under-absorption means that not enough overheads have been charged against profits, so we deduct the under-absorption from profit to make up for this.

Statement of profit or loss for April

	£
Sales	200,000
Less: production cost of sales	
direct costs	(60,000)
overheads	(15,000)
	125,000
Less: under-absorption of overheads	(1,000)
Profit	124,000

Note. Be very careful to calculate the under- or over-absorption based on actual vs absorbed costs; budgeted costs are not brought into this calculation. This is particularly relevant when the actual amounts of both overheads and activity are different from budget.

Let's say that **in May** the number of units produced and sold by Cowslip Ltd is 12,000, machine hours amounted to 38,000 and overheads actually incurred amount to £16,500. So this time both overheads and activity level are different from budget.

Calculate the overhead under- or over-absorbed as before, being careful to pick up the correct figures.

	£
Actual overheads	16,500
Absorbed overheads (38,000 hrs × £0.50)	19,000
Over-absorption	2,500

The profit calculation will take account of the over-absorption.

Statement of profit or loss for May

	£
Sales (12,000 × £20)	240,000
Less: production cost of sales	
direct costs (12,000 × £6)	(72,000)
overheads absorbed (38,000 hrs × £0.50)	(19,000)
	149,000
Add: over-absorption of overheads	2,500
Profit	151,500

Assessment focus point

An assessment question may ask you to calculate under- or over-absorption.

Activity 5: Overhead absorption rates (OAR) 3

Pumpkin Ltd provides you with the following budgeted information for its painting division.

Total overheads: £400,000.

Total budgeted direct labour hours: 3,200

Total budgeted machine hours: 10,000

Required

(a) **Calculate the budgeted fixed overhead absorption rate using a direct labour hours basis.**

(b) **Calculate the budgeted fixed overhead absorption rate using a machine hours basis.**

(c) The painting manager informs you that the painting division is highly automated and operates with expensive machinery which is run whenever possible on a 24 hour a day, 7 days a week basis.

   Which of the two OARs calculated in (a) and (b) above would be the most appropriate for absorption?

(d) At the end of the accounting period, the painting manager provides you with the following actual data for the painting division:

Total overheads   = £521,262

Total direct labour hours = 4,100

Total machine hours   = 12,562

Calculate the amount of overheads over- or under-absorbed for the period using the basis chosen in part (c).

(a)   OAR = £ [   ] per direct labour hour

(b)   OAR = £ [   ] per machine hour

(c)   OAR most appropriate for absorption is £ [   ] per [   ]

(d)   Overheads £ [   ] over/under* absorbed

*Delete the incorrect word ie over or under

Activity 6: Over- or under-absorption

The Assembly department recovers its fixed overheads on the basis of budgeted machine hours.

The Finishing department, however, recovers its fixed overheads on the basis of the budgeted direct labour hours.

The following information relates to these two departments for January 20X6.

	Assembly department	Finishing department
Budgeted fixed overhead absorption rate	£10.00 per hour	£7.50 per hour
Actual machine hours worked	775	810
Actual direct labour hours worked	1,200	1,250
Actual fixed overheads	£8,110	£9,000

Required

(a) Calculate the fixed overheads absorbed in January in the Assembly department.

(b) Calculate the fixed overhead absorbed in January in the Finishing department.

(c) Calculate the over- or under-absorption of fixed overheads during January, stating clearly whether overheads have been over- or under-absorbed, for:

(i) The Assembly department

(ii) The Finishing department

(a) £ [   ]   Assembly department overhead absorbed

(b) £ [   ]   Finishing department overhead absorbed

(c) (i) Assembly department   £ [   ]   over/under* absorbed

(ii) Finishing department   £ [   ]   over/under* absorbed

*Delete the incorrect word ie over or under

---

4 Advantages and disadvantages of absorption costing

4.1 Advantages

(a) Inventory valuation using absorption costing complies with IAS 2 (which requires that cost includes a fair share of production overheads based on normal activity levels).

(b) Fixed costs must be covered in the long run and absorption costing takes fixed costs into account (unlike marginal costing).

(c) Production cannot be divorced from fixed costs since without them production could not occur.

4.2 Disadvantages

(a) Unit cost includes costs which are not relevant for marginal decision making (see later chapters on marginal costing).

(b) The nature of cost behaviour is obscured.

(c) The method of absorption is to some extent arbitrary.

Activity 7: Mars Ltd

Mars Ltd has the following overhead absorption rates:

Mixing department   50p per labour hour

Stirring department   25p per machine hour

Mars Ltd has a product, the 'Venus', for which you obtain the following information.

Direct materials per unit	£5
Direct labour hours	
– mixing	2.0 hours
– stirring	0.5 hours
Direct machine hours	
– mixing	0.2 hours
– stirring	6.0 hours
Labour is paid £8.60 per hour	

Required

What is the total cost of this product?

	£	£
Direct costs		
Materials		
Labour		
Mixing		
Stirring		
Total direct costs		
Overheads		
Mixing department		
Stirring department		
Total overheads		
Total cost		

5 Accounting for overhead absorption

The absorbed overhead is part of the production cost of the cost units, and therefore it is debited to the work in progress control account together with the direct materials, direct labour and any direct expenses incurred to give the total production cost for the period.

The credit entry is to the production overhead control account, which will have been debited with the actual overhead incurred. Any balance on the production overhead control account is the transfer to the statement of profit or loss as under- or over-absorbed overhead.

Illustration 3: Accounting for overheads

We will return to the cost ledger accounts of Gilchrist Chemicals where neither the work in progress control account nor the production overhead control account were yet completed for the month of June. Gilchrist has incurred other expenses of £16,500 for royalties and £38,900 of indirect expenses. These are debited in the control accounts and credited to the bank account as shown. We are now going to look at how overheads are accounted for.

Work in progress control account

		£			£
30 June	Materials control	69,200			
30 June	Wages control	110,000			
30 June	Bank	16,500			

Production overhead control

		£			£
30 June	Materials control	3,600			
30 June	Wages control	30,000			
30 June	Bank	38,900			

The debits in the production overhead control account are the actual overheads incurred during the month. You are now told that the amount of overhead to be absorbed into production based upon the overhead absorption rate is £75,000.

This must be debited to the work in progress control account and credited to the production overhead control account.

Work in progress control account

	£		£
30 June Materials control	69,200		
30 June Wages control	110,000		
30 June Bank	16,500		
30 June Prod'n overhead control	75,000		

Production overhead control

	£		£
30 June Materials control	3,600	30 June WIP	75,000
30 June Wages control	30,000		
30 June Bank	38,900		

If we balance the production overhead control account we will find any under- or over-absorbed overhead to transfer to the statement of profit or loss.

Production overhead control

	£		£
30 June Materials control	3,600	30 June WIP	75,000
30 June Wages control	30,000		
30 June Bank	38,900		
30 June Statement of profit or loss	2,500		
	75,000		75,000

The overheads actually incurred total £72,500 (£3,600 + £30,000 + £38,900), whereas the overhead absorbed was £75,000. This is an over-absorption of overhead, which is debited in the production overhead control account and credited to the statement of profit or loss, thereby increasing profit. If the balance had been on the credit side of the production overhead control account this would have been an under-absorption which would then have been debited or charged to the statement of profit or loss.

Assessment focus point

Assessment questions may ask you whether over- or under-absorbed overheads will be debited or credited to the statement of profit or loss. Remember:

An **over**-absorption of overheads is credited to the statement of profit or loss. This will decrease expenses and will increase profit.

An **under**-absorption of overheads is debited to the statement of profit or loss. This will increase expenses and will decrease profit.

We will now finish the cost accounting process by considering the work in progress control account. The total on this account of £270,700 is the total production cost for the period. We are now told that during the period finished products with a production cost of £250,000 have been transferred to the warehouse ready for sale. The accounting entries reflect this with £250,000 being credited to work in progress and debited to a finished goods account.

Work in progress control account

	£		£
30 June Materials control	69,200	30 June Finished goods	250,000
30 June Wages control	110,000		
30 June Bank	16,500	30 June Closing balance	20,700
30 June Production o/h	75,000		
	270,700		270,700

Finished goods account

	£		£
30 June WIP	250,000		

The closing balance on the work in progress control account is the amount of work in progress at the end of the month, that is, cost units that have been started but not yet completed in the month.

6 Activity-based costing (ABC)

Activity-based costing (ABC) is an alternative approach to absorption costing. It involves the identification of the factors (called **cost drivers**) which cause the costs of an organisation's major activities.

6.1 The reasons for the development of ABC

In the past, most organisations used to produce only a few products. Direct labour costs and direct material costs accounted for the largest proportion of total costs and so it was these variable costs that needed to be controlled.

Overhead costs were only a very small fraction of total costs and so it did not particularly matter what absorption costing bases were used to apportion overheads to products.

Nowadays, a high proportion of total costs tend to be fixed and substantial.

Manufacturing is machine intensive rather than labour intensive and so direct labour might account for as little as 5% of a product's cost.

Advanced manufacturing technology has had a significant impact on the level of overheads. For example, the variable cost of producing a piece of computer software might be just a few pounds but the fixed (initial) cost of the software development might run into millions of pounds.

Many resources are used in support activities such as setting-up, production scheduling, first-item inspection and data processing. These support activities help with the manufacture of a wide range of products and are not, in general, affected by changes in production volume. They tend to vary instead in the long term according to the range and complexity of the products manufactured.

The wider the range and the more complex the products, the more support services will be required. Suppose factory X produces 10,000 units of one product, the Alpha. Factory Y also produces 10,000 units, made up of 1,000 units each of ten slightly different versions of the Alpha. Consider the setting-up activity.

- Factory X will only need to set up once.

- Factory Y will have to set up the production run at least ten times for the ten different products and so will incur more set-up costs.

6.2 Problems of using absorption costing in today's environment

Absorption costing assumes all products consume all resources in proportion to their production volumes.

- It tends to allocate too great a proportion of overheads to high-volume products (which cause relatively little diversity and hence use fewer support services).

- It tends to allocate too small a proportion of overheads to low-volume products (which cause greater diversity and therefore use more support services).

Activity-based costing (ABC) attempts to overcome these problems.

6.3 ABC and using it to calculate product costs

Activities cause costs	Activities include ordering and despatching.

The costs of an activity are caused or driven by factors known as cost drivers	The cost of the ordering activity might be driven by the number of orders placed, the cost of the despatching activity by the number of despatches made.

The costs of an activity are assigned to products on the basis of the number of the activity's cost driver products generate	If product A requires 5 orders to be placed, and product B 15 orders, ¼ (ie 5/(5 + 15)) of the ordering cost will be assigned to product A and ¾ (ie 15/(5 + 15)) to product B.

6.3.1 Cost drivers

> A **cost driver** is a factor influencing the level of cost.

For those costs that vary with production levels in the short term, ABC uses volume-related cost drivers such as labour hours or machine hours. The cost of oil used as a lubricant on machines would therefore be added to products on the basis of the number of machine hours, since oil would have to be used for each hour the machine ran.

For costs that vary with some other activity and not volume of production, ABC uses transaction-related cost drivers such as the number of production runs for the production scheduling activity.

	Output	Number of production runs in the period	Material cost per unit	Direct labour hours per unit	Machine hours per unit
	Units		£		
W	10	2	20	1	1
X	10	2	80	3	3
Y	100	5	20	1	1
Z	100	5	80	3	3
		14			

BPP
LEARNING MEDIA

6.3.2 Calculating product costs using ABC

Step 1
Identify an organisation's major activities

Step 2
Identify the factors (cost drivers) which cause the costs of the activities

Step 3
Collect the costs associated with each activity into cost pools

Cost pools are equivalent to cost centres used with traditional absorption costing.

Step 4
Charge the costs of activities to products on the basis of their usage of the activities. A product's usage of an activity is measured by the number of the activity's cost driver it generates

Suppose the cost pool for the ordering activity totalled £100,000 and that there were 10,000 orders (orders being the cost driver). Each product would therefore be charged with £10 for each order it required. A batch requiring five orders would therefore be charged with £50.

Illustration 4: ABC

Suppose that Cooplan Co manufactures four products, W, X, Y and Z. Output and cost data for the period just ended are as follows.

	Output	Number of production runs in the period	Material cost per unit	Direct labour hours per unit	Machine hours per unit
	Units		£		
W	10	2	20	1	1
X	10	2	80	3	3
Y	100	5	20	1	1
Z	100	5	80	3	3
		14			

Direct labour cost per hour is £5. Overhead costs are as follows.

	£
Short-run variable costs	3,080
Set-up costs	10,920
Production and scheduling costs	9,100
Materials handling costs	7,700
	30,800

Required

Calculate product costs using absorption costing and ABC.

Solution

Using **absorption-costing** and an absorption rate based on either direct labour hours or machine hours, the product costs would be as follows.

	W £	X £	Y £	Z £	Total £
Direct material	200	800	2,000	8,000	11,000
Direct labour	50	150	500	1,500	2,200
Overheads*	700	2,100	7,000	21,000	30,800
	950	3,050	9,500	30,500	44,000
Units produced	10	10	100	100	
Cost per unit	£95	£305	£95	£305	

* £30,800 ÷ 440 hours = £70 per direct labour or machine hour

Using **activity-based costing** and assuming that the number of production runs is the cost driver for set-up costs, production and scheduling costs and materials handling costs and that machine hours are the cost driver for short-run variable costs, unit costs would be as follows.

	W £	X £	Y £	Z £	Total £
Direct material	200	800	2,000	8,000	11,000
Direct labour	50	150	500	1,500	2,200
Short-run variable overheads (W1)	70	210	700	2,100	3,080
Set-up costs (W2)	1,560	1,560	3,900	3,900	10,920
Production and scheduling costs (W3)	1,300	1,300	3,250	3,250	9,100
Materials handling costs (W4)	1,100	1,100	2,750	2,750	7,700
	4,280	5,120	13,100	21,500	44,000
Units produced	10	10	100	100	
Cost per unit	£428	£512	£131	£215	

Workings

1 £3,080 ÷ 440 machine hours   =   £7 per machine hour
2 £10,920 ÷ 14 production runs   =   £780 per run
3 £9,100 ÷ 14 production runs   =   £650 per run
4 £7,700 ÷ 14 production runs   =   £550 per run

Summary

Product	Absorption costing Unit cost £	ABC Unit cost £	Difference £
W	95	428	+ 333
X	305	512	+ 207
Y	95	131	+ 36
Z	305	215	− 90

The figures suggest that the traditional volume-based absorption costing system is flawed.

- It under-allocates overhead costs to low-volume products (here, W and X) and over-allocates overheads to higher-volume products (here Z in particular).

- It under-allocates overhead costs to less complex products (here W and Y with just one hour of work needed per unit) and over-allocates overheads to more complex products (here X and particularly Z).

Activity 8: Activity-based costing

Having attended an AAT course on activity-based costing (ABC) you decide to experiment by applying the principles of ABC to the four products currently made and sold by your company. Details of the four products and relevant information are given below for one period.

	P1	P2	P3	P4
Output in units	120	100	80	120
Costs per unit:	£	£	£	£
Direct material	40	50	30	60
Direct labour	28	21	14	21

The total of the production overhead for the period has been analysed as follows.

	£
Set-up costs	5,250
Stores receiving	3,600
Inspection/quality control	2,100
Materials handling and despatch	4,620

You have ascertained that the following 'cost drivers' are to be used for the costs shown.

Cost	Cost driver
Set-up costs	Number of production runs
Stores receiving	Requisitions raised
Inspection/quality control	Number of production runs
Materials handling and despatch	Orders executed

	P1	P2	P3	P4	Total
Number of production runs	6	5	4	6	21
Number of requisitions raised	20	20	20	20	80
Number of orders executed	12	10	8	12	42

Required

(a) Fill in the table below to calculate the cost per driver for each overhead cost.

$\dfrac{\text{Set-up costs}}{\text{Number of production runs}}$		=	£	per production run
$\dfrac{\text{Stores receiving}}{\text{Number of requistions raised}}$		=	£	per requisition raised
$\dfrac{\text{Inspection / quality control}}{\text{Number of production runs}}$		=	£	per production run
$\dfrac{\text{Materials handling and despatch}}{\text{Number of orders executed}}$		=	£	per order executed

(b) Using your answers from (a), calculate the overhead costs for each product.

	P1	P2	P3	P4
Number of production runs	6	5	4	6
Cost per production run				
Set up costs per product				

	P1	P2	P3	P4
Number of requisitions raised	20	20	20	20
Cost per requisition raised				
Stores receiving costs per product				

	P1	P2	P3	P4
Number of production runs	6	5	4	6
Cost per production run				
Inspection/quality control costs per product				

	P1	P2	P3	P4
Number of orders executed	12	10	8	12
Cost per order executed				
Materials handling and despatch per product				

(c) Fill in the table below to calculate the total costs for each product.

	P1 £	P2 £	P3 £	P4 £
Direct material				
Direct labour				
Production overhead				
Set-up costs				
Stores receiving				
Inspection/quality control				
Material handling and despatch				
Total cost				
Unit costs				

Chapter summary

- In absorption costing, it is usual to add overheads into product costs by applying a predetermined overhead absorption rate. The predetermined rate is set annually, in the budget.

- The absorption rate is calculated by dividing the budgeted overhead by the budgeted level of activity. For production overheads, the level of activity is often budgeted direct labour hours or budgeted machine hours.

- Management should try to establish an absorption rate that provides a reasonably 'accurate' estimate of overhead costs for jobs, products or services.

- The use of separate departmental absorption rates instead of blanket (or single factory) absorption rates will produce more realistic product costs.

- The rate of overhead absorption is based on estimates and it is quite likely that either one or both of the estimates will not agree with what actually occurs. Actual overheads incurred will probably be either greater than or less than overheads absorbed into the cost of production.

    - Over-absorption means that the overheads charged to the cost of production are greater than the overheads actually incurred.

    - Under-absorption means that insufficient overheads have been included in the cost of production.

- Activity-based costing (ABC) is an alternative approach to absorption costing. It involves the identification of the factors (cost drivers) which cause the costs of an organisation's major activities.

Keywords

- **Activity-based costing:** An alternative approach to absorption costing using cost drivers to assign activity costs to units

- **Cost driver:** Factor influencing the level of cost

- **Overhead absorption rate:** The rate at which overheads are charged to cost units calculated by dividing budgeted overheads by the budgeted level of activity

- **Over-absorption:** More overheads are absorbed into production than have actually been incurred

- **Under-absorption:** Fewer overheads are absorbed into production than have actually been incurred

Test your learning

1 **Which of the following statements about overhead absorption rates are true?**

(i) They are predetermined in advance for each period
(ii) They are used to charge overheads to products
(iii) They are based on actual data for each period
(iv) They are used to control overhead costs

A (i) and (ii) only
B (i), (ii) and (iv) only
C (ii), (iii) and (iv) only
D (iii) and (iv) only

2 **Over-absorbed overheads occur when**

A absorbed overheads exceed actual overheads
B absorbed overheads exceed budgeted overheads
C actual overheads exceed budgeted overheads
D budgeted overheads exceed absorbed overheads

3 A company absorbs overheads on machine hours which were budgeted at 11,250 with overheads of £258,750. Actual results were 10,980 hours with overheads of £254,692.

Overheads were

A Under-absorbed by £2,152
B Over-absorbed by £4,058
C Under-absorbed by £4,058
D Over-absorbed by £2,152

The following information relates to questions 4 and 5

Budgeted labour hours	8,500
Budgeted overheads	£148,750
Actual labour hours	7,928
Actual overheads	£146,200

4 **Based on the data given above, what is the labour hour overhead absorption rate?**

A £17.20 per hour
B £17.50 per hour
C £18.44 per hour
D £18.76 per hour

5 **Based on the data given above, what is the amount of under-/over-absorbed overhead?**

A   £2,550 under-absorbed overhead
B   £2,550 over-absorbed overhead
C   £7,460 over-absorbed overhead
D   £7,460 under-absorbed overhead

Job, batch and service costing

7

Learning outcomes

2.5	Differentiate between and apply different costing systems
	• The appropriate choice of costing system for different business sectors and individual organisations.
	• How to record cost information using different costing systems. These are:
	– Job costing
	– Batch costing
	– Service costing

Assessment context

There is likely to be a task on this topic. For example, you may be asked to calculate a cost per batch.

Qualification context

This chapter introduces some tools that will be used throughout your studies and included within the later *Management Accounting* units, such as mark-ups and costing particular jobs.

Business context

Many businesses will use these techniques when calculating charges to clients for work performed.

Chapter overview

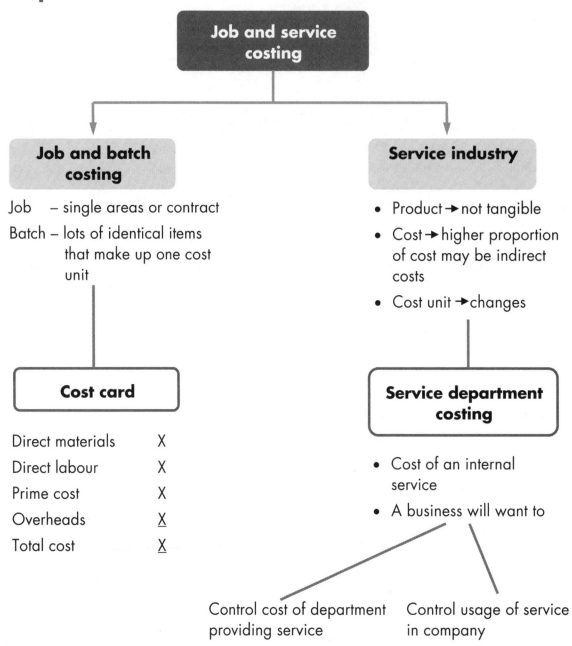

Job and service costing

Job and batch costing

Job   – single areas or contract

Batch – lots of identical items
that make up one cost
unit

Cost card

Direct materials	X
Direct labour	X
Prime cost	X
Overheads	X
Total cost	X

Service industry

- Product → not tangible
- Cost → higher proportion of cost may be indirect costs
- Cost unit → changes

Service department costing

- Cost of an internal service
- A business will want to

Control cost of department providing service

Control usage of service in company

- Methods of deciding the cost to charge for an internal service
    - Actual cost
    - Standard cost
    - Variable cost
    - Cost + margin

Introduction

So far we have concentrated on gathering together the costs for individual cost units – the products that a business makes. However, there are other costing systems depending upon the type of product or service that a business provides. We will now consider some alternative costing systems.

1 Job costing

1.1 What is a job?

It is a cost unit that consists of a single order or contract carried out to the special requirements of the customer.

> **Jobs** are customer orders which last a relatively short time.

Key term

Jobs differ and it is necessary to keep a separate record of each job and the costs incurred on that job.

Job costing is used by builders, electricians, plumbers and so on.

The problem with jobbing businesses is that there is no price list as such, as there is no standard product. Each individual job will be different with different costs.

When a customer approaches the business requesting a quote for a price for the job, they will provide details of the precise requirements they have for this particular job. The business must then decide how much the job is going to cost and how much profit it is to earn on the job and then come up with a price that satisfies this.

It is important to realise that not only must the price of the job cover the direct costs of materials, labour and any direct expenses, but it must also cover a portion of the overheads, so that all of the overheads for a period are covered by the prices of the jobs done in that period.

1.2 Collection of job costs

Materials requisitions are sent to stores requesting the necessary materials.

The materials requisition is used to cost materials allocated to a job. This is recorded on a job cost sheet or job cost card.

1.3 Labour costs

A **job card** or job ticket is completed by an employee recording start and finish times and then passed on to the employee who undertakes the next function and so on.

Direct labour is recorded on the job cost card.

Remember that where overtime is done at the specific request of the customer, it is treated as a direct cost. For job costing, it will be included on the job card.

1.4 Expenses

Direct expenses are recorded on the job cost card.

1.5 Overheads

Once direct costs have been recorded on the job cost card, the job needs to be charged with overheads.

Overheads are absorbed using predetermined overhead absorption rates. A job may pick up overheads from several departments.

If the overheads of the business are not included in the job quote then the overheads will never be covered by the income from jobs. Only by including the overheads before any profit element is added can the business be sure of earning enough to cover its overheads as well as the direct costs.

1.6 Reworking

Where reworking occurs as a one-off (ie specifically because of the job) rather than as an expected part of production, its cost should be included on the job card as a direct cost.

Activity 1: Job 4321

The following information is available for job 4321, which is being produced at the request of a customer.

	Department A	Department B	Department C
Materials consumed	£4,000	£1,000	£1,500
Direct labour: wage rate per hour	£6	£8	£5
Direct labour hours	300	200	400

In accordance with company policy, the following are chargeable to jobs:

Fixed production overheads £5 per labour hour
Fixed administration overhead 80% of total production cost
Profit 20% mark-up on cost

Required

Calculate the total cost and selling price of job 4321.

	Job 4321	
	£	£
Direct materials: department A		
B		
C		
Direct labour: department A		
B		
C		
Fixed production overhead:		
Total production cost		
Fixed administration overhead:		
Total cost		
Profit		
Selling price		

Activity 2: Splodge Ltd

Splodge Ltd has been asked to undertake a particular job for a customer. The relevant information is as follows:

- 40 kg of bricks will be used @ £5 per kg.

- Louis will need to work 2 hours and is paid £8.00 per hour.

- Ben will need to work 3 hours and is paid £8.50 per hour.

- Overtime is to be done if necessary as the customer wants the job completed ASAP.

- Overtime is paid at triple time.

- Due to unforeseen complexities, Louis had to stay late on Tuesday and work 2 hours' overtime to finish the job.

- Due to Ben's cold, he had to redo his work on Wednesday morning as he hadn't done it properly the first time.

- Ben had to use 10 kg extra of bricks to rework the job.

- Ben doesn't normally have to rework his tasks.

Required

Complete the job card below.

Job 08/10/04 No 111	Workings	£
Materials – bricks		
Issued		
Issued for rework		
Labour		
Louis		
Basic hours		
Overtime premium		
Ben		
Basic hours		
Reworked hours		
Total direct cost		
Overheads (£200 per job)		
Total job cost		

2 Batch costing

2.1 What is a batch?

A batch is a cost unit that consists of a separately, readily identifiable group of units. It is used in manufacturing businesses that make batches of different products rather than single products. For example, a shoe manufacturer may make a batch of 400 shoes of one style in size 4 and then a batch of 300 shoes of a different style in size 7.

Key term

Batch costing is a costing system that gathers together the costs of production of an entire batch of a similar product in order to find the cost of each individual item in that batch.

The costing is the same as for a job. The necessary information and procedures are set out below.

A batch card must be set up for each batch, carrying a unique identifying number. This card will be used to collect information on the costs of the batch.

2.2 Materials requisition document

Quantities of materials issued to each batch should be documented by some form of materials requisition document. This will be a record of materials issued from stores. A similar document should be used to record materials returned to stores, or transferred for use on other batches.

2.3 Perpetual inventory system

The materials issued from stores need to be priced in some way. One method is to maintain a perpetual inventory system on ledger cards. The cards would be updated for materials receipts from goods inward notes, which would have to be priced at actual cost. The materials requisition document would be the source for updating the cards for materials issues. A decision would have to be taken on the basis for pricing such issues; possible bases include LIFO, FIFO and AVCO.

2.4 Cost per unit

Once all of the costs of the batch have been determined the cost of each individual unit of product in that batch can be found as follows:

$$\text{Cost per unit} = \frac{\text{Cost of the batch}}{\text{Number of units in the batch}}$$

Assessment focus point

In your assessment, a task could ask you to calculate a cost per batch and then a cost per unit.

3 Service costing

3.1 Service organisations

Service organisations	
Profit seeking	**Non profit seeking organisations**
eg: accountancy firms, law firms, management consultancies, transport companies, banks and hotels	eg: hospitals, schools and libraries

Service organisations do not make or sell tangible goods.

Service costing is a costing system adapted for services or functions.

Key term

Service costing differs from product costing methods for a number of reasons.

(a) With many services, the cost of direct materials consumed will be relatively small compared to the labour, direct expenses and overheads cost. In product costing the direct materials are often a greater proportion of the total cost.

(b) The output of most service organisations is difficult to define and hence a unit cost is difficult to calculate.

(c) The service industry includes such a wide range of organisations which provide such different services and have such different cost structures that costing will vary considerably from one to another.

3.2 Charging customers for services

The procedure for charging customers for services is similar to that which applies in job costing. A mark-up will be added to the cost per unit to give a selling price that will provide the required level of profit.

The choice of the cost unit by the organisation is important to ensure that a fair charge is made to the users of the service.

3.3 Cost per unit

$$\text{Cost per unit} = \frac{\text{Total costs for a period}}{\text{Number of service consults in the period}}$$

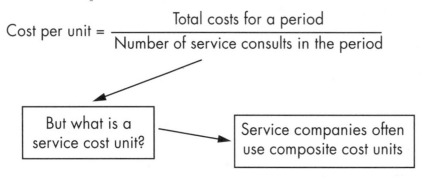

3.4 Composite cost units

Organisations in the service industry often use **composite cost units** to analyse and monitor their costs, particularly when a 'single' cost unit would not be appropriate. As an example, an airline may base a charge for paying for excess baggage on:

(a) How far in km the baggage will be transported
(b) The weight of the baggage

Both of these will have an impact on the airline's fuel cost, so it would be inappropriate to base the charge on distance or weight alone.

An appropriate composite cost unit would therefore be £X per kg per km.

Typical cost units used by companies operating in a service industry are shown below.

Service	Cost unit
Road, rail and air transport services	Passenger–kilometre, tonne–kilometre
Hotels	Occupied bed–night
Education	Full-time student
Hospitals	Patient–day
Catering establishments	Meal served

3.5 Service department costing

Service department costing is used to establish a specific cost for an 'internal service', which is a service provided by one department for another, rather than sold externally to customers. Service departments therefore include canteens and data-processing departments.

The purposes of service department costing:

(a)   To control the costs and efficiency in the service department

(b)   To control the costs of the user departments and prevent the unnecessary use of services

The 'cost' of support services charged to user departments could be based on any of the following:

(a)   No charge at all
(b)   Total actual cost
(c)   Standard absorption cost
(d)   Variable cost
(e)   Cost plus a mark-up for profit

Chapter summary

- Job costing is a costing system that is used in a business that provides individual, 'one-off' products for customers.

- In a job costing system the accounting function must first produce a schedule of the expected costs of the product that the customer wants; this schedule must include not only the direct costs of producing the product but also any overheads that need to be absorbed into the job to ensure that all of the overheads of the business for the period are eventually covered by the prices set for the jobs done.

- Once the price has been agreed and the job is started, all of the costs of the job must be gathered together by the accounting function. Any materials requisitions must quote the job number and all job cards for employees' hours must also show which job was worked on.

- The accounting function will then absorb overheads into the job according to the organisation's policies.

- Batch costing is used in businesses where instead of there being production runs of identical products there are a number of production runs of batches of different products.

- The purpose of batch costing is to find the cost of an entire batch of a product and then to divide that cost by the number of units produced in the batch; this will then give the unit cost of each unit of that product.

- Service costing is used in service businesses where services are provided rather than goods made. The measurement of activity often involves more than one activity as a composite cost unit.

Keywords

- **Batch costing:** A costing system that gathers together the costs of production of an entire batch of a similar product in order to find the cost of each individual item in that batch

- **Composite cost unit:** A cost unit where the service combines more than one activity

- **Job card:** An individual employee's record of the time spent on each job

- **Job costing:** A costing system that allocates costs to individual, 'one-off' jobs for customers

- **Service costing:** A costing system adapted for services or functions

1 A kitchen manufacturer has been asked to supply a kitchen to a customer. The estimates of costs are given below:

Materials for manufacturing the units – £12,500

Direct labour for fitting the units – 23 hours @ £8.60 per hour

Direct labour for redecorating – 5 hours @ £6.50 per hour

Overheads are absorbed on the basis of £12.40 per direct labour hour.

Profit on each job is taken at 25% of total costs.

How much will the kitchen cost the customer?

£ [   ]

2 A pie factory operates on a batch production system. The latest batch to have been produced is 1,200 cheese and mushroom pies. The costs of this batch are:

Ingredients   £840.00

Labour   7 hours @ £6.50

Overheads are absorbed on the basis of £1.20 per labour hour.

What is the cost of each pie (to one decimal place)?

[   ] pence

3 **Which of the following would be appropriate cost units for a transport business?**

(i)   Cost per tonne–kilometre
(ii)   Fixed cost per kilometre
(iii) Maintenance cost of each vehicle per kilometre

☐ (i) only
☐ (i) and (ii) only
☐ (i) and (iii) only
☐ All of them

4 **Which of the following organisations should NOT be advised to use service costing?**

☐ Distribution service
☐ Hospital
☐ Maintenance division of a manufacturing company
☐ An engineering company

Process costing
– losses

8

Learning outcomes

2.5	Differentiate between and apply different costing systems
	• How to record cost information, using different costing systems. These include:
	– Process costing (opening and/or closing WIP, value abnormal gains/losses transferred out of the process account and use of FIFO, and/or AVCO
	– Normal (scrap) losses, abnormal losses and gains, equivalent units, closing work progress and opening work in progress

Assessment context

An assessment question may ask you to calculate a loss or work in progress. However, there are no tasks on process costing in the sample assessments.

Qualification context

Modern costing techniques are tested in Level 4 *Management Accounting* papers and are often compared to traditional process costing techniques.

Business context

All businesses must keep track of their costs so that they can control them. Process costing is a type of costing system used by businesses that produce a continuous mass of similar units such as liquids, gases, paper, chemicals or food. Individual units, particularly liquids and gases, cannot be easily identified until the end of the production process.

Chapter overview

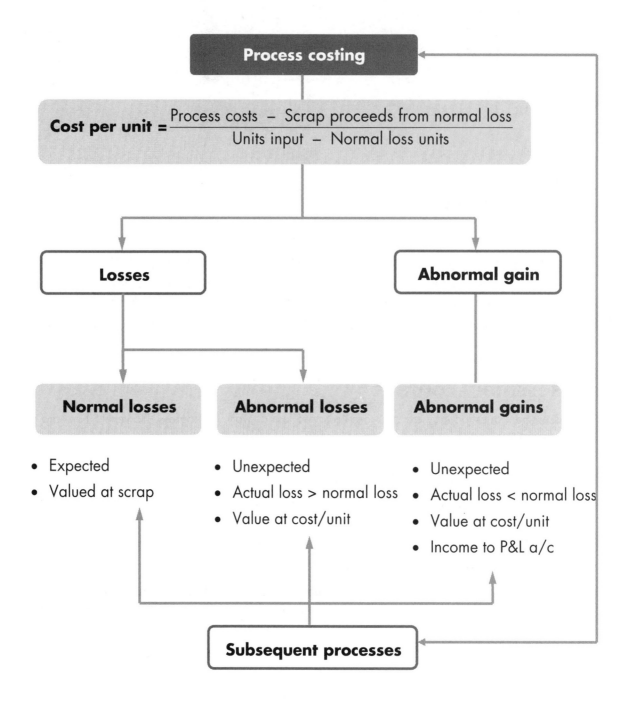

Process costing

$$\text{Cost per unit} = \frac{\text{Process costs} - \text{Scrap proceeds from normal loss}}{\text{Units input} - \text{Normal loss units}}$$

Losses

Abnormal gain

Normal losses

- Expected
- Valued at scrap

Abnormal losses

- Unexpected
- Actual loss > normal loss
- Value at cost/unit

Abnormal gains

- Unexpected
- Actual loss < normal loss
- Value at cost/unit
- Income to P&L a/c

Subsequent processes

Introduction

Process costing is a method of costing goods or services that are identical but not separately identifiable until the end of the production process due to the continuous nature of the process. Process costing involves spreading the total costs in a 'fair' way across the output.

The assessment for this paper may ask you to deal with a situation where there are losses or where there is work in progress but not both.

1 No losses

The aim of process costing is to gather together all of the costs incurred in a process in a period and divide these costs by the number of units produced in the period. As each of the units is identical, what we are effectively doing is finding the average cost for each unit produced in the period. This is simple when there are no losses and no work in progress.

$$\text{Cost per unit of output} = \frac{\text{Total process costs}}{\text{Output units}}$$

Illustration 1: Cost per unit and process account

Nuneaton Enterprises is a food processing manufacturer which makes a number of different types of product in a number of different processes.

The costs of the process VF1 for May were:

	£
Direct materials 120,000 kg	38,000
Direct labour (1,200 × £9)	10,800
Overheads absorbed	11,200
Total process cost	60,000

The cost per unit produced is the total process cost divided by the number of units produced:

$$\text{Cost per unit} = \frac{£60,000}{120,000\,\text{kg}}$$

$$= 50 \text{ pence per kg}$$

The costs and the production are normally shown in a process account. The process account for process VF1 for May would be made up as follows:

- The materials input into the process in both kilograms and value are debited to the process account.

- The labour and overhead costs are also debited to the account (sometimes these two costs are given together and called the **conversion costs**).

- The output is shown on the credit side as 120,000 kg each valued at 50 pence, therefore totalling £60,000, and the process account is balanced.

Process VF1

	kg	£		kg	£
Materials	120,000	38,000			
Labour		10,800			
Overheads		11,200	Output	120,000	60,000
	120,000	60,000		120,000	60,000

Key term

Conversion costs are labour costs plus overhead costs.

Activity 1: Process account – no losses

Input to Process I during a period was 1,000 units of raw materials, costing £40,000. Other costs were: labour £50,000, overheads £20,000. All output was transferred to Process II.

Required

Calculate the cost per unit of output and complete the process account.

Cost per unit = £ [   ]

PROCESS I

	Units	£		Units	£

2 Normal losses

Key term

Normal loss is the expected loss from the process.

In many processes the quantity of material put into the process is not the same as the quantity that is produced from the process as the process has losses during the processing time, for example due to evaporation or defective units. Over time an organisation will be able to judge the normal level of loss from a process. The normal loss is the amount of loss that is expected from a process. This is usually expressed as a percentage of the materials input to the process.

As the normal loss is part of the normal manufacturing process, no value is given to the normal loss units; instead the process costs are averaged out over the good units of production. Note that when there is a scrap value, this does not apply (see later in the chapter).

Illustration 2: Normal loss

Another of Nuneaton's processes is the GS3. There is a normal loss of 10% of materials input into this process. The costs incurred in this process and the output achieved for the month of May are:

Direct materials	50,000 kg	£22,500
Direct labour		£16,500
Overheads		£6,000
Output		45,000 kg

The steps to follow are:

Step 1   **Calculate the number of normal loss units:**
Kg input × normal loss %
   50,000 kg × 10% = 5,000 kg

Step 2   **Calculate the expected output from the process:**
Kg input less normal loss
   50,000 kg – 5,000 kg = 45,000 kg

Step 3   **Total the process costs:**
Materials + labour + overheads
   £22,500 + £16,500 + £6,000 = £45,000

Step 4   **Calculate the cost per unit of expected output**
Process costs/expected output

$$\frac{£45,000}{45,000 \text{ kg}} = £1 \text{ per kg}$$

This can then all be written up in the process account:

Process GS3

	kg	£		kg	£
Materials	50,000	22,500	Normal loss	5,000	–
Labour		16,500	Output	45,000	45,000
Overheads		6,000			
	50,000	45,000		50,000	45,000

Both the kg and the value columns must balance. No value has been assigned to the normal loss units: all of the process costs have been shared between the expected output units.

Assessment focus point

An assessment task may ask you to calculate a normal loss.

2.1 Normal loss with scrap value

In some instances the loss units are defective units or waste materials that can be sold for a scrap value. Any scrap value arising from selling the normal loss can be used to reduce the process cost, and the normal loss is valued at this scrap value. The net costs are then spread over the 'good' units of output.

Formula to learn

$$\text{Cost per 'good' unit} = \frac{\text{Total process costs} - \text{Scrap proceeds from normal loss}}{\text{Units input} - \text{Normal loss units}}$$

The scrap value of a normal loss is debited to the scrap account and credited to the process account. We have added the scrap account in the activity below for completeness, although it is unlikely that you will see it in your assessment.

Activity 2: Process account – normal loss

Input and costs are the same as Activity 1.

Losses normally account for 10% of input.

Output was 900 units.

BPP
LEARNING MEDIA

Required

Calculate the cost per unit of output and complete the Process I account assuming all scrapped units have a scrap value of £20 each.

Cost per unit = | £ | |

PROCESS I

	Units	£		Units	£
Raw materials	1,000	40,000	Normal loss		
Labour		50,000	To Process II		
Overheads		20,000			

SCRAP ACCOUNT

	Units	£		Units	£
Scrap value of normal loss	100	2,000	Cash received		2,000
		2,000			2,000

3 Abnormal losses and gains

Key term

Abnormal loss is any actual loss units in excess of the normal loss units.

Abnormal gain is any actual loss units that are less than the normal loss units.

In many processes the actual process loss will differ from the expected or normal loss. If the actual loss is greater than the expected loss the difference is known as an abnormal loss. If the actual loss is less than the expected loss the difference is known as an abnormal gain.

Whereas the normal loss units are expected and unavoidable, any abnormal losses or gains are not expected and are considered avoidable, therefore the accounting treatment of abnormal losses and gains is different from that of the normal loss. The normal loss units were assigned no value. However, any abnormal loss units are valued in the same way as the good output.

Illustration 3: Abnormal losses

The normal loss for another of Nuneaton's processes PE7 is 5%. The inputs, costs and output of this process in May are given below.

Direct materials	20,000 kg	£15,400
Direct labour		£6,200
Overheads		£1,200
Output		18,400 kg

Step 1   **Calculate the number of normal loss units:**

20,000 kg × 5% = 1,000 kg

Step 2   **Calculate the expected output from the process:**

20,000 kg – 1,000 kg = 19,000 kg

Step 3   **Total the process costs:**

£15,400 + £6,200 + £1,200 = £22,800

Step 4   **Calculate the cost per unit of expected output**

$$\frac{£22,800}{19,000\,kg} = £1.20 \text{ per kg}$$

The process account is now written up. This is where the units column becomes important. Our expected output was 19,000 kg but in fact only 18,400 kg was produced, so there is an abnormal loss of 600 kg which is valued at the same value as the good output, £1.20 per kg, so £720 in total. The good output of 18,400 kg is also valued at £1.20 per kg, totalling £22,080, and both the unit columns and value columns balance.

Process PE7

	kg	£		kg	£
Materials	20,000	15,400	Normal loss	1,000	–
Labour		6,200	Abnormal loss	600	720
Overheads		1,200	Output	18,400	22,080
	20,000	22,800		20,000	22,800

The abnormal loss has been credited to the process account and must be debited to an abnormal loss account:

Abnormal loss account

	kg	£		kg	£
Process PE7	600	720			

At the period end, the abnormal loss account is cleared to the statement of profit or loss. In this case it will be an expense of £720. In your assessment it is likely that you will only need to deal with the process T account, but we have shown you the abnormal loss account just to help your understanding.

Activity 3: Process account – abnormal loss

As per Activity 2, but output to Process II is 880 units not 900 units as expected.

Required

Calculate the cost per unit and complete the Process I account.

Cost per unit =   £ [   ]

PROCESS I

	Units	£		Units	£
Raw materials	1,000	40,000	Normal loss		
Labour		50,000	To Process II		
Overheads		20,000	Abnormal loss		

Illustration 4: Abnormal gains

Process RD4 in Nuneaton Enterprises has a normal loss of 10%. The inputs, costs and output for the month of May are given below:

Direct materials	10,000 kg	£11,200
Direct labour		£9,400
Overheads		£6,400
Output		9,350 kg

Step 1 **Calculate the number of normal loss units:**

10,000 kg × 10% = 1,000 kg

Step 2 **Calculate the expected output from the process:**

10,000 kg – 1,000 kg = 9,000 kg

Step 3 **Total the process costs:**

£11,200 + £9,400 + £6,400 = £27,000

Step 4 **Calculate the cost per unit of expected output:**

$$\frac{£27,000}{9,000\,kg} = £3 \text{ per kg}$$

Now we can write up the ledger accounts. In this case there is an abnormal gain as actual output is 350 kg more than the expected output. The abnormal gain units are debited to the process account and valued at the cost per unit of £3. The normal loss as usual has no value assigned to it and the output of 9,350 kg is also valued at £3.

Process RD4

	kg	£		kg	£
Materials	10,000	11,200	Normal loss	1,000	–
Labour		9,400	Output	9,350	28,050
Overheads		6,400			
Abnormal gain	350	1,050			
	10,350	28,050		10,350	28,050

The abnormal gain has been debited in the process account and therefore must be credited in an abnormal gain account.

Abnormal gain

	kg	£		kg	£
			Process RD4	350	1,050

This amount is then credited to the statement of profit or loss as an abnormal gain. Again, you will only need to worry about the process T account in your assessment.

Activity 4: Process account – abnormal gain

Continuing with the same example from Activity 2, but output to Process II is 920 units, not 900 units as expected.

Required

Calculate the cost per unit and complete the Process I account.

Cost per unit = £ [   ]

PROCESS I

	Units	£		Units	£
Raw materials	1,000	40,000	Normal loss		
Labour		50,000	To Process II		
Overheads		20,000			
Abnormal gain					

Chapter summary

- Where identical products are produced in a continuous process then a process costing system will be in operation.

- The costs of the process are divided by the expected output from the process to find the cost per unit of the good output; any normal losses are not assigned any value unless a scrap value is available.

- Abnormal losses or gains are valued at the full process cost per unit.

- Any scrap value for normal loss units is offset against the total process cost.

Keywords

- **Abnormal loss:** Any actual loss units in excess of the normal loss units

- **Abnormal gain:** Any actual loss units that are less than the normal loss units

- **Conversion costs:** Labour and overhead costs of the process

- **Normal loss:** The expected loss from the process

- **Process costing:** A costing system where the unit cost is found by averaging the period costs of the process over the expected good output from the process

1 **In a process account, abnormal losses are valued (please tick):**

☐ At their scrap value

☐ At the same rate as good production

☐ At the cost of raw materials

☐ At good production cost less scrap value

2 Sometimes materials are lost during processing and the materials may be scrapped. Sometimes scrap may have a value.

If this is the case, the accounting treatment for the scrap value of normal loss is:

Debit [▼] account

Credit [▼] account

Picklist:

Process

Scrap

3 Given below are the details for a process for the month of January:

Direct materials	50,000 kg	£350,000
Direct labour		£125,000
Overheads		£57,000
Normal loss		5%
Output		46,000 kg

Write up the process account to record the process results for the month.

Process account

	kg	£		kg	£
Materials			Normal loss		
Labour			Abnormal loss		
Overheads			Output		

4 Given below are the details for a process for week 18:

Direct materials	6,000 litres	£14,300
Direct labour		£7,200
Overheads		£11,980

The normal loss from the process is 10% and the output for the week was 5,600 litres.

Write up the process account to reflect the process costs for the week.

Process account

	ltr	£		ltr	£
Materials			Normal loss		
Labour					
Overheads					
Abnormal gain			Output		

5 Given below are the details of a process for the month of March. Any loss units can be sold for scrap for £1.00 per kg.

Direct materials	40,000 kg	£158,200
Direct labour		£ 63,500
Overheads		£ 31,740
Normal loss		8%
Output		35,000 kg

Write up the process account to reflect the process results for the month.

Process account

	kg	£		kg	£
Materials			Normal loss		
Labour			Abnormal loss		
Overheads			Output		

Process costing – work in progress (WIP)

Learning outcomes

2.5	Differentiate between and apply different costing systems
	• How to record cost information, using different costing systems. These include:
	– Process costing (opening and/or closing WIP, value abnormal gains/losses transferred out of the process account and use of FIFO, and/or AVCO
	– Normal (scrap) losses, abnormal losses and gains, equivalent units, closing work progress and opening work in progress

Assessment context

An assessment question may ask you to calculate a loss or work in progress. However, there are no tasks on process costing in the sample assessments.

Qualification context

Modern costing techniques are tested in Level 4 *Management Accounting* papers and are often compared to traditional process costing techniques.

Business context

All businesses must keep track of their costs so that they can control them. Process costing is a type of costing system used by businesses that produce a continuous mass of similar units such as paper, chemicals or food. It is typically used when dealing with liquids and gases as the individual units cannot be easily identified until the end of the production process.

Chapter overview

Process costing

Costing → where goods/services are product in a series of processes

Work in progress (WIP)

At the end of the accounting period partially completed units are called WIP units

- Restate WIP units in terms of equivalent whole units (EU)

Closing WIP

(no opening WIP)
(1) Unit calculation
(2) Set up T account
(3) Statement of EU
(4) Valuations
(5) Complete T account

Opening WIP

(and closing WIP)
Same steps

Which method?

FIFO
Assumes opening WIP completed first, need:
% complete materials
% complete conversion
Total cost b/f

Weighted average
All units equally likely to be completed, need: cost b/f broken down into materials and conversion

Opening WIP + Input units = Good output + Normal loss +/- Abnormal loss/gain + Closing WIP

Losses and WIP are unlikely to be tested in the same question in the exam

Subsequent/previous processes

- Output from process 1 becomes input to process 2

Introduction

At the end of the accounting period we may have two types of output from a process:

(a)   Fully completed good output

(b)   Output that is incomplete

This partially completed output is known as work in progress (WIP).

To spread the cost fairly between units we use a measure called **equivalent units (EU)**.

Key term

Equivalent units (EU) are the number of complete units to which the work in progress is equivalent.

1 Equivalent units

This will calculate how many finished units the WIP equates to in terms of materials and labour input. For example, two shirts each 50% complete have had the same amount of fabric and labour input as one finished shirt, so in this case the two work in progress units are one equivalent unit.

The number of equivalent units for each cost type is then used to calculate the cost per equivalent unit. This then allows a value to be given to the finished goods and the WIP in the process account.

Where there is WIP there may be a rounding difference as either a debit or a credit to make the account balance. This should be fairly small.

2 Work in progress

Illustration 1: Bank reconciliation

Nuneaton Enterprises has a process called SL4. During the month of May the costs of that process were £21,000 and the output was 10,000 completed units and 1,000 units that were half completed. How do we value each of the units of completed output and work in progress? We use equivalent units.

	Equivalent units
Completed production	10,000
Work in progress (1,000 × ½)	500
	10,500

Therefore during the period the equivalent of 10,500 completed units have passed through the process. The cost per equivalent unit (EU) can now be found.

$$\text{Cost per equivalent unit} \quad = \frac{£21,000}{10,500\,EU}$$

$$= £2 \text{ per equivalent unit}$$

In the process account the completed production will be valued at:

Completed production 10,000 × £2 = £20,000

The closing work in progress will be valued at £2 for each equivalent unit:

Closing work in progress 500 × £2 = £1,000

The process account will appear as follows:

Process account

	£		£
Input costs	21,000	Completed production	20,000
		Closing work in progress	1,000
	21,000		21,000

Later on we will look at two ways of calculating **opening work in progress**. Before that we will finish off looking at equivalent units where costs are incurred at different stages of the process.

3 Different stages of completion

Remember that in a process we not only have materials input to the process, but also labour costs and overheads. In practice it is common for the materials, labour and overheads to be incurred at different stages of the process. Therefore at the end of the period the **closing work in progress** may have had all of its material input but only half of the labour input. The method of dealing with this is to split out the costs into their different categories – materials and labour/overheads – and to calculate equivalent units of completion for each category of cost.

Illustration 2: Different stages of completion

Another of Nuneaton Enterprises processes is the KS2. The costs incurred in this process for the month of May are as follows:

Materials	£23,760
Labour and overheads	£10,200
(sometimes called conversion costs)	

At the end of the period there were 8,000 units of completed output and 1,000 units of closing work in progress. The work in progress has had 80% of its material input and 50% of the labour and overheads input.

We must now calculate the cost per equivalent unit for materials and labour/overheads.

	Units	Materials		Labour/overheads	
		Proportion complete	Equivalent units	Proportion complete	Equivalent units
Completed	8,000	100%	8,000	100%	8,000
Work in progress	1,000	80%	800	50%	500
Total equivalent units			8,800		8,500
Cost per equivalent unit		= £23,760		= £10,200	
		8,800		8,500	
		= £2.70 per EU		= £1.20 per EU	

Finally, we can find values for the completed output and the closing work in progress.

	£
Completed output	
Materials (8,000 × £2.70)	21,600
Labour/overhead (8,000 × £1.20)	9,600
	31,200
Work in progress	
Materials (800 × £2.70)	2,160
Labour/overhead (500 × £1.20)	600
	2,760

This can all then be entered into the process account.

Process account

	£		£
Materials	23,760	Completed output	31,200
Labour/overhead	10,200	Closing work in progress	2,760
	33,960		33,960

Activity 1: Process account – closing WIP

The following are introduced into Process I.

Raw materials	1,500 units	£12,975
Labour		£9,576
Overheads		£3,156

Closing WIP: 50 units – completed as below

Raw materials	100%	complete
Labour	60%	complete
Overheads	30%	complete

There are no losses in this process. Finished output is 1,450 units.

Required

Follow the instructions below to complete the tables.

(a) Complete the process account as far as possible and add to it as you complete parts (c) and (d).

PROCESS I					
	Units	**£**		**Units**	**£**
Raw materials			To Process II		
Labour			Closing WIP c/d		
Overheads			Rounding		

(b) Complete the statement of equivalent units.

	Total	**Materials**	**Labour**	**Overheads**
Finished output				
Closing WIP				

(c) The cost per equivalent unit is (to 2 decimal places):

	Cost ÷ equivalent units	**£**
Materials		
Labour		
Overheads		
Finished unit total cost		

(d) The value of finished goods is:

Finished goods (units) × Cost per finished unit =

The value of closing WIP is (to the nearest whole number):

Cost item	**Workings** **Closing WIP equivalent units × cost per equivalent unit**	**£**
Materials		
Labour		
Overheads		
Total closing WIP value		

4 Opening WIP using FIFO and weighted average methods

The closing WIP from one accounting period will become the opening WIP in the next. There are two methods that we can use when there is opening WIP.

(a) FIFO

- Assumes that opening WIP is completed first
- Spreads costs incurred in the period over work done in that period, ie
  - (i) Finished goods/output (started and finished)
  - (ii) Opening WIP (finished)
  - (iii) Closing WIP (started)

  and then adds on the opening WIP costs to the sum of (i) and (ii) to give the total costs of finished output

(b) Weighted average

- All items are equally likely to be completed
- Spreads all costs (including those brought forward in opening WIP) over all units

Illustration 3: Opening WIP

Alpha Ltd has the following costs in a period:

Raw materials	2,050 units	£22,550
Labour		£16,304
Overheads		£8,212

Opening WIP: 50 units with a value of £610. It was 100% complete for materials, 60% for labour and 30% for overheads.

The split of the £610 is:

Materials	£400
Labour	£180
Overheads	£30
	£610

Output from this process: 2,020 units

Closing WIP: 80 units with a value of £1,456. It was also complete as below

Raw materials	100%	complete
Labour	60%	complete
Overheads	60%	complete

There were no losses.

Required

Prepare a process account using (a) FIFO and (b) weighted average methods.

(a) FIFO

Unit calculation:

Opening WIP + Input = Good output + Closing WIP

Note. In the assessment you will not have to deal with WIP and losses at the same time. (If you did, the unit calculation would have to include losses and gains.)

Step 1 Prepare a statement of equivalent units

	Actual	Equivalent units		
	units	Materials	Labour	Overheads
Opening WIP W1	50	–	20	35
Goods started and finished	1,970	1,970	1,970	1,970
(= output – opening WIP)				
Good output	2,020	1,970	1,990	2,005
Closing WIP W2	80	80	48	48
Equivalent units	2,100	2,050	2,038	2,053

Step 2 Prepare a statement of cost per equivalent unit

	£	£	£
	Materials	Labour	Overheads
Input costs	22,550	16,304	8,212
Cost per equivalent unit	11.00	8.00	4.00
= Input costs/Equivalent units			

Step 3 Value the units

		£
Value of good output =	Costs b/f in opening WIP =	610
	Materials 1,970 × £11	21,670
	Labour 1,990 × £8	15,920
	Overheads 2,005 × £4	8,020
		46,220
Value of Closing WIP = 80 × £11 + 48 × £8 + 48 × £4 = £1,456		

Step 4 Prepare the process account

Process

	Units	£		Units	£
Opening WIP	50	610	Good output	2,020	46,220
b/f					
Raw Materials	2,050	22,550	(see st of equiv units)		
Labour		16,304	Closing WIP W2	80	1,456
Overheads		8,212			
	2,100	47,676		2,100	47,676

Workings

1 Opening WIP is 100% complete for materials but 60% for labour and 30% for overheads.

   To complete – Labour (100 – 60)% = 40% × 50 = 20

                  – Overheads (100 – 30)% = 70% × 50 = 35

2 Closing WIP –   100% complete for materials so 100% × 80 = 80

                  – 60% complete for labour so 60% × 80 = 48

                  – 60% complete for overheads so 60% × 80 = 48

(b) Weighted average

Step 1 Statement of equivalent units

	Actual	Equivalent units		
	units	Materials	Labour	Overheads
Good output	2,020	2,020	2,020	2,020
Closing WIP	80	80	48	48
Equivalent units	2,100	2,100	2,068	2,068

Step 2 Costs

	£	£	£
Costs b/f (£610) (from the example)	400	180	30
Input costs	22,550	16,304	8,212
	22,950	16,484	8,242
Cost per equivalent unit = Input costs/Equivalent units	10.93	7.97	3.99
		Total £22.89	

Step 3 Value the units

Value of good output = £22.89 × 2,020 = £46,238

Value of Closing WIP = 80 × £10.93 + 48 × £7.97 + 48 × £3.99 = £1,448

Step 4 Prepare the process account

Note. You can do the calculations for number of units and costs of the process easily as these are the same as the FIFO method.

Assessment focus point

It is unlikely that you will see both opening and closing work in progress together in an assessment task, but we have shown you it above to help your understanding.

Activity 2: Opening WIP – FIFO and weighted average method

This information relates to Process I.

Input:	Raw materials	2,050 units	£22,550
	Labour		£16,304
	Overheads		£8,212

Opening WIP: 50 units valued @ £610 as follows:

		£
Materials	100% complete	400
Labour	60% complete	180
Overheads	30% complete	30
		610

Output from Process I: 2,100 units

There were no losses.

Required

Using (a) FIFO and (b) weighted average methods, calculate the equivalent units and cost per equivalent unit under both the methods.

(a) FIFO

Statement of equivalent units

	Total Units	Equivalent Units		
		Materials	Labour	Overheads
Opening WIP				
Goods started and finished				
Good output				

Costs per equivalent unit

	Materials £	Labour £	Overheads £
Input costs			
Equivalent units			
Cost per equivalent unit			

The total cost per equivalent unit is   £

(b) Weighted average

Statement of equivalent units

	Actual units	Equivalent units		
		Materials	Labour	Overheads
Good output				

Cost per equivalent unit

Costs	Materials £	Labour £	Overhead £
Opening WIP costs b/f			
Input costs			
Total costs			
Equivalent units			
Cost per equivalent unit			

The total cost per equivalent unit is   £

Assessment focus point

An assessment task may ask you to calculate work in progress.

Chapter summary

- At the end of the period there may be some partially completed units, or closing work in progress.

- In order to value the completed units and the closing work in progress the total number of equivalent units must be calculated and the cost per unit determined.

- If the closing work in progress has different stages of completion for the different elements of input, materials and labour/overheads, then a cost per equivalent unit must be calculated for each element of the input.

Keywords

- **Closing work in progress:** Partially completed units from a process at the end of the period

- **Equivalent units:** The number of complete units to which the work in progress is equivalent

- **Opening work in progress:** Partially completed units brought forward at the beginning of the period

1 **In process costing an equivalent unit is (please tick):**

☐ A notional whole unit representing incomplete work

☐ A unit made at standard performance

☐ A unit which is identical to a competitor's product

☐ A unit being currently made which is the same as previously manufactured

☐ A unit made in more than one process cost centre

2 A process has the following inputs for the month of July:

	£
Materials	8,960
Labour/overheads	4,290

The output from the process consists of 2,000 completed units and 400 units of closing work in progress. The work in progress is 60% complete as to materials but only 50% complete for labour and overheads.

Calculate the value of the completed output and the closing work in progress, and prepare the process account for the month.

		Materials		Labour/overheads	
	Units	Proportion complete	Equivalent units	Proportion complete	Equivalent units
Completed units					
Closing work in progress					
Total equivalent units					
Cost per equivalent unit					

	£
Valuation	
Completed units	
Materials	
Labour/overheads	
Total	
Closing work in progress	
Materials	
Labour/overheads	
Total	

Process account

	£		£
Materials		Completed units	
Labour/overhead		Closing work in progress	

Budgeting – fixed and flexed budgets

10

Learning outcomes

4.1	Calculate variances
	• Students need to be able to compare budget/standard vs actual costs and revenues, and calculate variances using:
	– Fixed budgets
	– Flexible budgets

Assessment context

You should make sure that you are happy with using the information from a cost card to prepare simple cost and revenues budgets at different activity levels. Assessment tasks may ask you prepare a flexed budget and to calculate variances and indicate whether they are adverse or favourable.

Qualification context

The fundamental aspects of budgeting learnt in this paper give the ground work for Level 4 *Management Accounting* units. At the higher level budgetary control, types of budgets and behavioural aspects of budgeting are looked at and flexed budgets are prepared and used for variance analysis calculations.

Business context

A core part of any business is to determine its objectives and come up with a plan of how they will achieve these objectives (strategy). Budgeting provides details of how the business should operate in order to achieve its objectives.

Chapter overview

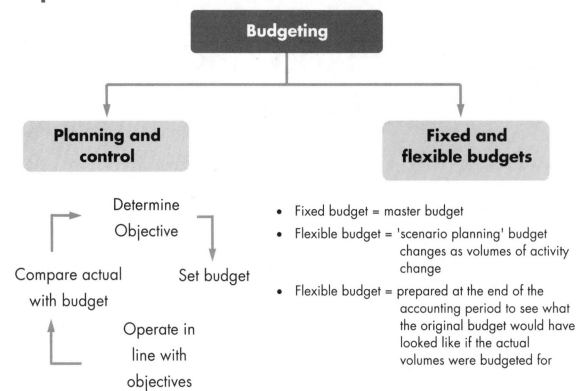

Budgeting

Planning and control

Determine Objective

Compare actual with budget

Set budget

Operate in line with objectives

Fixed and flexible budgets

- Fixed budget = master budget
- Flexible budget = 'scenario planning' budget changes as volumes of activity change
- Flexible budget = prepared at the end of the accounting period to see what the original budget would have looked like if the actual volumes were budgeted for

Introduction

A budget is a financial and/or quantitative plan of operations for a forthcoming period.

Budgeting is part of the overall process of planning and control. A budget is a plan which will assist in achieving objectives.

The cycle of planning and control:

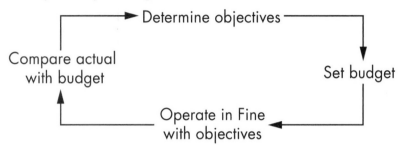

1 Fixed and flexible budgets

The **fixed budget** is the master budget prepared before the beginning of the budget period.

It is based on budgeted volumes, costs and revenues.

Illustration 1: Fixed budgets

Martin Engineering prepares detailed budgets for each quarter of the year. The budget for Quarter 4 of 20X8 was set as follows:

	Quarter 4 budget £
Sales 1,000 units	40,000
Material	(10,000)
Labour	(12,000)
Production overhead	(3,000)
Gross profit	15,000
Overheads	(8,000)
Operating profit	7,000

This budget was set on the basis of both production and sales of 1,000 units and no opening or closing inventory.

It is now the first week in January 20X9 and the actual results for Quarter 4 are being compared to the budget:

	Quarter 4 budget £		Quarter 4 actual £
Sales 1,000 units	40,000	1,200 units	45,600
Material	(10,000)		(12,480)
Labour	(12,000)		(13,800)
Production overhead	(3,000)		(3,200)
Gross profit	15,000		16,120
Overheads	(8,000)		(9,080)
Operating profit	7,000		7,040

As part of the process of control, the management accountant of Martin Engineering now prepares a report showing the variances between the budget and the actual results (remember from your earlier studies that variances will be described either as adverse or favourable).

Variance report

	Quarter 4 budget £	Units	Quarter 4 actual £	Variance £
Sales 1,000 units	40,000	1,200	45,600	5,600 Fav
Material	(10,000)		(12,480)	2,480 Adv
Labour	(12,000)		(13,800)	1,800 Adv
Production overhead	(3,000)		(3,200)	200 Adv
Gross profit	15,000		16,120	1,120 Fav
Overheads	(8,000)		(9,080)	1,080 Adv
Operating profit	7,000		7,040	40 Fav

It would appear that there are a mixture of variances with favourable variances for sales and profit but adverse variances for all of the costs.

The problem however is that the budget and the actual figures are not strictly comparable: the budget was based upon sales and production of 1,000 units whereas the actual activity level was production and sales of 1,200 units. This is where flexed budgets can be used.

Key term

Flexible budgets are budgets designed to change as volume of activity changes. This can be done by recognising the behaviour of different costs (fixed or variable).

Flexed budgets are budgets that have been prepared based on actual volumes for budgetary control purposes.

1.1 Purpose of flexible budgets

(a) Designed to cope with **different activity levels** to keep the budget meaningful and hence preserve the relevance of variances for effective control.

(b) Useful at the **planning** stage to show different results from possible activity levels. This is an example of 'what if?' analysis.

(c) Necessary as a **control** device because we can meaningfully compare actual results with relevant flexed/flexible budget, ie budgetary control. They are used at the end of a control period to aid with budgetary control – to compare actual results with what should have been achieved based on budgeted costs/revenues at the actual volumes.

When used within this context of budgetary control the **flexible** budget is referred to as the **flexed budget**. A flexed budget is a budget that has been prepared based on actual volumes for budgetary control purposes.

Differences between the flexible/flexed budget figures and actual results are called **variances**.

Illustration 2: Flexed budgets

Given below again is the Quarter 4 budget for Martin Engineering:

	£
Sales 1,000 units	40,000
Material	(10,000)
Labour	(12,000)
Production overhead	(3,000)
Gross profit	15,000
Overheads	(8,000)
Operating profit	7,000

The details of the cost behaviour of each of the costs is given below:

Materials	The materials cost is totally variable.
Labour	Each operative can only produce 250 units each quarter – the cost of each operative is £3,000 each quarter.
Production overhead	The production overhead is a totally fixed cost.
Overheads	The general expenses are made up of a budgeted fixed cost of £8,000.

We will now flex the budget to the actual activity level of 1,200 units.

Sales

Budgeted selling price	=	£40,000/1,000 units
	=	£40 per unit

Therefore the budgeted sales revenue for 1,200 units is:

Sales	=	1,200 × £40
	=	£48,000

Materials are totally variable

Budgeted materials per unit	=	£10,000/1,000 units
	=	£10 per unit
Budgeted materials cost for 1,200 units	=	1,200 × £10
	=	£12,000

Labour is a stepped cost

One operative is required for each 250 units; therefore for 1,200 units five operatives will be required. For 1,000 units, four operatives would be used. So the cost per operative = £12,000/4 = £3,000.

Budgeted labour cost	=	5 × £3,000
	=	£15,000

Production overheads is a fixed cost

Budgeted cost for 1,200 units	=	£3,000

General overheads is a fixed cost	=	£8,000

The flexed budget will appear as follows:

	Quarter 4 flexed budget £
Sales 1,200 units	48,000
Materials	(12,000)
Labour	(15,000)
Production overhead	(3,000)
Gross profit	18,000
Overheads	(8,000)
Operating profit	10,000

The flexed budget can then be compared to the actual figures in the form of an operating statement and the true variances calculated.

Martin Engineering: Quarter 4 operating statement

	Budget £	Units	Actual £	Variance £
Sales 1,200 units	48,000	1,200	45,600	2,400 Adv
Material	(12,000)		(12,480)	480 Adv
Labour	(15,000)		(13,800)	1,200 Fav
Production overhead	(3,000)		(3,200)	200 Adv
Gross profit	18,000		16,120	1,880 Adv
General expenses	(8,000)		(9,080)	1,080 Adv
Operating profit	10,000		7,040	2,960 Adv

We can now see that instead of an overall favourable profit variance being reported there is in fact a significant adverse profit variance with all the variances other than the labour variance being adverse. This is quite a different picture to the variances calculated using the fixed budget. Note that a report like this, that allows actual figures to be compared with budget figures and variances to be calculated, is called an **operating statement.**

Activity 1: Country soups

The marketing manager of Country Soups believes that the sales of mushroom soup next quarter will be between 350,000 and 450,000 cans. The budgeted cost schedule below contains cost information relevant over this range.

Required

Complete the budgeted cost schedule for the three possible levels of production shown below, calculating the cost per can in £ to 3 decimal places.

Cans made:		350,000 £	400,000 £	450,000 £
Cost element	**Cost**			
Direct materials	10p per can			
Direct labour	8p per can			
Canning costs	2p per can			
Depreciation	£16,000			
Rent and rates	£28,000			
Other overheads	£36,000			
Total cost (£)				
Cost per can (£)				

Note. Depreciation, rent and rates, and other overheads are all fixed costs.

Activity 2: Charter flights

The Charter Flights profit centre has just revised its forecasts for the number of miles it expects to fly during the next month on a particular charter contract. Originally it expected the contract would be for flights totalling 5,000 miles. It now expects that the total miles to be flown will increase to either 6,000 or 7,000 miles.

Notes

- The company chartering the flights has negotiated with Charter Flights a reduction on the sales price of 10% per mile, paid on all miles flown in excess of the 5,000 miles agreed in the original contract.

- Landing and servicing fee are a semi-variable cost. There is a fixed charge of £600,000 plus £50 per mile.

Required

Use the table below to estimate the profit per mile (in pounds, to 2 decimal places) of this contract at both 6,000 and 7,000 miles flown.

Likely miles	5,000 £000	6,000 £000	7,000 £000
Sales revenue	2,500		
Variable/semi-variable costs:			
Aviation fuel	400		
Landing and servicing fees	850		
Other variable overheads	135		
Fixed costs:			
Wages and salaries	420		
Other fixed overheads	625		
Total cost	2,430		
Total profit	70		
	£	£	£
Profit per mile flown	14.00		

Activity 3: TV dinners

A company has produced three forecasts of activity levels for the next three months for its TV dinners range. The original budget involved producing 5,000 batches but, due to an increase in demand, production levels of between 6,000 and 7,000 batches now seem likely.

Overheads are semi-variable and they should be calculated using the high–low method. If 8,000 batches are sold the total overheads will be £20,800 and the unit variable cost is constant up to this volume. At 5,000 units total overheads are £16,300.

Required

Complete the table below to estimate the profit per batch (to 3 decimal places) of the TV dinners range at the different activity levels.

Batches made and sold	5,000	6,000	7,000
	£	£	£
Sales revenue	30,000		
Costs:			
Direct materials	1,250		
Direct labour	3,000		
Overheads			
Variable element			
Fixed element			
Total cost			
Total profit			
Profit per batch			

Assessment focus point

An assessment task may ask you to flex a budget, calculate variances and indicate whether they are adverse or favourable.

Chapter summary

- A budgeted costing system which allows the budgeted cost of production to be compared to the actual costs and variances calculated can help management perform their three main roles of decision making, planning and control.

- A fixed budget is set in advance of a budgeting period as a predetermined plan of activity for all areas of a business.

- A flexed budget is used in the control aspect of the budgetary system as the actual results are compared to the flexed budget in order to determine any variances.

- In order to flex a budget a distinction must be drawn between variable costs and fixed costs. The variable elements of cost will increase or decrease with changes in activity level whereas the fixed elements of cost do not vary with changes in activity levels.

Keywords

- **Budgeted costing system:** A system that assigns budgeted costs to each cost unit and allows a comparison of budgeted costs to actual costs and the calculation of variances

- **Variance:** The difference between the budgeted costs and the actual costs for a period

- **Fixed budget:** A budget set in advance of a period in order to act as a plan of action for the whole organisation

- **Flexed budget:** A budget prepared for the actual activity level for the period

- **Operating statement:** A report allowing actual figures to be compared with budget figures and variances calculated

1   The budget for a production company for the month of December and the actual results for the month are given below:

	Budget 4,000 units £	Actual 3,600 units £
Sales	96,000	90,000
Materials	18,000	15,120
Labour	27,200	25,200
Production overhead	5,700	5,900
Gross profit	45,100	43,780
General expenses	35,200	32,880
Operating profit	9,900	10,900

The materials and labour costs are variable costs, the production overhead is a fixed cost and the general expenses are fixed.

(a)   **Calculate variances between the fixed budget and the actual results and state whether they are adverse or favourable.**

	Budget 4,000 units £	Actual 3,600 units £	Variance £	Adv/Fav
Sales	96,000	90,000		
Materials	18,000	15,120		
Labour	27,200	25,200		
Production overhead	5,700	5,900		
Gross profit	45,100	43,780		
General expenses	35,200	32,880		
Operating profit	9,900	10,900		

(b) **Prepare a flexed budget for the actual activity level and show the variances for each of the figures.**

	Flexed budget 3,600 units £	Actual 3,600 units £	Variance £	Adv/Fav
Sales		90,000		
Materials		15,120		
Labour		25,200		
Production overhead		5,900		
Gross profit		43,780		
General expenses		32,880		
Operating profit		10,900		

2   Vanquish Ltd has the following original budget and actual performance for its product zephyr for the year ending 31 December.

	Budget	Actual
Volume sold	50,000	72,000
	£000	£000
Sales revenue	1,000	1,800
Less costs:		
Direct materials	175	265
Direct labour	200	240
Overheads	350	630
Operating profit	275	665

Both direct materials and direct labour are variable costs, but the overheads are fixed.

Complete the table below to show a flexed budget and the resulting variances against this budget for the year. Show the actual variance amount, for sales and each cost, in the column headed 'Variance' and indicate whether this is Favourable or Adverse by entering F or A in the final column. If neither F nor A enter 0.

	Flexed budget	Actual	Variance	Favourable F or Adverse A
Volume sold		72,000		
	£000	£000	£000	
Sales revenue		1,800		
Less costs:				
Direct materials		265		
Direct labour		240		
Overheads		630		
Operating profit		665		

Variance analysis 11

Assessment context

Variance calculation is a very important part of your *Management Accounting* studies and it is vital that you are able to calculate all of the different types of variance included in the syllabus for this unit.

Qualification context

Variances examined in this unit are also examinable in the Level 4 *Management Accounting* units. This is taken a step further by including a few further calculations and the interpretation and behavioural aspects of variances.

Business context

Actual costs and revenues are compared against forecasts within a business on a frequent basis. This is part of the budgetary control process and helps to identify problems within the production process.

Chapter overview

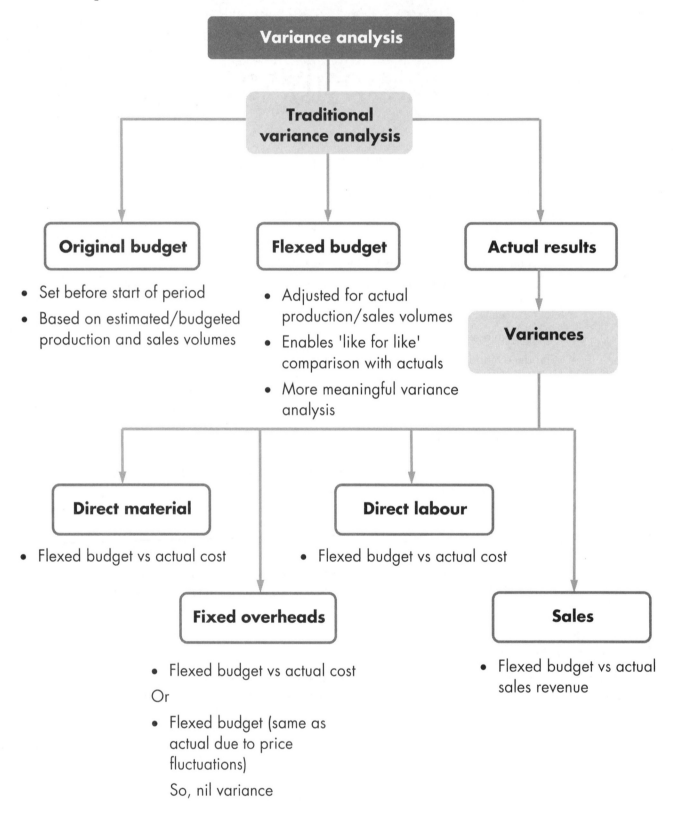

Variance analysis

Traditional variance analysis

Original budget

- Set before start of period
- Based on estimated/budgeted production and sales volumes

Flexed budget

- Adjusted for actual production/sales volumes
- Enables 'like for like' comparison with actuals
- More meaningful variance analysis

Actual results

Variances

Direct material

- Flexed budget vs actual cost

Direct labour

- Flexed budget vs actual cost

Fixed overheads

- Flexed budget vs actual cost
Or
- Flexed budget (same as actual due to price fluctuations)
So, nil variance

Sales

- Flexed budget vs actual sales revenue

Introduction

As you know, **variances** can be either favourable (F), ie better than expected, or adverse (A), ie worse.

Overview

	Fixed (original) budget	Flexed budget		Actual results
Sales volume	X	X		X
	£	£		£
Sales revenue	X	X	Sales variance	X
Cost of sales:				
Materials	X	X	Material variance	X
Labour	X	X	Labour variance	X
Overheads	X̲	not flexed	Overhead variance	see note below
Profit	X̲	X̲		X̲

Budget	Actual units × standard cost or selling price per unit	Actual units × actual cost or selling price per unit

Fixed overhead variances will just be the difference between actual and budgeted (original) fixed overheads.

Fixed overheads should not be flexed. Hence the variance will not be due to under/over absorption.

1 Calculating variances

You need to know how to flex a budget and show the resulting variances.

Illustration 1: Flexed budgets and variances

Vanquish Ltd has the following original budget and actual performance for product ZT4 for the year ending 31 December.

	Budget	Actual
Volume sold	100,000	144,000
	£000	**£000**
Sales revenue	2,000	3,600
Less costs:		
Direct materials	350	530
Direct labour	400	480
Overheads	980	980
Operating profit	270	1,610

Both direct materials and direct labour are variable costs, but the overheads are fixed.

Complete the table below to show a flexed budget and the resulting variances against this budget for the year. Show the actual variance amount, for sales and each cost, in the column headed 'Variance' and indicate whether this is Favourable or Adverse by entering F or A in the final column. If neither F nor A enter 0.

	Flexed budget	Actual	Variance	Favourable F or Adverse A
Volume sold		144,000	–	
	£000	**£000**	**£000**	
Sales revenue		3,600		
Less costs:				
Direct materials		530		
Direct labour		480		
Overheads		980		
Operating profit		1,610		

	Flexed budget	Actual	Variance	Favourable F or Adverse A
Volume sold	144,000	144,000	–	
	£000	£000	£000	
Sales revenue	2,880	3,600	720	F
Less costs:				
Direct materials	504	530	26	A
Direct labour	576	480	96	F
Overheads	980	980	0	0
Operating profit	820	1,610	790	F

Workings

Sales revenue

Budgeted sales price per unit = £2,000,000/100,000 units = £20 per unit

So, 144,000 units of revenue should have been 144,000 × £20 = £2,880,000

Direct materials

Budgeted material cost per unit = £350,000/100,000 = £3.5 per unit

So, 144,000 units of material should have cost 144,000 × £3.5 = £504,000

Direct labour

Budgeted labour cost per unit = £400,000/100,000 = £4 per unit

So, 144,000 units of material should have cost 144,000 × £4 = £576,000

Fixed overheads

Fixed overheads do not change as volume/activity changes. Actual fixed overheads were £980,000.

Operating profit

Operating profit = £2,880,000 – £504,000 – £576,000 – £980,000 = £820,000

In the illustration above, we calculated the sales price variance, the total direct material variance, the total direct **labour variance** and the fixed overhead variance. So you now know that:

(a) The sales price variance is the difference between the actual revenue received and the budgeted sales revenue for the actual level of sales.

(b) The total direct **materials variance** is the difference between the actual cost of materials used in production and the budgeted cost for the actual level of production.

(c) The total direct labour variance is the difference between the actual cost of labour for the period and the budgeted cost of labour for the actual production in the period.

(d) The total fixed overhead cost variance is the difference between the actual fixed overhead and the budgeted fixed overhead.

Activity 1: Protec Ltd

Protec Ltd has the following original budget and actual performance for product PT5 for the year ending 31 December.

	Budget	Actual
Volume sold	100,000	100,000
	£000	**£000**
Sales revenue	3,000	5,400
Less costs:		
Direct materials	525	795
Direct labour	600	720
Overheads	1,470	1,842
Operating profit	405	2,043

Both direct materials and direct labour are variable costs, but the overheads are fixed.

Required

Complete the table below to show a flexed budget and the resulting variances against this budget for the year. Show the actual variance amount, for sales and each cost, in the column headed 'Variance' and indicate whether this is Favourable or Adverse by entering F or A in the final column. If neither F nor A enter 0.

	Flexed budget	Actual	Variance	Favourable F or Adverse A
Volume sold				
	£000	£000	£000	
Sales revenue				
Less costs:				
Direct materials				
Direct labour				
Overheads				
Operating profit				

Fixed overheads do not change as volume/activity changes. But actual fixed overheads may change due to price effects.

Activity 2: Zetec Ltd

Zetec Ltd has the following original budget and actual performance for product ZT4 for the year ending 31 December.

	Budget	Actual
Volume sold	10,000	12,350
	£	£
Sales revenue	300,000	407,550
Less costs:		
Direct materials	50,000	53,000
Direct labour	40,000	49,000
Overheads	110,000	178,000
Operating profit	100,000	127,550

Both direct materials and direct labour are variable costs, but the overheads are fixed.

Required

Complete the table below to show a flexed budget and the resulting variances against this budget for the year. Show the actual variance amount for sales and each cost in the column headed 'Variance' and indicate whether this is Favourable or Adverse by entering F or A in the final column. If neither F nor A enter 0.

	Flexed budget	Actual	Variance	Favourable F or Adverse A
Volume sold				
	£	£	£	
Sales revenue				
Less costs:				
Direct materials				
Direct labour				
Overheads				
Operating profit				

2 Investigating variances

2.1 Causes of variances

When reporting variances to management a simple table is a useful starting point. However, management will also wish to know the reasons for the variances. In this unit we only look at total material, labour, fixed overhead and sales variances.

Variance	Favourable	Adverse
Material	Unforeseen discounts received	Price increase
	Greater care in purchasing	Careless purchasing
	More efficient use of material	Defective material
	Errors in allocating material to jobs	Excessive waste or theft
		Stricter quality control
		Errors in allocating material to jobs

Variance	Favourable	Adverse
Labour	Use of workers at a lower rate of pay Output produced more quickly than expected because of worker motivation, better quality materials etc	Wage rate increase Output lower than standard set because of lack of training, sub-standard materials etc Idle time – waiting for materials, machine breakdown etc
Fixed overhead	Savings in costs incurred More economical use of services	Increase in cost of services used Excessive use of services Change in type of service used
Sales revenue	Units sold at a higher selling price More units sold than budgeted due to increase in demand	Lower price charged due to competition Demand has fallen as better product available in the market

2.2 Interdependence of variances

You may have noticed from some of the possible causes of variances given above that many of these are likely to be inter-related. This is known as the **interdependence of variances**.

For example, if lower-grade material is purchased at a cheaper price than standard, this would lead to a favourable material variance. However, this **favourable variance** may be cancelled out by an **adverse variance**, if the lower grade of material means that there is greater wastage than standard.

2.3 Responsibility for variances

Investigating the causes of variances and determining any interdependence between them is an important aspect of management control, as in a system of responsibility accounting the managers responsible for various elements of the business will be held accountable for the relevant variances.

Take the example of a favourable material price variance caused by purchasing a lower grade of material, which leads directly to an adverse materials usage variance. The initial reaction might be to praise the purchasing manager for the favourable variance and to lay blame for the adverse usage variance on the production manager. However, the true picture is that, in the absence of any further reasons for the variance, the responsibility for both variances lies with the purchasing manager.

2.4 Other reasons for variances

Further causes of variances may be one-off events such as a power cut, breakdown of machinery or annual staff holidays.

Assessment focus point

An assessment task may ask you to flex a budget, calculate variances and indicate whether they are adverse or favourable. You could also be given variances and asked which one has the greatest impact on profit. You could also be asked about the likely cause of a particular variance.

Chapter summary

- The sales variance is the difference between the actual revenue received and the budgeted sales revenue for the actual level of sales.

- The materials variance is the difference between the actual cost of materials used in production and the budgeted cost for the actual level of production.

- The labour variance is the difference between the actual cost of labour for the period and the budgeted cost of labour for the actual production in the period.

- The fixed overhead cost variance is the difference between the actual fixed overhead and the budgeted fixed overhead.

- Management like to know the causes of variances as well as see the numbers. This helps them understand why variances have arisen and how they might avoid them in the future.

Keywords

- **Adverse variance:** Where the actual cost is greater than the budgeted cost, or the actual sales were less than budgeted sales

- **Favourable variance:** Where the actual cost is less than the budgeted cost, or the actual sales were more than budgeted sales

- **Interdependence of variances:** Causes of variances are often inter-related. This is called the interdependence of variances

- **Labour variance:** The difference between the budgeted labour cost for the actual production and the actual cost

- **Materials variance:** The difference between the budgeted materials cost for the actual production and the actual cost

- **Fixed overhead variance:** The difference between the budgeted and actual fixed overhead for the period

- **Variance:** The difference between the budgeted costs or sales and the actual costs or sales for a period

Test your learning

1 Flower budgeted to sell 200 units and produced the following budget.

	£	£
Sales		71,400
Variable costs		
Labour	31,600	
Material	12,600	
		44,200
Contribution		27,200
Fixed costs		18,900
Profit		8,300

Actual sales turned out to be 230 units, which were sold for £69,000. Actual expenditure on labour was £27,000 and on material £24,000. Fixed costs totalled £10,000.

Prepare a flexible budget that will be useful for management control purposes

	Budget 200 units £	Budget per unit £	Flexed budget 230 units £	Actual 230 units £	Variance £ (A)/(F)
Sales					
Variable costs					
Labour					
Material					
Fixed costs					
Profit					

Cost bookkeeping

12

2.2	**Analyse and use appropriate cost information**
	• Prepare cost accounting journal entries for direct materials or indirect materials; direct or indirect labour; or overhead costs.
3.4	**Demonstrate understanding of the under or over recovery of overheads**
	• Account for under or over recovered overhead costs in accordance with established procedures. These include: – Making cost journal postings

Assessment context

There is likely to be a task on this topic. For example, you could be asked to complete labour cost journals to record payroll payments.

Qualification context

The understanding of journal entries is important for cost accounting and also to eventually understand the links with financial accounting.

Business context

Most businesses use computerised accounting packages to maintain their cost ledgers and financial ledgers and so the understanding of cost bookkeeping will help to analyse the reports that these accounting systems produce.

Chapter overview

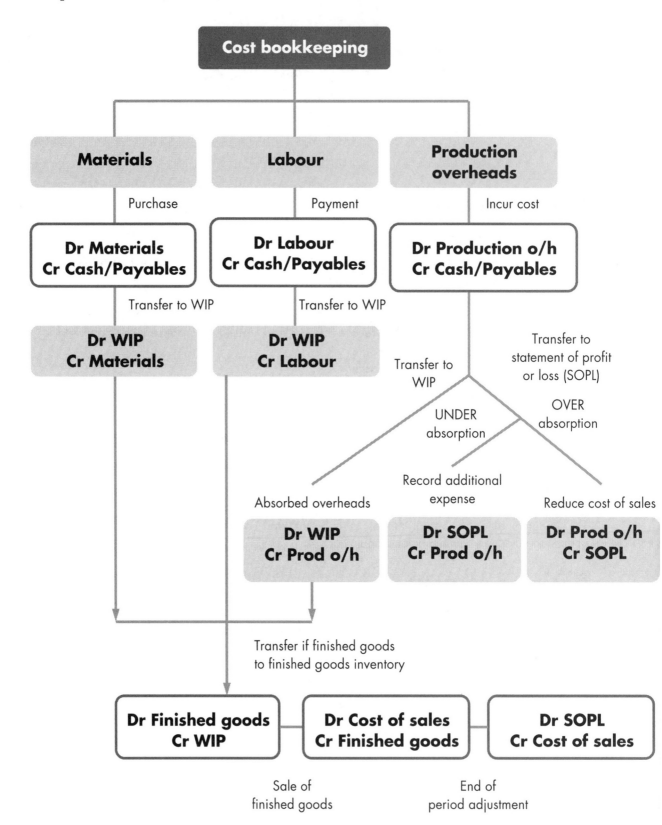

Introduction

This unit requires some ability with double entry bookkeeping. The assessment may require:

(a) Recording purchases, wages or movements of inventory as a double entry

(b) How to deal with under/over absorption of overheads

A cost bookkeeping system will need to be able to cope with a great deal of detail. For example, it won't be enough to record all items purchased as 'purchases'. We need to be able to distinguish between direct and indirect items, and each type of material will need its own record. Similarly, each product, batch, job or process will need its own account to record the materials, labour and production overheads incurred on it. To help organise the information into a manageable system we use control accounts.

1 Control accounts

These show the total values and are part of the overall double entry system. They may be backed up by more detailed listings (ledger accounts) which are covered in *Financial Accounting* units.

The following control accounts appear in a cost bookkeeping system:

- **Materials control account**. This will record the total purchases of materials and issues to WIP, summarising the individual materials or stores ledger accounts.

- **Wages control account**. This will record the total payroll costs, the total direct labour charged to each individual product, job, batch or process in WIP and indirect labour charged to appropriate cost centres.

- **Production overhead control account**. This will record the total production overheads incurred by different cost centres and the total charged to each individual product, job, batch or process in WIP.

- **Work in progress control account**. This will summarise each individual product, job, batch or process in WIP, recording the total costs of direct materials, direct labour and production overheads that have been charged and the transfer of items to finished goods.

2 Basic double entry

First, consider how a single purchase of materials works through into the final accounts. The relevant double entries are as follows.

(a)   DEBIT   Materials   £X
      CREDIT   Cash (or payables)   £X

Being the purchase of materials which are put into raw materials inventory.

(b)   DEBIT   Work in progress   £X
      CREDIT   Materials   £X

Being the issue of materials to production for use in work in progress.

(c)   DEBIT   Finished goods   £X
      CREDIT   Work in progress   £X

Being the transfer of units that are now finished to finished goods inventory.

(d)   DEBIT   Cost of sales   £X
      CREDIT   Finished goods   £X

Being the taking of units out of finished goods inventory and selling them.

(e)   DEBIT   Statement of profit or loss   £X
      CREDIT   Cost of sales   £X

Being the closing off of ledger accounts and the drawing up of financial statements.

This entry would be made at the end of a period.

The process of accounting for labour is similar.

Sometimes the materials which are issued to production for use in work in progress are not actually used. They are therefore returned to stores. The double entry for this is:

      DEBIT   Materials   £X
      CREDIT   Work in progress   £X

Being the return of materials to stores.

Activity 1: Control accounts – Bodger & Co

Bodger & Co spends the following in 20X2:

	£
Raw materials bought on credit	5,000

Required

Show how this cost would be initially recorded in the following accounts.

Payables control account
Raw materials control account

Payables control account

	£		£

Raw materials control account

	£		£

Activity 2: Payment to supplier – Bodger & Co

Bodger & Co makes the following payment in 20X2:

	£
Payment to supplier for raw materials bought on credit	5,000

Required

Show how this cost would be recorded in the following accounts.

Payables control account
Bank account

Payables control account

	£		£

Bank account

	£		£

Activity 3: Issuing materials – Bodger & Co

Bodger & Co issues all the materials to production for use in work in progress.

Required

Show how the issue of materials would be recorded in the following accounts.

Raw materials control account
WIP control account

Raw materials control account

	£		£
Payables	5,000		

WIP control account

	£		£

---

3 Production overheads

The process of accounting for production overheads is slightly different.

The initial entry is similar to that for labour and materials:

DEBIT	Production overheads	£X	
CREDIT	Cash (or payables)		£X

The subsequent entry is:

DEBIT	Work in progress	£X	
CREDIT	Production overheads		£X

The amount we debit WIP and credit production overheads is the amount absorbed into production (overhead absorption rate × actual activity level).

This leaves a balance on the production overheads account which is taken to the statement of profit or loss account. This is known as the under- or over-absorption. This calculation is covered in the chapter on absorption costing.

If under-absorption occurs this will be an additional cost in the statement of profit or loss account. Under-absorbed overheads mean that actual overheads incurred are greater than the amount absorbed into the statement of profit or loss account during the period.

Under-absorption accounting double entry is:

DEBIT	Statement of profit or loss	£X	
CREDIT	Production overheads		£X

If over-absorption occurs this will reduce the cost in the statement of profit or loss account. Over-absorbed overheads mean that actual overheads incurred are less than the amount absorbed into the statement of profit or loss account during the period.

Over-absorption accounting double entry is:

DEBIT	Production overheads	£X	
CREDIT	Statement of profit or loss		£X

Activity 4: Recording production overheads – Bodger & Co

Bodger & Co incurs production overheads of £6,000.

The production overhead to be absorbed into WIP is:

	£
Manufacturing department	4,000
Finishing department	600
Quality control	500

Required

Show how the production overheads will be recorded in the following accounts:

Payables control account, Production overheads control account, WIP control account

Payables control account

	£		£
		Raw materials	5,000

Production overheads control account

	£		£

WIP control account

	£		£
Materials	5,000		

4 Summary of cost bookkeeping double entries

1 Production costs are recorded	Debit: Materials Debit: Wages Debit: Production o/h	Credit: Cash/payables Credit: Cash/HMRC Credit: Cash/payables
2 Direct costs issued to production	Debit: WIP Debit: WIP	Credit: Materials Credit: Wages
3 Indirect labour transferred to production overheads	Debit: Production o/h	Credit: Wages
4 Production overheads absorbed into production	Debit: WIP	Credit: Production o/h
5 Completed WIP transferred to finished goods	Debit: Finished goods	Credit: WIP
6 Finished goods are sold	Debit: Cost of sales Debit: Cash/receivables Debit: Sales	Credit: Finished goods Credit: Sales Credit: Statement of profit or loss
7 Non-production overheads charged to statement of profit or loss	Debit: Non-production overheads Debit: Statement of profit or loss	Credit: Payables/cash Credit: Non-production overheads

5 Coding

Each control account may be given its own code number to aid identification.

Activity 5: Coding and inventory – Spice Ltd

Spice Ltd provides you with the information about the inventory movements of Component C.

Required

Identify the inventory issue method being used for valuing issues to production and complete the inventory record card for June 20X9.

	Receipts			Issues			Balance	
Date 20X9	Quantity kg	Cost per kg £	Total cost £	Quantity kg	Cost per kg £	Total cost £	Quantity kg	Balance £
1 June							25,000	50,000
9 June	30,000	2.30	69,000				55,000	119,000
12 June				40,000	25,000 × 2.00 15,000 × £2.30	84,500	15,000	34,500
18 June	20,000	2.50	50,000				35,000	84,500
27 June				10,000				

Inventory record card for Steel Component C

The issue of Component C on 12 June was for the production of Product P1. The issue of Component C on 27 June was for the production of Product P2.

The following cost accounting codes are used:

Code	Description
300	Raw material control account – Component C
400	Work in progress Product P1
405	Work in progress Product P2
600	Payables control account

Required

Complete the journal entries below to record separately the four cost accounting entries in respect of the two receipts and two issues during the month of June.

Journal entries

		Cost accounting code	£
9 June	Debit		
9 June	Credit		
12 June	Debit		
12 June	Credit		
18 June	Debit		
18 June	Credit		
27 June	Debit		
27 June	Credit		

Assessment focus point

In your assessment, a task could ask you to complete journal entries from a drop down list of codes and accounts.

Illustration 1: Bookkeeping

The information below relates to Shieldbug Limited for the month of April 20X6. (Note that VAT has been ignored for the purpose of this example.)

Opening trial balance at 1 April 20X6

Account	Debit £	Credit £
Inventory:		
Raw materials	150	
Work in progress	380	
Finished goods	600	
Receivables	937	
Payables		502
HMRC (PAYE and NIC owing)		250
Cash at bank	1,634	
Plant and equipment	3,000	
Allowance for depreciation of plant and equipment		500
Share capital		2,000
Retained earnings		3,449
	6,701	6,701
Transactions in April		
Summary of bank transactions		
Receivables cheques received	3,000	
Cheques paid to payables		1,900
Wages paid		810
HMRC		250
Pension scheme		50
Production overheads		660
Administration overheads		140
Selling overheads		120
Total	3,000	3,930

Other information	Debit £	Credit £
Invoices for materials received		1,840
Materials requisitions:		
Production		1,790
Administration		95
Payroll:		
Net	810	
PAYE & NIC	186	
Pension scheme contributions	50	
Total		1,046
Payroll analysis:		
Direct labour (100 hours)	920	
Indirect: production salaries	100	
Indirect: admin salaries	26	
		1,046
Sales invoices issued		3,170
Production transferred to finished goods in the period		2,100
Value of closing inventory of finished goods		200
Overhead absorption rate per direct labour hour		10.50
Depreciation of plant and equipment for the month (factory plant: £80, office equipment: £25)		

Work through the accounts below, checking that you understand each double entry. You may find it useful to begin by checking the opening balances from the trial balance, and then working down the transactions as listed.

Note that you will not be required to use T accounts in the assessment. You will have to prepare journal entries instead. We have written up the T accounts to make it easier for you to follow the entries.

Raw materials account

	£		£
Balance b/d	150	WIP (direct materials)	1,790
Payables	1,840	Administration overheads	95
		Balance c/d	105
	1,990		1,990
Balance b/d	105		

Wages and salaries account

	£		£
Cash at bank	810	WIP (direct labour)	920
HMRC	186	Production overheads	100
Pension scheme contributions	50	Administrative overheads	26
	1,046		1,046

Production overheads account

	£		£
Wages and salaries	100	WIP (absorbed: 100 hrs @ £10.50)	1,050
Plant depreciation	80		
Cash at bank	660		
Statement of profit or loss (over-absorbed)	210		
	1,050		1,050

WIP account

	£		£
Balance b/d	380	Finished goods	2,100
Raw materials	1,790		
Wages and salaries	920		
Production overheads	1,050	Balance c/d	2,040
	4,140		4,140
Balance b/d	2,040		

Finished goods account

	£		£
Balance b/d	600	Statement of profit or loss:	
WIP	2,100	cost of sales	2,500
		Balance c/d	200
	2,700		2,700
Balance b/d	200		

Administration overheads account

	£		£
Materials	95	Statement of profit or loss	286
Wages and salaries	26		
Equipment depreciation	25		
Cash at bank	140		
	286		286

Selling overheads account

	£		£
Cash at bank	120	Statement of profit or loss	120
	120		120

Sales account

	£		£
Statement of profit or loss	3,170	Receivables	3,170
	3,170		3,170

Statement of profit or loss for April

	£		£
Cost of sales	2,500	Sales revenue	3,170
Administration overheads	286	Over-absorbed overheads	210
Selling overheads	120		
Net profit (transfer to retained earnings)	474		
	3,380		3,380

Cash at bank account

	£		£
Balance b/d	1,634	Payables	1,900
Receivables	3,000	Wages and salaries	810
		HMRC	250
		Pension scheme	50
		Production overheads	660
		Administration overheads	140
		Selling overheads	120
		Balance c/d	704
	4,634		4,634
Balance b/d	704		

Receivables account

	£		£
Balance b/d	937	Cash at bank	3,000
Sales	3,170	Balance c/d	1,107
	4,107		4,107
Balance b/d	1,107		

Payables account

	£		£
Cash at bank	1,900	Balance b/d	502
Balance c/d	442	Raw materials	1,840
	2,342		2,342
		Balance b/d	442

HMRC payables account

	£		£
Cash at bank	250	Balance b/d	250
Balance c/d	186	Wages and salaries for April	186
	436		436
		Balance b/d	186

Pension scheme payables

	£		£
Cash at bank	50	Wages and salaries for April	50
	50		50

Plant and equipment account

	£		£
Balance b/d	3,000	Balance c/d	3,000
	3,000		3,000
Balance b/d	3,000		

Allowance for depreciation of plant and equipment account

	£		£
		Balance b/d	500
		Production overhead (plant depn)	80
Balance c/d	605	Administration overheads (office equipment depn)	25
	605		605
		Balance b/d	605

Share capital account

	£		£
Balance c/d	2,000	Balance b/d	2,000
	2,000		2,000
		Balance b/d	2,000

Retained earnings account

	£		£
		Balance b/d	3,449
		Profit for April (transferred from statement of profit or loss for the month)	474
Balance c/d	3,923		3,923
	3,923	Balance b/d	3,923

Chapter summary

- Control accounts are used in a cost bookkeeping system in order to summarise information about the major elements of production – materials purchased and issued, wages, production overheads and work in progress.

- Each cost incurred must be correctly coded to ensure that it is posted to the correct account in the cost bookkeeping ledger.

- The production overheads account is debited with the overheads actually incurred in the period and credited with the overheads that are to be absorbed into the work in progress for the period; any balance on the account is an under- or over-absorption of overheads and is taken to the statement of profit or loss.

Keywords

- **Materials control account:** Records all purchases of materials and issues to WIP

- **Production overhead control account:** Records the actual overhead incurred, the amount of overhead absorbed into WIP and any under- or over-absorption

- **Wages control account:** Records the total payroll costs and the transfers of direct labour to WIP and indirect labour to overheads

- **Work in progress control account:** Records the total direct materials, direct labour and production overhead used in the production process in the period

1 **What would be the double entry for materials purchased on credit for the production process?**

Debit [_____] ▾

Credit [_____] ▾

Picklist:

Materials control account
Payables control account
Production overheads account
Work in progress account

2 The overhead absorption rate for a factory is £3.24 per direct labour hour. During the month of July 20X1 the number of direct labour hours worked was 1,050 and the overheads incurred were £3,690.

Write up the production overheads account.

Production overheads account

	£		£
Overheads incurred		Overheads absorbed	
		Under-absorbed overheads	

3 Given below are extracts from the trial balance of a business at 1 July 20X6:

	Debit £	Credit £
Inventory:		
Raw materials	550	
Work in progress	680	
Finished goods	1,040	
Receivables	3,700	
Payables		2,100
Cash at bank	2,090	

You are also given a summary of some of the transactions of the business for the month of July:

Materials purchased on credit	£5,300
Materials requisitions	
– factory	£4,670
– administration	£760
Wages cost	
– direct factory labour (360 hours)	£2,520
– indirect factory labour	£640
Sales invoices issued	£12,000
Cheques received from receivables	£11,000
Cheques paid to payables	£5,140
Production transferred to finished goods	£10,000
Production overheads paid by cheque	£2,700
Administration overheads paid by cheque	£1,580
Closing inventory of finished goods	£2,010

Production overheads are absorbed at the budgeted overhead absorption rate of £7.80 per direct labour hour.

You are required to write up the following ledger accounts to reflect these transactions and to balance each of the accounts at the end of the month:

Materials control account

	£		£

Wages control account

	£		£

Production overhead control account

	£		£

Work in progress control account

	£		£

Finished goods control account

	£		£

Receivables control account

	£		£

Payables control account

	£		£

Cash at bank account

	£		£

Administration overheads account

	£		£

Sales account

	£		£

Marginal costing

13

Learning outcomes

1.4	Explain and demonstrate the differences between marginal and absorption costing
	• How to calculate prime, marginal and full absorption costs
	• The difference between product and period costs
	• The impact on reported performance of marginal vs absorption costing in both the short run and the long run
	• When each method is appropriate

Assessment context

Look out for questions in your examination which require you to calculate profit or losses using absorption and marginal costing. The concept of contribution is frequently tested in the assessment and is used when making decisions involving limiting factors.

Qualification context

At Level 4, costing techniques in the modern business environment will be studied. These are often compared with the more traditional techniques of absorption costing and marginal costing.

Business context

Marginal costing is an alternative to absorption costing. The marginal cost is the part of the cost of one unit of product that would be avoided if the unit were not produced. This information is extremely useful for making decisions such as pricing decisions or whether to continue producing a particular type of unit.

Chapter overview

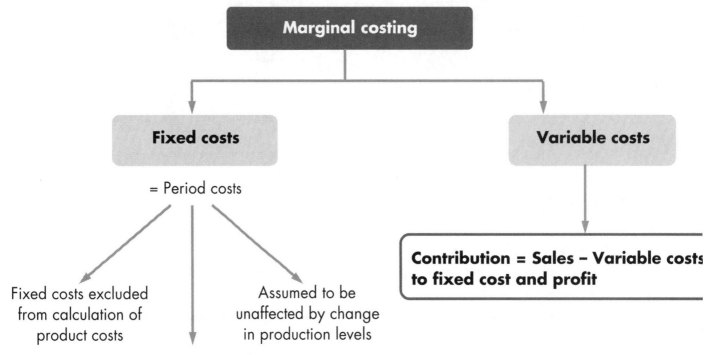

Introduction

In an earlier chapter we mentioned that there were a number of approaches we could apply to calculate the cost of producing an item or providing a service. So far we have seen how all of the production overheads can be allocated, apportioned and then absorbed into the cost of the product giving a total production cost for each cost unit. This is known as **absorption costing** (or **full costing**).

However, there is a different method of costing known as **marginal costing** (or **variable costing**), which may be preferred by some organisations and can be more useful for some reporting purposes.

Under a marginal costing system the cost unit is valued at just the variable (or marginal) cost of production. The fixed production costs for the period are charged to the statement of profit or loss as an expense for the period rather than being included as part of the cost of the cost unit.

1 Marginal costing

1.1 Contribution

Marginal costing treats all fixed costs as **period costs**. The fixed costs are not included when calculating **product costs**.

Only variable costs are therefore charged as a cost of sale. Instead of profit, a figure known as **contribution** is calculated:

	£
Sales revenue	X
Less: all variable costs	(X)
Contribution to fixed cost and profit	X

> **Contribution** – Contribution = Sales value – Variable cost of sales.
>
> Key term **Period costs** are costs relating to a time period rather than to the output of products.
>
> **Product costs** are costs of a product made up from its cost elements.

Activity 1: Contribution

Required

Calculate the contribution for the following products:

	J	K	L
Sales price	£10.00	£5.00	£3.00
Costs:			
Materials	£3.00	£2.50	£0.50
Labour	£1.00	£1.50	£1.25
Variable sales costs	£0.25	£0.15	£0.30
Variable overheads	£0.75	£0.10	£0.25
Fixed overheads	£1.00	£1.00	£1.00

	J	K	L
Contribution per unit	£	£	£

If we sell one extra unit:

- We will generate additional revenue for one extra unit
- We will incur variable costs of one extra unit
- Profit will increase by the contribution (sales price – variable costs) of that one extra unit
- There will be no impact on fixed overheads

Illustration 1: Absorption costing and marginal costing

Graham Associates produce just one product in their factory. The factory has two production departments, assembly and packaging. The anticipated production for the next month, March, is 50,000 units and the expected costs are as follows:

Direct materials	£20 per unit
Direct labour	3 hours assembly at £8.00 per hour
	1 hour packaging at £6.00 per hour
Assembly variable overheads	£240,000
Assembly fixed overheads	£120,000
Packaging variable overheads	£100,000
Packaging fixed overheads	£40,000

Overheads are absorbed on the basis of labour hours.

We will start by calculating the cost of each cost unit using absorption costing.

Absorption costing

		Assembly	Packaging
Total overhead (variable + fixed)		£360,000	£140,000
Total labour hours	50,000 × 3	150,000	
	50,000 × 1		50,000
Overhead absorption rate		£360,000	£140,000
		150,000	50,000
Total overhead/Total labour hours	=	£2.40 per	£2.80 per
		labour hour	labour hour

Unit cost

		£
Direct materials		20.00
Direct labour	assembly 3 hours × £8.00	24.00
	packaging 1 hour × £6.00	6.00
Overheads	assembly 3 hours × £2.40	7.20
	packaging 1 hour × £2.80	2.80
Total unit cost		60.00

Marginal costing

Now we will calculate the same unit cost using marginal costing and therefore only including the variable costs, which are direct materials, direct labour and variable overheads.

		Assembly	Packaging
Variable overhead		£240,000	£100,000
Total labour hours		150,000	50,000
Variable overhead cost per hour		£240,000	£100,000
		150,000	50,000
	=	£1.60 per	£2.00 per
		labour hour	labour hour

Unit cost

		£
Direct materials		20.00
Direct labour	assembly	24.00
	packaging	6.00
Variable overhead	assembly 3 hours × £1.60	4.80
	packaging 1 hour × £2.00	2.00
Prime cost		56.80

Activity 2: Unit cost

A factory produces a single product with the following budgeted costs:

Direct materials	£3.40
Direct labour	£6.80
Variable overheads	£1.20
Fixed overheads	£340,000

Overheads are absorbed on the machine hour basis and it is estimated that in the next accounting period machine hours will total 100,000. Each unit requires two hours of machine time.

What is the cost per unit using:

(a) Absorption costing?
(b) Marginal costing?

(a)

Absorption costing – unit cost	£
Direct material	
Direct labour	
Variable overhead	
Total variable cost	
Fixed overhead	
Absorption cost	

(b)

Marginal costing – unit cost	£
Direct material	
Direct labour	
Variable overhead	
Marginal cost	

Activity 3: MC v AC cost per unit

The following information relates to the manufacture of product E during the month of December 20X6:

Direct materials per unit	£12.00
Direct labour per unit	£13.50
Total variable overheads	£88,000
Total fixed overheads	£110,000
Number of units produced	11,000

Required

Calculate the cost per unit of product E under:

(a) Marginal costing
(b) Full absorption costing

(a)

Marginal costing	£
Direct materials	
Direct labour	
Variable overheads per unit	
Total variable (marginal) cost	

(b)

Full absorption costing	£
Total variable cost	
Add: overhead absorption rate	
Full product cost	

1.2 Absorption versus marginal costing – effect on profit

We can now have a look at what effect the two different accounting methods have on the profits that are reported. Under absorption costing the full production cost of the units actually sold in the period is charged as part of cost of sales. The only other entry may be some adjustment for under- or over-absorption of overheads.

However, under marginal costing the lower, variable, cost per unit is charged as part of cost of sales and deducted from sales. This resulting figure is called contribution – it is sales minus variable costs of production and is the contribution towards the fixed costs and any profit. The fixed overheads are then charged to the statement of profit or loss as a period cost.

In the long run, the total profit for a company will be the same whether marginal costing or absorption costing is used. Different accounting conventions merely affect the profit of individual accounting periods.

Illustration 2: Effect on profit

Returning to Graham Associates the budgeted sales and production for each of the next three months, March, April and May, are 50,000 units. The budgeted cost figures for each month remain the same at:

Direct materials	£20.00 per unit
Direct labour	3 hours assembly at £8.00 per hour
	1 hour packaging at £6.00 per hour
Assembly variable overheads	£240,000
Assembly fixed overheads	£120,000
Packaging variable overheads	£100,000
Packaging fixed overheads	£40,000

The actual production and sales for each of the three months turned out to be:

	March	April	May
Sales	50,000	45,000	52,000
Production	50,000	50,000	50,000

There were no inventories of the product at the beginning of March. In each month both variable and fixed overheads were exactly as budgeted. Sales were at a selling price of £70.00 per unit.

Remember that the cost per unit for absorption costing is £60.00 and for marginal costing is £56.80.

Statement of profit or loss for March

Absorption costing

	£000	£000
Sales (50,000 × £70.00)		3,500
Less: cost of goods sold		
Opening inventory	–	
Cost of production (50,000 × £60.00)	3,000	
	3,000	
Less: closing inventory	–	
		3,000
Profit		500

Marginal costing

	£000	£000
Sales		3,500
Less: cost of goods sold		
Opening inventory	–	
Cost of production (50,000 × 56.80)	2,840	
	2,840	
Less: closing inventory	–	
		2,840
Contribution		660
Less: fixed costs (120,000 + 40,000)		160
Profit		500

In this month the profits under absorption costing and under marginal costing are exactly the same. The reason for this is that there has been no change in inventory levels. There was no opening inventory and as production and sales were for equal amounts there is also no closing inventory. **When opening and closing inventory amounts are equal then absorption costing profit and marginal costing profit will be equal.**

Statement of profit or loss for April

In April sales were 45,000 units and production was 50,000 units leaving closing inventory of 5,000 units.

Absorption costing

	£000	£000
Sales (45,000 × £70.00)		3,150
Less: cost of goods sold		
Opening inventory	–	
Cost of production (50,000 × £60.00)	3,000	
	3,000	
Less: closing inventory (5,000 × £60.00)	300	
		2,700
Profit		450

Marginal costing

	£000	£000
Sales		3,150
Less: cost of goods sold		
Opening inventory	–	
Cost of production (50,000 × 56.80)	2,840	
	2,840	
Less: closing inventory (5,000 × 56.80)	284	
		2,556
Contribution		594
Less: fixed costs (120,000 + 40,000)		160
Profit		434

In this month there is a difference in profit:

		£000
Absorption costing profit		450
Marginal costing profit		434
Difference		16

The difference in reported profit under the two costing methods is due to the fixed overheads absorbed into inventory. Under marginal costing the entire fixed overhead for the month is charged to the statement of profit or loss. However, under absorption costing the fixed overhead is included in the cost per unit and therefore any fixed overhead in the closing inventory is carried forward to the next period rather than being charged in this period.

As inventory levels have risen from zero opening inventory to 5,000 units of closing inventory this means that the fixed overhead amount included in the inventory valuation for those 5,000 units has been deducted from this month's cost of sales and carried forward to the next month. This has not happened under marginal costing, therefore the absorption costing profit is higher.

The two profit figures can be reconciled as **the difference is due solely to the increase in inventories and the fixed overhead included in that inventory valuation.**

Fixed overheads per unit $= \dfrac{£120,000 + £40,000}{50,000} = £3.20$

Remember that the difference in profit was £16,000. This has been caused by:

Fixed overhead included in increase in inventory

(5,000 units × £3.20)   £16,000

Statement of profit or loss for May

Absorption costing

	£000	£000
Sales (52,000 × £70.00)		3,640
Less: cost of goods sold		
Opening inventory (5,000 × £60.00)	300	
Cost of production (50,000 × £60.00)	3,000	
	3,300	
Less: closing inventory (3,000 × £60.00)	180	
		3,120
Profit		520

Marginal costing

	£000	£000
Sales		3,640
Less: cost of goods sold		
Opening inventory (5,000 × 56.80)	284	
Cost of production (50,000 × 56.80)	2,840	
	3,124	
Less: closing inventory (3,000 × 56.80)	170.4	
		2,953.6
Contribution		686.4
Less: fixed costs (120,000 + 40,000)		160.0
Profit		526.4

	£000
Absorption costing profit	520.00
Marginal costing profit	526.40
Difference	6.40

In May the marginal cost profit is £6,400 higher than the absorption cost profit as in this month inventory levels have decreased from 5,000 units to 3,000 units. Therefore under absorption costing more of the brought forward fixed costs have been charged to the statement of profit or loss in the month than have been carried forward to the following month in closing inventory.

The difference is made up of:

Fixed overhead in inventory decrease 2,000 × £3.20 = £6,400

Activity 4: Marginal costing profit statement

Sanctuary Catering has established the following budgeted annual sales and cost information meal types.

'STANDARD' and 'VEGETARIAN'

Meal type	Standard	Vegetarian
Meals prepared and sold	130,000 meals	200,000 meals
Staff hours required	3,250	6,000
Sales revenue	£1,040,000	£1,500,000
Direct materials (ingredients etc)	£468,000	£600,000
Direct labour	£260,000	£400,000
Variable overheads	£260,000	£300,000

The fixed costs attributable to Standard and Vegetarian meals are budgeted to be £212,000.

Required

Complete the table below to show the budgeted contribution per type of meal and Sanctuary Catering's budgeted profit or loss for the year from these two meals.

	Standard £	Vegetarian £	Total £
Selling price per meal			
Less: variable costs per meal			
Direct materials			
Direct labour			
Variable overheads			
Contribution per unit			
Sales volume (units)			
Total contribution			
Less: fixed costs			
Budgeted profit or loss			

1.3 Absorption versus marginal costing – Advantages & disadvantages

- Absorption costing has the advantage of allowing managers to see whether the sales of their products are covering all of the production costs of those products.

- However, it is argued that contribution is a much more useful figure for management decision-making purposes.

- Under absorption costing, we have seen that it is possible to report a higher profit figure by increasing the closing inventory levels. Although this will increase absorption costing profit, it is not in the best interests of the organisation. It is unethical behaviour.

  - It is argued, however, that **absorption costing is preferable to marginal costing in management accounting, in order to be consistent with the requirement of current accounting standards and financial reporting**.

  - It is also argued that absorption costing is more appropriate for a business which uses cost plus pricing.

It is, however, important to appreciate that the differences in reported profits occur only in the short run, ie in reporting the profit of individual accounting periods. This is because, in the long run, total costs will be the same using either method of accounting. Short-term differences are the results of changes in the level of inventory.

Activity 5: MC v AC

CPL is considering what the effect would be of costing its products under marginal costing (MC) principles, instead of under the full absorption costing (FAC) principles that it currently follows.

The following information relates to one of the company's products:

Selling price per unit	£12
Prime cost per unit	£4
Variable production overhead per unit	£3
Budgeted fixed production overhead	£30,000 per month
Budgeted production	15,000 units per month
Budgeted sales	12,000 units per month
Opening inventory	2,000 units

Required

(a) Calculate the contribution per unit (on a MC basis).

	£
Selling price/unit	
Prime cost/unit	
Variable production cost/unit	
Marginal cost (MC)/unit	
= Contribution/unit	

(b) Calculate the profit per unit (on a FAC basis).

	£
Selling price/unit	
Marginal cost/unit	
Fixed production cost/unit	
FAC cost/unit	
= Profit/unit	

(c) Complete the table below to produce a statement of profit or loss for the product for the month under marginal costing (MC) principles.

	£	£
Sales		
Less: cost of sales		
Opening inventory		
Variable production costs		
Closing inventory		
Cost of sales (MC basis)		
Contribution		
Fixed costs		
Profit		

(d) Complete the table below to produce a statement of profit or loss for the product for the month under full absorption costing (FAC) principles.

	£	£
Sales		
Less: cost of sales		
Opening inventory		
Production costs		
Closing inventory		
Cost of sales (FAC basis)		
Profit		

(e) Explain why the two profit figures differ by selecting the correct words from the brackets in the statement below.

The two profit figures differ by £ [ ] because under FAC the _____(decrease/increase) in the valuation of inventory during the month is _____(higher/lower) than the _____(decrease/increase) under MC.

This is because fixed overhead cost has been carried forward in the statement of financial position in the inventory valuation as an asset under FAC principles, but written off against profit under MC principles.

Assessment focus point

In your assessment, a task could ask you to calculate the marginal cost of a batch or the marginal cost of a unit.

Chapter summary

- Under absorption costing all production overheads are allocated and apportioned to production cost centres and then absorbed into the cost of the products on some suitable basis.

- Under marginal costing the cost of the products is the variable cost of production with all fixed production costs being charged to the statement of profit or loss as a period charge.

- If inventory levels are constant then both absorption costing and marginal costing will report the same profit figure.

- If inventory levels are increasing, absorption costing profit will be higher as more fixed overheads are carried forward to the following period in closing inventory than those brought forward in opening inventory.

- If inventory levels are falling, marginal costing profit will be higher as less fixed overheads are carried forward under absorption costing in the closing inventory figure than those brought forward in opening inventory.

- The difference in profit will be the fixed production overhead included in the increase/decrease in inventory levels under absorption costing.

- The contribution figure shown in marginal costing can be argued to be more use to management than the full absorption costing profit figure.

- It is possible to manipulate profit reporting under absorption costing by increasing inventory levels and thereby increasing reported profit. However, differences in reported profits occur only in the short run, and in the long run total costs will be the same by either method of accounting.

Keywords

- **Absorption (full) costing:** Both variable and fixed production overheads are included in unit cost

- **Contribution:** Sales value less variable cost of the goods sold

- **Marginal (variable) costing:** Unit cost includes only variable production costs

- **Period cost or a cost relating to a time period:** Usually, fixed overheads which aren't affected by changes in production level

- **Production or product cost:** The cost of a finished product built up from its cost elements

1   Given below is the budgeted information about the production of 60,000 units of a single product in a factory for the following quarter:

Direct materials		£12.50 per unit
Direct labour	– assembly	4 hours @ £8.40 per hour
	– finishing	1 hour @ £6.60 per hour
Assembly production overheads		£336,000
Finishing production overheads		£84,000

It is estimated that 60% of the assembly overhead is variable and that 75% of the finishing overhead is variable.

What is the budgeted cost of the product using:

(a) Absorption costing?

£ [   ]

(b) Marginal costing?

£ [   ]

Short-term decision making

14

Assessment context

Cost-volume-profit (CVP) analysis is an important tool that management accountants can use in decision making. Most assessment questions will require that you can recall the formulae included in this chapter – make sure you learn them so that you can apply them when you need to.

Qualification context

CVP analysis is a basic tool that a company can use for decision making, particularly for short-term decision making. It is therefore a tool that can be useful at all levels of your studies.

Business context

When using a marginal costing system, there is more risk that fixed costs will not be covered. Using CVP, the business can plan to ensure fixed costs are covered and target profit figures can also be calculated.

Chapter overview

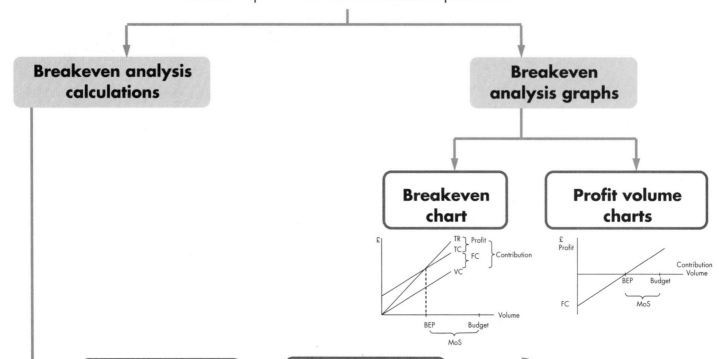

CVP analysis

- Breakeven point = Sales volume where profit is £0

Breakeven analysis calculations

Breakeven analysis graphs

Breakeven chart

Profit volume charts

Breakeven point (BEP)

$$BEP = \frac{\text{Fixed costs}}{\text{Contribution per unit}}$$

(volume of units)

- May need high–low method

C/S ratio

$$\text{Breakeven revenue} = \frac{\text{Fixed costs}}{\text{C/S ratio}}$$

$$\text{C/S ratio} = \frac{\text{Contribution}}{\text{Sales}}$$

Required profit calculations

Sales volume to reach required profit

$$= \frac{\text{Fixed costs + Required profit}}{\text{Contribution/unit}}$$

Margin of safety

(1) In units = budgeted sales volume – breakeven sales volume

(2) As a % =

$$\frac{\text{Budgeted SV – Breakeven SV}}{\text{Budgeted SV}} \times 100$$

Limitations

- Split cost into VC + FC
- FC/VC/unit SP/unit = constant
- Production = sales
- Only for single production or single production mixes

Introduction

This chapter considers a useful technique for making decisions that will affect the business in the next few months (in the short term). It is commonly examined.

Cost-volume-profit (CVP) analysis is concerned with the relationship between sales volume and profit level. CVP analysis identifies the **breakeven point** for a company and the **margin of safety**.

Limiting factor analysis considers situations where only a certain amount of some resource is available in the short term and therefore the management must decide how to allocate it in the most profitable way.

1 Relevant future income and costs for short-term decision making

When providing management information for decision making, you must work out which costs and revenues are **relevant** to the decision.

In the context of short-term decision making, the **relevant cost** is **contribution**. The fixed costs do not affect the decision made and are **irrelevant costs**.

A relevant cost (sometimes known as an **avoidable cost**) is a future, incremental cash flow arising as a direct consequence of a decision. In other words, relevant costs are those costs that are changed by a decision.

2 Breakeven analysis and contribution

2.1 Assumption

We will assume that selling price per unit, variable cost per unit and fixed costs are all constant, that is, they do not change with varying output. This is a reasonable assumption for short-term decisions although, of course, in the long term or for very high levels of output this might not apply.

2.2 Contribution

As discussed in the previous chapter, **contribution** shows us how much profit increases as sales increase.

Contribution per unit = Selling price per unit less all variable costs per unit

We will need this definition to set up the breakeven formula.

BPP
LEARNING MEDIA

3 Breakeven point

Key term

> The **breakeven point** is the volume of sales which will give a company a profit of £nil.

If sales exceed the breakeven point the company will make a profit.

Breakeven analysis is often referred to as **cost-volume-profit analysis**.

> **Formula to learn**
>
> Breakeven point = Number of units of sale required to breakeven
>
> $$= \frac{\text{Fixed costs}}{\text{Unit contribution}}$$

When calculating the breakeven point, always round the number of units **up** to the next whole unit.

> **Illustration 1: Breakeven point**
>
> Reardon Enterprises sells a single product with a selling price of £10 per unit. The variable costs of producing the product are £6 per unit and the fixed costs of the business are £200,000.
>
> What is the breakeven point in units?
>
> $$\text{Breakeven point} = \frac{£200,000}{£10 - £6}$$
>
> $$= 50,000 \text{ units}$$
>
> We can prove that this is the point where no profit or loss is made.
>
> | | £ |
> | --- | --- |
> | Sales (50,000 × £10) | 500,000 |
> | Variable costs (50,000 × £6) | 300,000 |
> | Contribution | 200,000 |
> | Fixed costs | (200,000) |
> | Profit | – |
>
> Therefore the management of Reardon Enterprises will know that they must ensure that sales volumes exceed 50,000 units per annum in order for the business to cover its total costs and make any profit.

Activity 1: Breakeven units

A business has a single product that it sells for £28. The variable costs of producing the product are £19 per unit and the fixed costs of the business are £360,000.

Required

What is the breakeven point in units?

Breakeven point = [   ] units

Activity 2: Breakeven revenue

A company has different output levels, and incurs different total production costs at each level, as follows:

Output Units	Total costs £
6,000	44,700
8,000	57,700

Required

If the selling price is £8 per unit at all levels, what is the breakeven point?
What is the breakeven revenue? (Use a rough sheet for workings.)

Breakeven point = [   ] units

Breakeven revenue = £ [   ]

4 The contribution/sales (C/S) ratio

Key term

The **C/S ratio** (or **profit–volume P/V ratio**) is a measure of how much contribution is earned from each £1 of sales. C/S ratio = contribution ÷ sales

The ratio of contribution to sales is an alternative method of finding the breakeven point.

Formula to learn

$$\text{Breakeven revenue} = \frac{\text{Fixed costs}}{\text{C/S ratio}}$$

$$\text{C/S ratio} = \frac{\text{Contribution}}{\text{Sales}}$$

Activity 3: Contribution/sales ratio

Required

Using details from the breakeven revenue activity (Activity 2) above, find the C/S ratio and breakeven revenue.

C/S ratio = [   ] %

Breakeven revenue = £ [   ]

5 The margin of safety

As well as being interested in the breakeven point, management may also be interested in the amount by which actual sales can fall below anticipated sales without a loss being made. This measure, of the amount by which sales must fall before we start making a loss, is the **margin of safety**.

A loss is made if sales volume is less than the breakeven point.

Margin of safety = Budgeted sales volume less breakeven sales volume

Or, as a percentage:

Formula to learn

$$\text{Margin of safety} = \frac{\text{Budgteted sales volume} - \text{Breakeven sales volume}}{\text{Budgeted sales volume}} \times 100$$

Activity 4: Margin of safety

Required

Using details as per the breakeven revenue example above, and with budgeted sales being 5,000 units, calculate the margin of safety.

Margin of safety = [   ] units

Margin of safety = [   ] %

6 Target profit

The approach used to find an expression for the breakeven sales volumes can be extended to find the volume needed to attain a required or **target profit** level.

Formula to learn

Sales volume to reach required profit level = $\dfrac{\text{Fixed costs} + \text{Required profit}}{\text{Unit contribution}}$

The required profit is like an additional fixed cost which must be covered before the company 'breaks even'.

Activity 5: Target profit level

Required

Using the data from the breakeven revenue example above, if we need to make a profit of £10,000, calculate the required sales volume.

Sales volume to achieve target profit = ⬚ units

---

7 Breakeven charts and profit–volume graphs

7.1 Breakeven chart

A breakeven chart shows the profit or loss at different levels of sales.

It shows, in diagrammatic form, the relationship between sales volume or value, total revenue, and total costs. Breakeven occurs when total costs are equal to total revenue.

The horizontal axis is used for sales volume or value and the vertical axis for money (costs and revenue).

Three lines are plotted on the graph:

- First the sales revenue line (which will pass through the origin, since when sales volume is nil, revenue is nil);

- Then the fixed costs line (which will be parallel to the horizontal axis);

- And finally the total costs line.

Illustration 2: Breakeven chart

The following information relates to Reardon Enterprises.

Selling price per unit	£10
Variable cost per unit	£6
Contribution per unit	£4
Fixed costs	£200,000
Breakeven point	50,000 units or £500,000
Budgeted sales	70,000 units

Breakeven chart

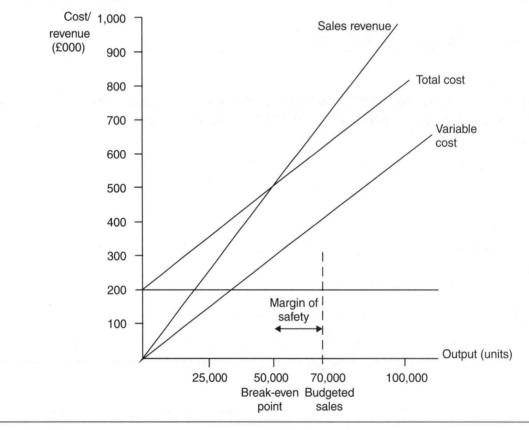

This chart shows variable costs, fixed costs, total costs and sales revenue at various different activity levels.

Assessment focus point

You will not be asked to sketch a graph in the computer based assessment but you could be asked to label one.

7.2 How to interpret the breakeven chart

- The fixed cost line is a horizontal line at £200,000.

- Variable costs start at the origin – if there are no sales then there are no variable costs. You can see, for example, variable costs at 100,000 units are £600,000.

- The total cost line is parallel to the variable cost line but starts at £200,000, the level of the fixed costs.

- Sales revenue again starts at the origin. You can see that the revenue is £1,000,000 if sales are 100,000 units.

7.3 What the breakeven chart shows

- The breakeven point is the point where the sales revenue line crosses the total costs line.

- The margin of safety is the horizontal distance between budgeted sales of 70,000 units and breakeven sales of 50,000 units.

- The amount of profit or loss at each activity level is the vertical distance between the sales revenue line and the total cost line.

7.4 Profit–volume chart

Illustration 3: Profit–volume chart

Profit–volume chart

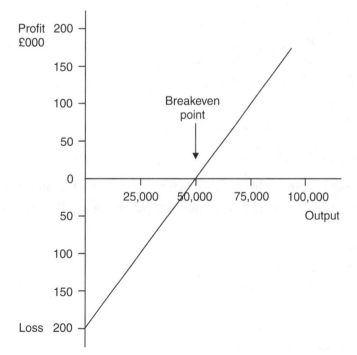

The profit–volume chart simply shows the level of profit or loss at any given level of activity.

7.5 How to interpret a P/V chart

- The loss when there are zero sales is equal to the fixed costs, £200,000.
- The profit at the 100,000 units activity level is £200,000.

7.6 What the P/V chart shows

- The profit or loss at any level of activity can be read off the chart.

- The breakeven point is where the profit line crosses the horizontal axis – where profit is zero.

- The horizontal axis could alternatively have shown sales revenue rather than activity level.

---

8 Limitations of breakeven analysis

CVP analysis is a useful technique for managers. It can provide simple and quick estimates, and breakeven charts provide graphical representations of breakeven arithmetic. It does, however, have a number of limitations.

The limitations are the assumptions that it makes.

8.1 Assumptions

(a) All costs can be split into fixed and variable elements
(b) Fixed costs are constant
(c) Variable cost per unit is constant
(d) Selling price is constant
(e) Constant inventory levels (sales = production)
(f) Analysis only possible for single products or for single product mixes

9 Limiting factor analysis

9.1 Single product

The production and sales plans of a business may be limited by a limiting factor/scarce resource. There are a number of potential limiting factors.

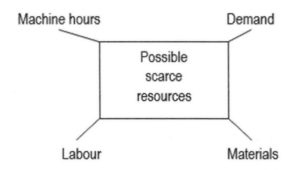

The plans of the business must be built around the limiting factor.

Assessment focus point

An assessment question could ask you to make recommendations in a limiting factor scenario based on the contribution per unit of limiting factor.

Illustration 4: Limiting factor

A business sells a single product for £35.00. The variable costs of the product are:

Direct materials   3 kg per unit @ £3.00 per kg
Direct labour   2 hours per unit @ £7.50 per hour

The fixed costs of the business are £800,000.

Materials as limiting factor

If the supply of materials is limited to 360,000 kg, how many units can the business produce and how much profit will be made?

Number of units that can be produced   = 360,000 kg/3 kg per unit
     = 120,000 units

	£
Sales (120,000 × £35.00)	4,200,000
Variable costs (120,000 × (£9.00 + £15))	2,880,000
Contribution	1,320,000
Fixed costs	800,000
Profit	520,000

Labour hours as limiting factor

If materials are now not restricted, but the business only has 280,000 labour hours available for production, how many units can be made and what is the profit at this production level?

Number of units that can be produced   = 280,000 hours/2 hours per unit
     = 140,000 units

	£
Sales (140,000 × £35.00)	4,900,000
Variable costs (140,000 × £24.00)	3,360,000
Contribution	1,540,000
Fixed costs	800,000
Profit	740,000

9.2 More than one product

If the business makes more than one product, it will want to find the product mix which will maximise profit given the limiting factor.

- In order to maximise overall profit, maximise contribution per unit of scarce resource.

- Concentrate upon the production of the product with the highest contribution per limiting factor unit.

Step 1   Identify limiting factor

Step 2   Calculate contribution per unit

Step 3   Calculate contribution per unit of limiting factor

Step 4   Rank the products

Step 5   Produce production plan based on rankings

Illustration 5: More than one product

Farnham Engineering makes three products A, B and C. The costs and selling prices of the three products are:

	A £	B £	C £
Direct materials @ £4 per kg	8	16	12
Direct labour @ £7 per hour	7	21	14
Variable overheads	3	9	6
	18	46	32
Selling price	22	54	39
Contribution	4	8	7

Sales demand for the coming period is expected to be as follows:

Product A   3,000 units
Product B   7,000 units
Product C   5,000 units

The supply of materials is limited to 50,000 kg during the period and the labour hours available are 28,000.

Step 1   Identify limiting factor

We have to decide first if there is a limiting factor other than sales demand. Consider the materials usage for each product if the maximum sales demand is produced. (You are not given the actual usage of materials of each product but you can work it out – for example, the materials cost for A is £8 and as the materials are £4 per kg, product A must use 2 kg etc).

	A	B	C	Total
Materials	6,000 kg	28,000 kg	15,000 kg	49,000 kg
Labour	3,000 hours	21,000 hours	10,000 hours	34,000 hours

As 50,000 kg of materials are available for the period and only 49,000 kg are required for the maximum production level, materials are not a limiting factor.

However, only 28,000 labour hours are available whereas in order to produce the maximum demand 34,000 hours are required. Therefore labour hours are the limiting factor.

Step 2   Calculate contribution per unit &

Step 3   Calculate contribution per unit of limiting factor

The contribution per limiting factor unit in this case is the contribution per labour hour for each product.

Step 4   Rank the products

Then rank the products according to how high the contribution per labour hour is for each one.

	A	B	C
Contribution	£4	£8	£7
Labour hours per unit	1 hour	3 hours	2 hours
Contribution per labour hour			
£4/1	£4.00		
£8/3		£2.67	
£7/2			£3.50
Ranking	1	3	2

Therefore in order to maximise contribution we must concentrate first on production of A up to the maximum sales demand, then on C, and finally, if there are any remaining hours available, on B.

Step 5   Produce production plan based on rankings

The optimal production plan in order to maximise contribution is:

	Units produced	Labour hours required
A	3,000	3,000
C	5,000	10,000
B (balance)	5,000	15,000 (balancing figure)
		28,000

The contribution earned from this production plan is:

		£
A	(3,000 × £4)	12,000
B	(5,000 × £8)	40,000
C	(5,000 × £7)	35,000
Total contribution		87,000

Activity 6: Sanctuary Catering

Sanctuary Catering's fixed costs for the year have been split as follows:

Standard meals	Vegetarian meals	Total
£32,500	£179,500	£212,000

The latest sales forecast is for 100,000 standard meals and 200,000 vegetarian meals.

It takes 0.025 hours to make a standard meal and 0.03 hours to cook a vegetarian meal.

Calculations have shown meal-type contributions to be as follows:

Standard meals	Vegetarian meals
40p	£1

Required

(a) Complete the table below to calculate:

(i) The breakeven sales, in meals, for standard and vegetarian meals

(ii) The margin of safety for each of the two types of meal

(iii) The margin of safety as a percentage

	Standard	Vegetarian
Fixed costs		
Meal contribution		
Breakeven sales (meals)		
Forecast sales (meals)		
Margin of safety (meals)		
Margin of safety (%)		

As a result of staff shortages planned for the year, the number of labour hours available has been reduced to 8,000 for the year.

Required

(b) Complete the table below to recommend how many standard and vegetarian meals should now be served in order to maximise the profits of Sanctuary Catering for the year.

	Standard	Vegetarian	Total
Contribution per meal			
Labour hours per meal			
Contribution per labour hour			
Ranking priority			
Labour hours allocated to type of meal			
Total contribution earned			
Less: fixed costs			£212,000
Profit			

Activity 7: Limiting factor decisions

SA Co sells two products, T and J, for which the following details are available.

	T £	J £
Direct labour (@ £5 per hr)	15	10
Direct materials (@ £2 per kg)	2	5
Variable overheads	2	2
Fixed overheads	3	3
	22	20
Selling price	25	22
	Units	**Units**
Maximum demand per month	10,000	8,000

Required

If only 40,000 labour hours are available per month, what is the best use of labour to generate the maximum possible contribution?

	T	J
Contribution per unit		
Hours taken		
Contribution per labour hour		
∴ Ranking		

Optimal production plan:

	Units	Hours used		Contribution £
J				
T			β	
Total				

Chapter summary

- In the context of short-term decision making, the relevant cost is contribution. Fixed costs are generally irrelevant.

- The breakeven point in units is found by dividing the fixed costs by the contribution per unit.

$$\text{Breakeven point} = \frac{\text{Fixed costs}}{\text{Unit contribution}}$$

- If a target profit is required the unit sales to achieve this can be found by dividing the fixed costs plus target profit by the contribution per unit.

- The difference between budgeted or actual sales and the breakeven point is the margin of safety, which can be expressed as a percentage of budgeted or actual sales.

- The contribution/sales ratio can be used to find the breakeven point in terms of sales revenue.

- Sales revenue, costs, contribution, profit and breakeven point can be illustrated by a breakeven chart or a profit–volume chart.

- Normally production is limited by sales demand; however, in some instances a factor such as the availability of material, labour hours or machine hours is the limiting factor.

- Where there is more than one product and a limiting factor, overall profit is maximised by concentrating production on the products with the highest contribution per limiting factor unit.

Keywords

- **Avoidable costs:** Costs that would not be incurred if the activity to which they relate did not exist

- **Breakeven analysis:** Calculations to determine the breakeven point

- **Breakeven point:** Level of sales whereby sales revenue is equal to total costs

- **Contribution:** Sales revenue or selling price per unit less variable costs

- **Cost-volume-profit analysis:** Analysis of the relationships between activity levels, costs and profits

- **Incremental cost:** The increase in costs that occur as a result of a decision

- **Irrelevant cost:** A cost incurred in the past (a past cost or **sunk cost**) that is irrelevant to any decision being made now; it includes committed costs which are future cash flows that will be incurred anyway, regardless of the decision taken now

- **Limiting factor:** A factor of production or sales that limits the amount of a product that can be produced or sold

- **Margin of safety:** Excess of budgeted or actual sales over the breakeven point sales

- **Profit–volume (P/V) ratio:** Ratio of contribution to sales, also known as the contribution to sales (C/S) ratio

- **Relevant cost:** A future incremental cash flow arising as a direct consequence of a decision

- **Target profit:** A planned level of profit, and from this the target profit units can be worked out

Test your learning

1   A business has budgeted sales of its single product of 38,000 units. The selling price per unit is £57 and the variable costs of production are £45. The fixed costs of the business are £360,000.

Calculate the breakeven point in units [   ] units

and the margin of safety (to the nearest whole per cent) [   ] %

2   A business has fixed costs of £910,000. It sells a single product at a selling price of £24 and the variable costs of production and sales are £17 per unit.

How many units of the product must the business [   ] units
sell in order to make a profit of £500,000?

3   A business sells its single product for £40. The variable costs of this product total £32. The fixed costs of the business are £100,000.

What is the sales revenue required in order to make £ [   ]
a profit of £200,000?

Long-term decision making

15

Learning outcomes

5	Apply management accounting techniques to support decision making

5.3	**Use long-term future income and costs**
	• The appropriate choice of techniques for long-term decision-making:
	    – Payback
	    – Net present value
	    – Internal rate of return
	• interpret the results from a capital investment appraisal (using techniques above)

Assessment context

Long-term decision making techniques will feature in the assessment. For example, in Task 10 you may be asked to make recommendations based on the payback period, net present value and internal rate of return.

Qualification context

You will find these techniques useful for making decisions about long-term projects such as whether to invest in new equipment.

Business context

Many decisions that the managers of a business will have to make will affect the business over a fairly long time period. In particular the purchase of buildings, machinery or equipment will be expected to bring benefits to the business over a number of future years. The decisions that managers will have to take are:

'Should this capital item, which is often a significant amount of expenditure, be purchased?' and

'Are the future benefits from this current expenditure enough to justify the investment?'

Most businesses use techniques such as payback, net present value or internal rate of return for appraising investments.

Chapter overview

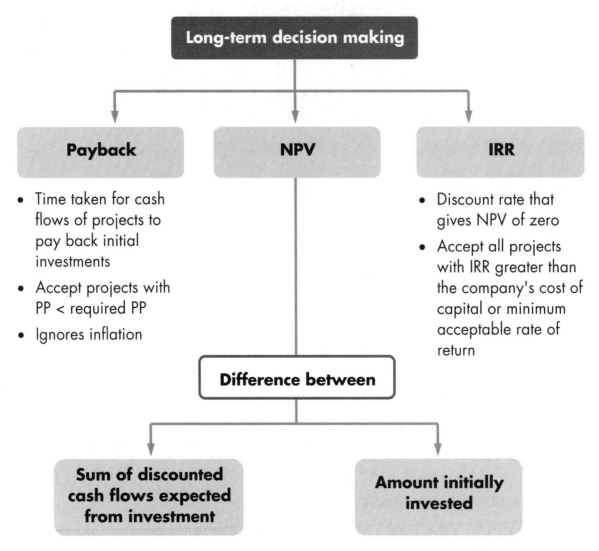

Long-term decision making

Payback

- Time taken for cash flows of projects to pay back initial investments
- Accept projects with PP < required PP
- Ignores inflation

NPV

Difference between

Sum of discounted cash flows expected from investment

Amount initially invested

- Accept all projects with NPV > zero

IRR

- Discount rate that gives NPV of zero
- Accept all projects with IRR greater than the company's cost of capital or minimum acceptable rate of return

Introduction

In the previous chapter we looked at techniques for making short-term decisions about production and sales. In this chapter we will consider longer-term decisions that have to be made, namely investment decisions. This means comparing initial capital expenditure with the future benefits that are to be received from that expenditure. Do the future benefits give a sufficient return on the initial investment?

To determine whether a future investment opportunity (project) is worthwhile, a number of appraisal methods may be used. Your assessment requires knowledge of the following methods:

(a) **Payback period (PP)**
(b) **Net present value (NPV)**
(c) **Internal rate of return (IRR)**

1 Payback period (PP)

Suppose a large amount of money is to be spent now on a project, such as the purchase of a major non-current asset. Management want to know whether the decision to purchase the non-current asset is a sensible one. One way that they could do this is keeping the length of time over which the benefits from this asset 'pay back' the original cost within acceptable limits. This is what is meant by the payback period.

Key term

Payback period is the number of years necessary for the cash flows of the project to pay back the initial investment.

Illustration 1: Payback

Uckport Industrials is considering investment in new plant for their factory which will cost £250,000 if purchased now, 1 January 20X6. It will provide major cost savings in future production.

The production manager has estimated that the cost savings for each year will be:

20X6	£80,000
20X7	£80,000
20X8	£80,000
20X9	£60,000
20Y0	£40,000

The payback period can be calculated by considering the cumulative cost savings:

Year	Cost saving £	Cumulative cost savings £
20X6	80,000	80,000
20X7	80,000	160,000
20X8	80,000	240,000
20X9	60,000	300,000

We assume that the cost savings occur evenly throughout the year and we can see that by the end of 20X8 we have almost recovered the cost with cumulative savings of £240,000. In 20X9 the cost savings total £60,000 but in order to pay back the initial cost we only need a further £10,000 of this. Therefore the payback period can be calculated as:

Payback period   =   3 years + (£10,000/£60,000 × 12 months)
                        =   3 years and 2 months

1.1 Decision rule

(a)   Accept projects with a payback period of less than the company's required payback period.

(b)   When deciding between two projects, the one with the shorter payback period is preferred.

Note that payback should not be used on its own to choose between projects. To choose between projects, other techniques would be needed too.

1.2 Advantages of payback period

(a)   Quick, simple calculation. The payback period is one of the most widely used methods of project appraisal. It is a fairly simple calculation.

(b)   Easily understood concept, especially by non-financial managers.

(c)   Considers liquidity, ie cash flow. It considers the **risk** of a business being parted from its money as it is considering the time period between the cash outflow for the initial cost and the cash inflow from income or cost savings.

1.3 Disadvantages of payback period

(a)   The maximum period set is arbitrary.

(b)   It ignores the timing of flows within the payback period.

(c)   It does not take account of all of the cash flows associated with the project, only those up to the end of the payback period, and it does not take any account of how those cash flows occur over the period.

(d)   It ignores the **time value of money** (explained later in this chapter).

Assessment focus point

An assessment question may tell you that a business is particularly interested in limiting its risk. If the business is choosing a project based on limiting risk, then it should choose the project with the quickest payback period.

Activity 1: Payback period – Kirby plc

Kirby plc is considering a five-year project that requires an initial cash outlay of £550,000 on equipment. At the end of the project the equipment is expected to have a scrap value of £25,000.

The equipment will produce annual cash operating revenues of £150,000 for five years.

Kirby has a required payback period of five years.

Required

Calculate the payback period of the project and state whether Kirby plc should accept or reject the project on the basis of payback period?

Simple payback = _____ Accept/Reject project

Year	Simple payback cash flow £	Cumulative cash flow £
0		
1		
2		
3		
4		
5		

2 Net present value (NPV)

2.1 Time value of money

For long-term decision making an important factor is the time value of money. The time value of money is all to do with our preference to receive money sooner rather than later. If we are offered £100 now or in a year's time then we would prefer to have the money now rather than wait. There are three main reasons for this:

Risk preference	If the money is received now then it is ours and there is no risk that it might not be paid in one year's time
Consumption preference	If the money is received now then we can spend it now rather than having to wait for a year (when it may be worth less in real terms)
Investment preference	If the money is received now then we can invest it and earn interest on it so that in one year's time it is worth more than £100

2.2 Present values

If we are offered £100 now or £100 in one year's time we are not comparing like with like. If the interest rate is, say, 10% per annum then if the £100 were received now it could be invested for a year at 10% interest. After one year the amount that we would have would be:

$$£100 \times 1.10 \quad = £110$$

We would therefore definitely prefer the £100 now.

We would only be indifferent if we were offered the option of £100 now or £110 in one year's time. By turning it around we can say that the **present value** of £110 in one year's time is £100 now (if the interest rate is 10%) – the equivalent sum now of that future income. We can calculate the present value (PV) as:

$$PV = \frac{£110}{1.10} = £100$$

Let's now suppose that if we had £100 now we would invest it for two years at 10% interest without removing the interest – this is known as **compound interest**

After one year our investment would be	£100 × 1.10	=	£110
After two years our investment would be	£110 × 1.10	=	£121
This can be simplified to:			
Investment after two years	£100 × 1.10 × 1.10	=	£121
OR	$£100 \times 1.10^2$		

We can therefore also say that the present value of £121 arising after two years is £100. This would have been calculated as:

$$\frac{£121}{1.10^2}$$

OR $£121 \times \dfrac{1}{1.10^2}$

The element that the cash flow is multiplied by, in this case

$\dfrac{1}{1.10^2}$ or 0.8264

is known as the **discount factor** or the present value factor (PV factor). The 10% interest rate is known as the **cost of capital**.

Let's summarise where we've got to. To calculate the value in today's money of a future cash flow, a discount factor is applied. This can be calculated using the cost of capital and is expressed as a decimal or a percentage. To calculate the present value the cash flow is multiplied by the discount factor. This means that a fair comparison is possible as it gives a value for what the cash flows are worth at time zero, ie now.

2.3 Net present value method

The computation of a present value is a discounted cash flow (DCF) technique. We are finding the discounted (present) value of each individual cash flow or annuity.

If we are appraising a project then the technique that we can use is to find the net present value of all of the cash flows of the project. This involves calculating the present value of each individual cash flow and then totalling them all, remembering that the initial cost of the project is a cash outflow and any income or cost savings are cash inflows. The total of the present value of the inflows minus the outflows is the net present value (NPV).

Net present value is the net total of the discounted cash flows of the project.

Key term

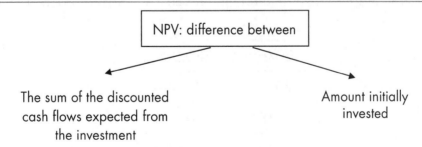

(a) Calculate/list the expected cash flows (per year) that result from the investment or decision.

(b) Discount each cash flow at the cost of capital.

(c) Total up the discounted cash flows, adding cash inflows and subtracting cash outflows.

2.4 Purpose of net present value

The purpose of net present value is to establish the maximum amount that an investor would be willing to pay for a given set of future cash flows, given the investor's cost of capital. This takes into account the time value of money.

2.5 Decision rule

If the net present value is a positive figure, a positive NPV, then the project should be accepted as this means that after taking account of the time value of money, the cash inflows from the project exceed the cash outflows. If, however, the net present value is a negative figure, a negative NPV, then the project should be rejected.

It is important to note when making recommendations in the assessment that NPV calculation is the most important factor when assessing projects. If the NPV of a project is negative you would always reject the project even when all other appraisal methods are favourable.

Assessment focus point

An assessment question may ask you whether a project should be accepted or not. You need to remember these rules:

Accept projects with a NPV greater than zero.

In deciding between two projects, accept the one with the higher NPV.

Illustration 2: Net present value

We will return to Uckport Industrials.

Uckport Industrials is considering investment in new plant for their factory that will cost £250,000 if purchased now, 1 January 20X6. It will provide major cost savings in future production.

The production manager has estimated that the cost savings for each calendar year will be:

20X6	£80,000
20X7	£80,000
20X8	£80,000
20X9	£60,000
20Y0	£40,000

The **discount rate**, or cost of capital to be used, is 10%.

We can now use discounted cash flow (DCF) techniques to determine the net present value of this project. When using DCF techniques we have to be very careful about our assumptions about the timing of cash flows.

We assume that the cost savings all occur on the last day of each year, but the investment occurs immediately, now, which we shall call year 0. Therefore the timings are

1 January 20X6	=	Year 0
31 December 20X6	=	Year 1
31 December 20X7	=	Year 2

and so on.

We can now build up the net present value of these cash flows:

Year	Cash flow £	Discount factor @ 10%	Present value £
0	(250,000)	1.0000	(250,000)
1	80,000	0.9091	72,728
2	80,000	0.8264	66,112
3	80,000	0.7513	60,104
4	60,000	0.6830	40,980
5	40,000	0.6209	24,836
Net present value			14,760

There are a number of points to note here:

- The initial cost occurs at Year 0 or now, therefore the discount factor is 1.0000 as £250,000 is the present value of the outflow now.

- Although the cost savings are not actual income, they are the saving of an outflow, ie they are reducing the cash costs of the business, and this is why they are treated as cash inflows.

- The initial cost of the machinery is a cash outflow and is therefore traditionally shown in brackets to distinguish it from the cost savings and cash inflows.

The layout above shows clearly how the net present value is arrived at. An alternative layout is as follows:

	Year 0 £000	Year 1 £000	Year 2 £000	Year 3 £000	Year 4 £000	Year 5 £000
Capital expenditure	(250)					
Cash inflows		80	80	80	60	40
Net cash flows	(250)	80	80	80	60	40
PV factors	1.0000	0.9091	0.8264	0.7513	0.6830	0.6209
Discounted cash flows	(250.000)	72.728	66.112	60.104	40.980	24.836
Net present value	14.760					

So for Uckport Industrials, at their cost of capital or discount rate of 10% the project cash flows have a positive net present value and therefore the project should be accepted.

Activity 2: NPV – Kirby plc

Kirby plc is considering a five-year project that requires an initial cash outlay of £550,000 on equipment. At the end of the project the equipment is expected to have a scrap value of £25,000.

The equipment will produce annual cash operating revenues of £150,000 for five years.

Kirby has a cost of capital of 10%.

Required

Calculate the NPV of Kirby's project (to 2 decimal places) and advise Kirby whether to accept or reject the project.

Year	Cash flow £	DF @ 10%	PV £
0		1.0000	
1		0.9091	
2		0.8264	
3		0.7513	
4		0.6830	
5		0.6209	
			NPV=

2.6 Advantages of NPV method

(a) It correctly accounts for the time value of money (discounting of future cash flows gives greater 'weight' to earlier cash flows).

(b) It is based on cash flows which are less subjective than profit.

(c) It is consistent with the objective of maximising shareholders' wealth. Shareholders will benefit if a project with a positive NPV is accepted.

2.7 Disadvantages of NPV method

(a) It can be difficult to identify an appropriate discount rate.

(b) It is a tricky concept. Some managers are unfamiliar with the concept of NPV.

(c) It does not allow for the risk of the project.

2.8 Net present cost

Sometimes there will be no income associated with a decision and projects will have a **net present cost** overall. The net present cost of a project is the sum of the present value of all costs over the period of interest. If a number of options are being considered then the option with the lowest net present cost will be the most favourable financial option.

Activity 3: NPV and PP

The following are the relevant cash flows of a project.

	0 £000	1 £000	2 £000	3 £000
Capital expense	720			
Indirect labour cost saving		340	348	448
Operating cost saving		264	272	270

Required

Calculate the NPV and payback period using the information below. Work to the nearest whole thousand in the NPV table.

	0 £000	1 £000	2 £000	3 £000
Capital expense				
Indirect labour cost saving				
Operating cost saving				
Net cash flow				
PV factors 14%	1	0.8772	0.7695	0.6750
Discounted				
NPV				

The payback period is _____ years (to 2 decimal places)

3 Internal rate of return (IRR)

Key term

> **Internal rate of return (IRR)** is the discount rate that gives an NPV of zero. It can also be defined as the percentage return from an investment.

If the internal rate of return of a project is higher than the organisation's cost of capital or higher than its required return from investments, the project should be accepted. If it is lower, then it should be rejected.

Illustration 3: IRR

A project might have the following NPVs at the following discount rates.

Discount rate %	NPV £
5	5,300
10	2,900
15	(1,700)
20	(3,200)

You can see that the NPV changes from a positive value to a negative value somewhere between 10% and 15%. The IRR is the discount rate which gives an NPV of zero. So the IRR is somewhere between 10% and 15%.

It might help you to see this on a graph, but just ignore the graph if it is not helpful for you. The important points to note are:

- The IRR is the discount rate that gives a zero NPV.

- The IRR must be greater than the organisation's cost of capital for the project to be acceptable.

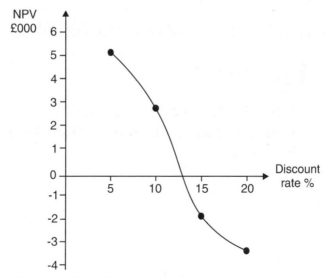

3.1 Method of calculation (linear interpolation)

(a) Take a project and calculate the NPV at two different discount factors.

The approximation is better if the second interest rate used is estimated closer to the IRR, ie if the first NPV is +ve, choose a higher interest rate for the second NPV to bring it as close to zero as possible.

(b) Use the interpolation formula below to calculate the approximate IRR, where a and b represent the chosen discount factors and NPVa and NPVb are their respective NPVs.

Formula to learn

$$IRR = a + \frac{NPVa}{NPVa - NPVb} \times (b - a)$$

Where a and b are the discount rates used.

Note. The formula will work even if both NPVs are +ve or –ve.

Illustration 4: IRR with linear interpolation

A project has the following NPVs at discount rates of 10% and 20%.

Discount rate %	NPV £
9	6,235
11	755
13	–4,430

Use linear interpolation to estimate the IRR.

$$IRR = a + \left[\frac{NPVa}{NPVa - NPVb} \times (b - a) \right]$$

We will use a = 11% and b = 13% (so NPVa = 755 and NPVb = –4,430)

$$IRR = 11 + \left[\frac{755}{755 - -4,430} \times (13 - 11) \right]$$

Look very carefully at NPVa – NPVb. As NPVb = –4,430 we have two minus signs next to each other. Note the rule of maths that says that two minuses make a plus. So we can re-write the formula as:

$$IRR = 11 + \left[\frac{755}{755 + 4,430} \times (13 - 11) \right]$$

$$\therefore IRR = 11 + \left[\frac{755}{5,185} \times 2 \right]$$

$$\therefore IRR = 11.29\%$$

Activity 4: IRR

The NPV of a project is 1,679 when the cost of capital is 10% and -49 when the cost of capital is 20%.

Required

Calculate the IRR of the project to two decimal places.

The IRR of the project is _____%

3.2 Advantages

(a) Results are expressed as a simple percentage and are more easily understood than some other methods.

(b) It does not require an exact cost of capital.

(c) It takes into account the time value of money, unlike other approaches such as payback period.

(d) It indicates how sensitive calculations are to changes in interest rates.

3.3 Disadvantages

(a) It cannot accommodate changing interest rates.

(b) It can sometimes rank projects incorrectly. Projects with unconventional cash flows can produce negative or multiple IRRs.

(c) It is complex to calculate.

Chapter summary

- Long-term decisions are often of the nature of large initial capital expenditure followed by benefits in terms of additional revenue or cost savings.

- The payback period is a method of assessing a project based upon how quickly the inflows from the project repay the initial investment.

- If the payback period for a project is shorter than the organisation's payback period limit then the project will be accepted.

- The main disadvantage of the payback period is that it takes no account of the time value of money – if cash is to be received in the future it must be discounted to take account of the time value of money.

- The net present cost of a project is the sum of the present value of all costs over the period of interest.

- One method of using discounted cash flow techniques for project appraisal is to calculate the net present value of the project cash flows – if the net present value at the organisation's cost of capital is positive then the project should be accepted but if it is negative it should be rejected.

- If the internal rate of return of the project is greater than the organisation's cost of capital the project should be accepted.

Keywords

- **Compound interest:** A system where interest is accumulated rather than being withdrawn – interest is then paid on the interest

- **Consumption preference:** Money received sooner rather than later can be used earlier

- **Cost of capital:** The discount rate used by an organisation to appraise projects, this represents the required rate of return

- **Discount factor:** The factor applied to a future cash flow to find its present value

- **Discount rate:** The interest rate used to discount cash flows

- **Internal rate of return (IRR):** The discount rate which when applied to project cash flows gives a zero net present value

- **Investment preference:** Money received sooner rather than later can be invested to earn interest

- **Net present cost:** The sum of the individual present costs over the project life

- **Net present value (NPV):** The total of the individual present values of the cash flows of a project

- **Payback period (PP):** The time it takes for the cash inflows from a project to repay the initial investment cost

- **Present value (PV):** The discounted value of a future cash flow to put it in terms of what it is worth in today's money

- **Risk preference:** Money received sooner rather than later carries less risk of not materialising

- **Time value of money:** The fact that money received or paid in the future is worth less than money received or paid now due to risk, consumption and investment preferences

1   A business is considering investment in new machinery at a cost of £100,000 now, 1 January 20X6. The machinery will be used to make a new product that will provide additional cash inflows as follows:

Year ending

31 December 20X6	£30,000
31 December 20X7	£40,000
31 December 20X8	£40,000
31 December 20X9	£20,000

The cash inflows occur evenly throughout the year.

What is the payback period?

The payback period is [_____] years and [_____] months.

2   Today's date is 1 January 20X6.

What are the present values of each of the following cash flows?

(a)   A receipt of £3,100 on 31 December 20X7 – discount factor 0.7972

£ [_____]

(b)   A payment of £15,000 on 1 January 20X6 – discount factor 1.0000

£ [_____]

(c)   A receipt of £1,000 on 31 December 20X6 and 20X7 – discount factors 0.8929 and 0.7972

£ [_____]

(d)   A payment of £4,400 on 31 December 20X8 – discount factor 0.8734

£ [_____]

3   A business is considering investment in new machinery at a cost of £340,000 on 1 April 20X6. This machinery will be used to produce a new product which will give rise to the following net cash inflows:

31 March 20X7	£80,000
31 March 20X8	£70,000
31 March 20X9	£90,000
31 March 20Y0	£120,000
31 March 20Y1	£60,000

The discount factors to use are 0.9346, 0.8734, 0.8163, 0.7629 and 0.7130.

What is the net present value of this project?

£ [_____]

4   A business is considering investment in new plant and machinery on
     1 January 20X6 at a cost of £90,000. The cash cost savings are estimated to be:

31 December 20X6	£23,000
31 December 20X7	£31,000
31 December 20X8	£40,000
31 December 20X9	£18,000

The business has a cost of capital of 11%. The discount factors to use are 0.9009,
0.8116, 0.7312 and 0.6587. The business has a payback limit of four years.

(a) **What is the net present value of this project? (Round your
     present values to the nearest whole pound.)**

£ [   ]

(b) **Advise the business as to whether it should invest in the new
     plant and machinery and justify your advice.**

	✓
Management should accept the project because the net present value is negative	
Management should not accept the project because the net present value is negative	
Management should accept the project because the payback period is less than 4 years	
Management should not accept the project because the payback is less than 4 years	

6   A project has the following NPVs at the following discount rates.

Discount rate %	NPV £
9	22
10	−4

What is the approximate IRR of the project?

☐   9.15%

☐   9.85%

☐   10.15%

☐   10.85%

Activity answers

CHAPTER 1 Introduction to management accounting

Activity 1: Information for management

Management accountants may provide information for management on the following:

	✓
Cost of goods and services	✓
Actual costs compared to expected costs	✓
Expected profits and production plans	✓

Activity 2: Production and service cost centres

Production cost centres	Service cost centres
Assembly	Canteen
Packing	Maintenance
Finishing	Stores

CHAPTER 2 Cost classification and cost behaviour

Activity 1: Fixed cost per unit

(a) | £ | 20 |

Working £20,000/1,000 = £20

(b) | £ | 2 |

Working £20,000/10,000 = £2

(c) | £ | 1 |

Working £20,000/20,000 = £1

(d) | £ | 0.20 |

Working £20,000/100,000 = £0.20

As the number of units increase, the fixed cost per unit decreases.

Activity 2: Fixed and variable elements of cost

The fixed element of the overhead cost is £580,000 × 55% = | £ | 319,000

The fixed element of the overhead cost is £580,000 × 55% = | £ | 319,000

The variable element of the overhead cost is £580,000 × (100% – 55%) =

| £ | 261,000

Activity 3: High–low method – manufacturing business

| £ | 110,500

Workings

	Units		£
High output	8,000	Total cost	115,000
Low output	6,000	Total cost	97,000
Difference	2,000		18,000

Variable cost per unit £18,000/2,000 = £9

Substituting in high volume:

	£
Total cost	115,000
Variable cost (8,000 × £9)	(72,000)
Fixed costs (balance)	43,000

At output of 7,500 units:

	£
Fixed costs	43,000
Variable costs (7,500 × £9)	67,500
Estimated total cost	110,500

Activity 4: High–low method – service business

£	210

Workings

	Units		£
High output	3,000	Total cost	220
Low output	2,100	Total cost	184
Difference	900		36

Variable cost per unit £36/900 = £0.04

Substituting in high volume:

	£
Total cost	220
Variable cost (3,000 × £0.04)	(120)
Fixed costs (balance)	100

	£
Total cost in June	
Fixed costs	100
Variable cost (2,750 × £0.04)	110
	210

CHAPTER 3 Materials costs and inventory valuation

Activity 1: Holding inventory

	✓
To avoid production stoppages due to a shortage of materials	✓
To take advantage of quantity discounts	✓
To avoid the detrimental effect of price fluctuations	✓
To provide a buffer or fail-safe in times of general shortage or heavy demand	✓

Activity 2: Inventory control levels

(a) Reorder level = Buffer inventory + (Max usage × Max lead time)
        = 0 + (420 parts × 15 days)
        = 6,300 parts

(b) Minimum inventory level = Reorder level – (Average usage per day × Average lead time)

$$= 6{,}300 \text{ parts} - (350 \text{ parts} \times 13 \text{ days})$$

$$= \boxed{1{,}750 \text{ parts}}$$

(c) Maximum inventory level = Reorder level + Reorder Quantity – (Min usage × Min lead time)

$$= 6{,}300 \text{ parts} + 6{,}500 \text{ parts} - (180 \times 11)$$

$$= \boxed{10{,}820 \text{ parts}}$$

Activity 3: EOQ

$$\text{EOQ} = \sqrt{\frac{2 \times 32 \times 150 \times 12}{25 \times 0.18}} = \sqrt{\frac{115{,}200}{4.5}} = \sqrt{25{,}600} = \boxed{160 \text{ parts}}$$

Activity 4: CCS Ltd

(a) The highest reported profit would be arrived at by using FIFO. This is because the earliest inventory with the lower costs are assumed to be issued first. This results in a lower cost of sales and therefore a higher profit.

(b) Inventory record card for potatoes

| Date | Receipts | | | Issues | | | Balance | |
	Quantity tonnes	Cost per tonne £	Total cost £	Quantity tonnes	Cost per tonne £	Total cost £	Quantity tonnes	Total cost £
Balance as at: 1 June							72	10,512
2 June	70	150.00	10,500				142	21,012
3 June				90	72 at £146.00 18 at £150.00	13,212	52	7,800
4 June	50	152.00	7,600				102	15,400
5 June				70	52 at £150.00 18 at £152.00	10,536	32	4,864

CHAPTER 4 Labour costs

Activity 1: Overtime premium

Basic pay   £ | 120.00

Overtime premium £ | 7.50

Mark's total wage £ | 127.50   for the day

			£	
Basic pay	=	8 hours @ £15	120.00	(direct cost)
Overtime premium	=	1 hour @ ½ × £15	7.50	(indirect cost)
			127.50	

Activity 2: Job 146

Basic pay   £ | 315,000

Overtime premium £ | 57,750

Direct labour cost of Job 146 is £ | 372,750

		£
Basic pay	= 45,000 hours @ £7	315,000
Overtime premium	= 33,000 hours @ 25% × £7	57,750
Total direct labour cost		372,750

Activity 3: Component C

Cost at normal rate:	5,000 hours @ £10	=	£50,000
	2,000 hours @ £10	=	£20,000
	1,000 hours @ £10	=	£10,000
			£80,000

Cost at time and a half:	2,000 hours @ £10 × 0.5 =	£10,000

Cost at double time:	1,000 hours @ £10 × 1	£10,000

(a) Total cost of direct labour   = £100,000

(b) Cost per unit = $\dfrac{£100,000}{500,000 \text{ units}}$ = 20p per unit

Activity 4: Piecework system

	£
First 4,000 units: 4,000 × 10p	400.00
Next 500 units: 500 × 12p	60.00
Last 230 units: 230 × 14p	32.20
Gross pay	492.20

Activity 5: Remuneration systems

	Time rate	Piecework rate
Easy/complicated to calculate an employee's pay	Easy	Complicated
Can/can't be used for all direct labour employees	Can	Can't
More efficient workers are paid **more than/the same as** less efficient workers	The same as	More than
The quality of the goods produced **is/is not** affected by workers being tempted to rush a job so that they earn more	Is not	Is
The employees' pay **fluctuates/remains the same** if output fluctuates	Remains the same	Fluctuates
More supervisors/more inspectors may be needed for this system	More supervisors	More inspectors
Production problems **can/cannot** lead to a cut in pay	Cannot	Can
Systems **do/do not** need to be set up to check the amount of work produced by each employee	Do not	Do

Activity 6: Tristan Ltd

Wages Calculation Sheet

Employee name: James Declan
Clock number: H63
Week beginning: 9 June (20X6)

	Mon	Tues	Wed	Thurs	Fri	Total
Hours worked	7.5	8.0	9.0	8.5	9.5	
Standard pay	63.75	63.75	63.75	63.75	63.75	318.75
Overtime hours	–	0.5	1.5	1.0	2.0	
Overtime payment	–	6.38	19.13	12.75	25.50	63.76
Units produced	191	197	225	204	245	
Extra units	11	5	9	–	17	
Bonus payable	1.95	0.89	1.59	–	3.01	7.44
Total payable for the day	65.70	71.02	84.47	76.50	92.26	389.95

Total wages payable for the week:

	£
Direct wages	382.51
Indirect wages	7.44
Total wages	389.95

CHAPTER 5 Allocation and apportionment

Activity 1: Allocation

Cost	
Wages of the supervisor of department A	Allocate to department A
Wages of the supervisor of department B	Allocate to department B
Indirect materials consumed in department A	Allocate to department A
Rent of the factory shared by departments A and B	Cannot be allocated

Both the wages of the supervisor of department A and the materials consumed by department A can be charged to the cost centre department A because they relate to that cost centre only.

The wages of the supervisor of department B can be charged to the cost centre department B because they relate to that cost centre only.

The cost of rent relates to both of the cost centres so it would be unfair to charge the cost to one of the cost centres only. Instead we need to charge a fair share of the cost of rent to both cost centres. This is called apportionment.

Activity 2: Apportionment bases

Cost	Basis of apportionment
Rent, rates and insurance	Floor space (square metres)
Light, heat and power	Floor space (square metres)
Depreciation charge of machinery	Carrying amount
Canteen costs	Number of employees

Activity 3: Allocation and apportionment basis

Overhead	Basis of apportionment
Rent/rates	Floor area
Depreciation	NBV or cost of equipment
Staff canteen costs	Number of employees
Heat, light	Volume of space occupied/floor area
Insurance of equipment	Value of equipment insured
Stores costs	Allocate to stores cost centre

Activity 4: Overhead apportionment

Allocation and apportionment

	Total £	Processing dept £	Packing dept £	Canteen £
Canteen	18,000	–	–	18,000
Processing dept supervisor	15,000	15,000	–	–
Packing dept supervisor	10,000	–	10,000	–
Rent (50:25:5)	20,000	12,500	6,250	1,250
Heat (50:25:5)	5,040	3,150	1,575	315
Depreciation (3:3:1)	7,000	3,000	3,000	1,000
Welfare (5:4:1)	5,000	2,500	2,000	500
Total	80,040	36,150	22,825	21,065

Activity 5: Overhead reapportionment – direct method

Reapportionment – inter-service centre work is ignored here.

Direct method

| | Production depts | | | Service centres | |
	X £	Y £	Stores £	Maintenance £	General admin overheads £
Overheads	70,000	30,000	20,000	15,000	6,000
Reapportion Stores (62.5% and 37.5%)	12,500	7,500	(20,000)		
Reapportion Maintenance (8,000/15,000) and (7,000 / 15,000)	8,000	7,000		(15,000)	
Reapportion General admin overheads (50:50)	3,000	3,000			(6,000)
Total	93,500	47,500			

Activity 6: Overhead reapportionment – step down method

Step-down method – inter-service work is taken into account in the first step only.

| | Production Depts | | Service Centre | |
	X £	Y £	Stores £	Canteen £
Allocated overhead	70,000	30,000	20,000	15,000
Apportion stores (50:30:20)	10,000	6,000	(20,000)	4,000
			–	19,000
Apportion canteen (45:50)	9,000	10,000	–	(19,000)
Total	89,000	46,000	–	–

Activity 1: Overhead absorption bases

	Mixing	Stirring
Direct labour hours	20,000	5,000
Direct machine hours	2,000	60,000

Mixing department: OAR should be based on | Budgeted direct labour hours |

Stirring department: OAR should be based on | Budgeted direct machine hours |

As we can see from the table, the mixing department has a higher proportion of labour hours than machine hours meaning it is labour intensive and therefore labour hours would be an appropriate basis for absorption. The stirring department has a higher proportion of machine hours compared to labour hours meaning it is machine intensive and therefore machine hours would be an appropriate basis for absorption.

Activity 2: Overhead absorption rates (OAR) 1

Budgeted OAR = Budgeted overheads / budgeted machine hours

Budgeted OAR = £40,000 / 2,000 = £20 per machine hour

Activity 3: Overhead absorption rates (OAR) 2

As units are not identical the units basis of absorption is not appropriate.

The Mixing department is labour intensive, therefore a suitable

$$OAR = \frac{£10,000}{20,000 \, \text{labour hours}} = 50p \text{ per labour hour}$$

The Stirring department is machine intensive, therefore a suitable

$$OAR = \frac{£15,000}{60,000 \, \text{machine hours}} = 25p \text{ per machine hour}$$

Activity 4: Overhead absorption rates in the service sector

OAR = £130,000/325,000 miles = 40p per mile

Activity 5: Overhead absorption rates (OAR) 3

(a) $OAR = \dfrac{\text{Budgeted overheads}}{\text{Budgeted direct labour hours}} = \dfrac{£400,000}{3,200 \text{ hours}}$

$$= £125 \text{ per labour hour}$$

(b) $\text{OAR} = \dfrac{\text{Budgeted overheads}}{\text{Budgeted machine hours}} = \dfrac{£400,000}{10,000\,\text{hours}}$

$$= £40 \text{ per machine hour}$$

(c) As the painting division is machine intensive a machine hour based OAR is more appropriate for calculations (£40 per machine hour).

(d) Absorbed overheads = £40 × 12,562 machine hours

$$= £502,480$$

Overheads actually incurred = £521,262

Therefore, overheads were under-absorbed by £521,362 – £502,480 = £18,782.

Activity 6: Over- and under-absorption

(a) Fixed overheads absorbed in Assembly department

775 actual machine hours × £10 = overheads absorbed of £7,750

(b) Fixed overheads absorbed in Finishing department

1,250 direct labour hours × £7.50 = overheads absorbed of £9,375

(c) **(i)** Under-absorption in Assembly department

Overheads absorbed <   Actual overheads
£7,750   £8,110

There is an under-absorption of (£8,110 – £7,750) = £360

(ii) Over-absorption in Finishing department

Overheads absorbed >   Actual overheads
£9,375   £9,000

There is an over-absorption of £375.

Activity 7: Mars Ltd

	£	£
Direct costs		
Materials		5.00
Labour		
Mixing (2.0 × £8.60)		1117.20
Stirring (0.5 × £8.60)		4.30
Total direct costs		26.50
Overheads		
Mixing department (2.0 × £0.50)	1.00	
Stirring department (6.0 × £0.25)	1.50	
Total overheads		2.50
Total cost		29.00

Activity 8: Activity-based costing

(a)

$\dfrac{\text{Set-up costs}}{\text{Number of production runs}}$	$\dfrac{£5,250}{21}$	=	£250	per production run
$\dfrac{\text{Stores receiving}}{\text{Number of requistions raised}}$	$\dfrac{£3,600}{80}$	=	£45	per requisition raised
$\dfrac{\text{Inspection/quality control}}{\text{Number of production runs}}$	$\dfrac{£2,100}{21}$	=	£100	per production run
$\dfrac{\text{Materials handling and despatch}}{\text{Number of orders executed}}$	$\dfrac{£4,620}{42}$	=	£110	per order executed

(b)

	P1	P2	P3	P4
Number of production runs	6	5	4	6
Cost per production run	£250	£250	£250	£250
Set-up costs per product	£1,500	£1,250	£1,000	£1,500

	P1	P2	P3	P4
Number of requisitions raised	20	20	20	20
Cost per requisition raised	£45	£45	£45	£45
Stores receiving costs per product	£900	£900	£900	£900

	P1	P2	P3	P4
Number of production runs	6	5	4	6
Cost per production run	£100	£100	£100	£100
Inspection/quality control costs per product	£600	£500	£400	£600

	P1	P2	P3	P4
Number of orders executed	12	10	8	12
Cost per order executed	£110	£110	£110	£110
Materials handling and despatch per product	£1,320	£1,100	£880	£1,320

(c)

	P1 £	P2 £	P3 £	P4 £
Direct material	4,800	5,000	2,400	7,200
Direct labour	3,360	2,100	1,120	2,520
Production overhead				
Set-up costs	1,500	1,250	1,000	1,500
Stores receiving	900	900	900	900
Inspection/quality control	600	500	400	600
Material handling and despatch	1,320	1,100	880	1,320
Total cost	12,480	10,850	6,700	14,040
Unit costs	(÷ 120) £104	(÷ 100) £108.50	(÷ 80) £83.75	(÷ 120) £117

Activity 1: Job 4321

		Job 4321 £	£
Direct materials: department	A	4,000	
	B	1,000	
	C	1,500'	
			6,500
Direct labour: department	A	1,800	
	B	1,600	
	C	2,000	
			5,400
Fixed production overhead:	900 hrs × £5		4,500
Total production cost			16,400
Fixed administration overhead:	80% × £16,400		13,120
Total cost			29,520
Profit	20% × £29,520		5,904
Selling price			35,424

Activity 2: Splodge Ltd

Job 08/10/04 No 111	Workings	£
Materials – bricks		
– Issued	40 kg @ £5.00	200.00
– Issued for rework	10 kg @ £5.00	50.00
Labour		
• Louis		
– Basic hours	4 hrs @ £8.00	32.00
– Overtime premium	2 hrs @ £16.00	32.00
• Ben		
– Basic hours	3 hrs @ £8.50	25.50
– Reworked hours	3 hrs @ £8.50	25.50
Total direct cost		365.00
Overheads (£200 per job)		200.00
Total job cost		565.00

CHAPTER 8 Process costing – losses

Activity 1: Process account – no losses

Cost per unit $= \dfrac{\text{Total process costs}}{\text{Output units}} = \dfrac{£110,000}{1,000} = £110 \text{ per unit}$

PROCESS I

	Units	£		Units	£
Raw materials	1,000	40,000	To Process II	1,000	110,000
Labour		50,000			
Overheads		20,000			
	1,000	110,000		1,000	110,000

Activity 2: Process account – normal loss

Cost per unit $= \dfrac{\text{Total process costs} - \text{Scrap value normal loss}}{\text{Units input} - \text{Normal loss units}}$

$= \dfrac{£110,000 - £2,000}{1,000 - 100} = £120 \text{ per unit}$

PROCESS I

	Units	£		Units	£
Raw materials	1,000	40,000	Normal loss	100	2,000
Labour		50,000	To Process II	900	108,000
Overheads		20,000			
	1,000	110,000		1,000	110,000

Activity 3: Process account – abnormal losses

$$\text{Cost per unit} = \frac{\text{Total process cost} - \text{Scrap value normal loss}}{\text{Units input} - \text{Normal loss units}}$$

$$= \frac{£110,000 - £2,000}{1,000 - 100}$$

$$= £120 \text{ per unit}$$

Cost of output = 880 units × £120 = £105,600

Cost of abnormal loss = 20 units × £120 = £2,400

PROCESS I

	Units	£		Units	£
Raw materials	1,000	40,000	Normal loss	100	2,000
Labour		50,000	To Process II	880	105,600
Overheads		20,000	Abnormal loss	20	2,400
	1,000	110,000		1,000	110,000

Activity 4: Process account – abnormal gain

$$\text{Cost per unit} = \frac{\text{Total process costs} - \text{Scrap value normal loss}}{\text{Units input} - \text{Normal loss units}}$$

$$= \frac{£110,000 - £2,000}{1,000 - 100}$$

$$= £120 \text{ per unit}$$

Cost of output = 920 units × £120 = £110,400

Cost of abnormal gain = 20 units × £120 = £2,400

PROCESS I

	Units	£		Units	£
Raw materials	1,000	40,000	Normal loss	100	2,000
Labour		50,000	To Process II	920	110,400
Overheads		20,000			
Abnormal gain	20	2,400			
	1,020	112,400		1,020	112,400

CHAPTER 9 Process costing – work in progress (WIP)

Activity 1: Process account – Closing WIP

(a) Process account

PROCESS I

	Units	£		Units	£
Raw Materials	1,500	12,975	To Process II	1,450	25,042
Labour		9,576	Closing WIP	50	659
Overheads		3,156	Rounding		6
	1,500	25,707		1,500	25,707

(b) Statement of equivalent units

	Total	Materials	Labour	Overheads
Finished output	1,450	1,450	1,450	1,450
Closing WIP	50	50	30	15
	1,500	1,500	1,480	1,465

(c) Cost per equivalent unit

	Cost ÷ equivalent units				£
Materials	£12,975	÷	1,500	=	8.65
Labour	£9,576	÷	1,480	=	6.47
Overheads	£3,156	÷	1,465	=	2.15
Finished unit total cost					17.27

(d) Value of finished goods

Finished goods (units) × cost per finished unit = (£17.27 × 1,450) = £25,042

Cost item	Workings Closing WIP equivalent units × cost per equivalent unit	£
Materials	(50 × £8.65)	433
Labour	(30 × £6.47)	194
Overheads	(15 × £2.15)	32
Total closing WIP value		659

Activity 2: Opening WIP – FIFO and AVCO method

(a) FIFO

Statement of equivalent units

	Total	Equivalent units		
	units	Materials	Labour	Overheads
Opening WIP	50	–	20	35
Goods started and finished	2,050	2,050	2,050	2,050
Good output	2,100	2,050	2,070	2,085

Costs per equivalent unit

	Materials £	Labour £	Overheads £
Input costs	22,550	16,304	8,212
Equivalent units	2,050	2,070	2,085
Cost per equivalent unit	£11.00	£7.88	£3.94

The total cost per equivalent unit is | £ | 22.82

(b) Weighted average

Statement of equivalent units

	Total	Materials	Labour	Overheads
Good output	2,100	2,100	2,100	2,100

Cost per equivalent unit

Costs	Materials £	Labour £	Overhead £
Opening WIP costs b/f	400	180	30
Input costs	22,550	16,304	8,212
Total costs	22,950	16,484	8,242
Equivalent units	2,100	2,100	2,100
Cost per equivalent unit	10.93	7.85	£3.92

The total cost per equivalent unit is £ 22.70

CHAPTER 10 Budgeting: fixed and flexed budgets

Activity 1: Country soups

Cans made		350,000 £	400,000 £	450,000 £
Cost element	Cost			
Direct materials	10p per	35,000	40,000	45,000
Direct labour	8p per can	28,000	32,000	36,000
Canning costs	2p per can	7,000	8,000	9,000
Depreciation	£16,000	16,000	16,000	16,000
Rent and rates	£28,000	28,000	28,000	28,000
Other overheads	£36,000	36,000	36,000	36,000
Total cost (£)		150,000	160,000	170,000
Cost per can (£)		0.429	0.400	0.378

Activity 2: Charter flights

Likely miles	5,000	6,000	7,000
	£000	£000	£000
Sales revenue	2,500	2,950	3,400
Variable/semi-variable costs:			
Aviation fuel	400	480	560
Landing and servicing fees	850	900	950
Other variable overheads	135	162	189
Fixed costs:			
Wages and salaries	420	420	420
Other fixed overheads	625	625	625
Total cost	**2,430**	**2,587**	**2,744**
Total profit	70	363	656
	£	£	£
Profit per mile flown	14.00	60.50	93.71

Workings

Sales revenues £2,500 + (0.45 × 1,000 miles) = £2,950;

£2,500 + (0.45 × 2,000 miles) = £3,400

Landing & servicing fees = £600 + (0.05 × 6,000 miles) = £900;

£600 + (0.05 × 7,000 miles) = £950

Activity 3: TV dinners

Batches made and sold	5,000	6,000	7,000
	£	£	£
Sales revenue	30,000	36,000	42,000
Costs:			
Direct materials	1,250	1,500	1,750
Direct labour	3,000	3,600	4,200
Overheads			
Variable element	7,500	9,000	10,500
Fixed element	8,800	8,800	8,800
Total Cost	20,550	22,900	25,250
Total profit	9,450	13,100	16,750
Profit per batch	1.890	2.183	2.393

Workings

$$\text{Variable cost per unit} = \frac{£20,800 - £16,300}{8,000 - 5,000\text{units}} = £1.50 \text{ per unit}$$

Fixed cost = £20,800 − (£1.50 × 8,000 units) = £8,800

CHAPTER 11 Variance analysis

Activity 1: Protec Ltd

	Flexed budget	Actual	Variance	Favourable F or Adverse A
Volume sold	100,000	100,000	–	
	£000	£000	£000	
Sales revenue	3,000	5,400	2,400	F
Less costs:				
Direct materials	525	795	270	A
Direct labour	600	720	120	A
Overheads	1,470	1,842	372	A
Operating profit	405	2,043	1,638	F

The flexed budget is the same as original budget because the volume produced and sold is the same for budget and actual.

Activity 2: Zetec Ltd

	Flexed budget	Actual	Variance	Favourable F or Adverse A
Volume sold	12,350	12,350	–	
	£	£	£	
Sales revenue	370,500	407,550	37,050	F
Less costs:				
Direct materials	61,750	53,000	8,750	F
Direct labour	49,400	49,000	400	F
Overheads	110,000	178,000	68,000	A
Operating profit	149,350	127,550	21,800	A

Workings

Sales revenue

Budgeted sales price per unit = £300,000/10,000 units = £30 per unit

So, 12,350 units of revenue should have been 12,350 × £30 = £370,500

Direct materials

Budgeted material cost per unit = £50,000/10,000 = £5 per unit

So, 12,350 units of material should have cost 12,350 × £5 = £61,750

Direct labour

Budgeted labour cost per unit = £40,000/10,000 = £4 per unit

So, 12,350 units of material should have cost 12,350 × £4 = £49,400

Fixed overheads

Fixed overheads do not change as volume/activity changes. But actual fixed overheads have changed to £110,000.

Operating profit

Operating profit = £370,500 – £61,750 – £49,400 – £110,000 = £149,350

CHAPTER 12 Cost bookkeeping

Activity 1: Control accounts – Bodger & Co

Payables control account

	£		£
		Raw materials	5,000

Raw materials control account

	£		£
Payables	5,000		

Activity 2: Payment to supplier – Bodger & Co

Payables control account

	£		£
Bank	5,000		

Bank account

	£		£
		Payables	5,000

Activity 3: Issuing materials – Bodger & Co

Raw materials control account

	£		£
Payables	5,000	WIP	5,000

WIP control account

	£		£
Materials	5,000		

Activity 4: Recording production overheads – Bodger & Co

Payables control account

	£		£
		Raw materials	5,000
		Production overheads	6,000

Production overheads control account

	£		£
Payables	6,000	Overheads absorbed:	
		Manufacturing dept	4,000
		Finishing dept	600
		Quality control	500
		Statement of profit or loss	900
	6,000		6,000

WIP control

	£		£
Materials	5,000		
Production overheads absorbed (mfg, finishing & quality control)	5,100		

Activity 5: Coding and inventory – Spice Ltd

FIFO method

Inventory record card for Steel Component C								
	Receipts			Issues			Balance	
Date 20X9	Quantity kg	Cost per kg £	Total cost £	Quantity kg	Cost per kg £	Total cost £	Quantity kg	Balance £
1 June							25,000	50,000
9 June	30,000	2.30	69,000				55,000	119,000
12 June				40,000	25,000 × 2.00 15,000 × £2.30	84,500	15,000	34,500
18 June	20,000	2.50	50,000				35,000	84,500
27 June				10,000	£2.30	23,000	25,000	61,500

Journal entries

		Cost accounting code	£
9 June	Debit	300	69,000
9 June	Credit	600	69,000
12 June	Debit	400	84,500
12 June	Credit	300	84,500
18 June	Debit	300	50,000
18 June	Credit	600	50,000
27 June	Debit	405	23,000
27 June	Credit	300	23,000

CHAPTER 13 Marginal costing

Activity 1: Contribution

	J	K	L
Sales price	10.00	5.00	3.00
Less: all variable costs:			
Materials	(3.00)	(2.50)	(0.50)
Labour	(1.00)	(1.50)	(1.25)
Sales	(0.25)	(0.15)	(0.30)
Overheads	(0.75)	(0.10)	(0.25)
Contribution/unit	5.00	0.75	0.70

Activity 2: Unit cost

(a)

Absorption costing – unit cost	£
Direct material	3.40
Direct labour	6.80
Variable overhead	1.20
Prime cost	11.40
Fixed overhead ((£340,000/100,000) × 2)	6.80
Absorption cost	18.20

(b)

Marginal costing – unit cost	£
Direct material	3.40
Direct labour	6.80
Variable overhead	1.20
Marginal cost	11.40

Activity 3: MC v AC cost per unit

(a)

Marginal costing	£
Direct materials	£12.00
Direct labour	£13.50
Variable overheads per unit = £88,000/11,000 units	£8.00
Total variable (marginal cost)	£33.50

(b)

Full absorption costing	£
Total variable cost	£33.50
Add: Overhead absorption rate £110,000/11,000 units	£10.00
Full product cost	£43.50

Activity 4: Marginal costing profit statement

	Standard £	Vegetarian £	Total £
Selling price per meal	$\frac{£1,040,000}{130,000}$ = £8.00	$\frac{£1,500,000}{200,000}$ = £7.50	
Less: variable costs per meal			
Direct materials	$\frac{£468,000}{130,000}$ = £3.60	$\frac{£600,000}{200,000}$ = £3.00	
Direct labour	£2.00	£2.00	
Variable overheads	£2.00	£1.50	
Contribution per unit	£0.40	£1.00	
Sales volume (units)	130,000	200,000	
Total contribution	£52,000	£200,000	£252,000
Less: fixed costs			£212,000
Budgeted profit or loss			£40,000

Activity 5: MC v AC

(a)

	£
Selling price/unit	12
Prime cost/unit	4
Variable production cost/unit	3
Marginal cost (MC)/unit	7
= Contribution/unit	5

(b)

	£
Selling price/unit	12
Marginal cost/unit	7
Fixed production cost/unit (30,000/15,000 units)	2
FAC cost/unit	9
= Profit/unit	3

(c)

	£	£
Sales (12,000 units at £12)		144,000
Opening inventory (2,000 units at £7)	14,000	
Variable production costs (15,000 units at £7)	105,000	
Closing inventory (5,000 units at £7)	(35,000)	
Cost of sales (MC basis)		(84,000)
Contribution		60,000
Fixed costs		(30,000)
Profit		30,000

(d)

	£	£
Sales (12,000 units at £12)		144,000
Less: cost of sales		
Opening inventory (2,000 units at £9)	18,000	
Production costs (15,000 units at £9)	135,000	
Closing inventory (5,000 units at £9)	(45,000)	
Cost of sales (FAC basis)		(108,000)
Profit		36,000

(e) The two profit figures differ by **£6,000** because under FAC the **increase** in the valuation of inventory during the month is **higher** than the **increase** under MC.

This is because fixed overhead cost has been carried forward in the statement of financial position in the inventory valuation as an asset under FAC principles, but written off against profit under MC principles.

CHAPTER 14 Short-term decision making

Activity 1: Breakeven units

Breakeven point $= \dfrac{£360,000}{£28 \quad £19}$

$= \boxed{40,000}$ units

Activity 2: Breakeven revenue

BEP in units $= \boxed{3,800}$ units

Breakeven revenue $= \boxed{£ \quad 30,400}$

$BEP = \dfrac{\text{Fixed costs}}{\text{Unit contribution}}$

First we need to find the fixed and variable costs and the unit contribution

	Output	Total costs
	Units	**£**
High	8,000	57,700
Low	6,000	44,700
Difference	2,000	13,000

Variable cost per unit $=$ £13,000/2,000

$=$ £6.50

Substituting in high volume

	£
Total cost	57,700
Variable cost (8,000 × £6.50)	52,000
Fixed costs (balance)	5,700

Unit contribution = Selling price – Variable cost $=$ £8.00 – £6.50

$=$ £1.50

$BEP = \dfrac{\text{Fixed costs}}{\text{Unit contribution}}$

$= \dfrac{£5,700}{£1.50} = \underline{3,800 \text{ units}}$

Breakeven revenue = BEP × selling price

= 3,800 × £8

= £30,400

Activity 3: Contribution/sales ratio

C/S ratio $\quad = \quad \dfrac{\text{Contribution}}{\text{Sales}} \quad = \dfrac{£1.50}{£8} = 0.1875 = \boxed{18.75}$ %

BE Revenue $\quad = \quad \dfrac{\text{Fixed costs}}{\text{C/S ratio}} \quad = \dfrac{£5,700}{0.1875} = \boxed{£ \quad 30,400}$

Activity 4: Margin of safety

Margin of safety in units $\quad$ = Budgeted sales volume – Breakeven sales volume

$$= 5,000 \text{ units} - 3,800 \text{ units} = \boxed{1,200} \text{ units}$$

Margin of safety $\quad = \quad \dfrac{\text{Budgeted sales volume} - \text{BE sales volume}}{\text{Budgeted sales volume}} \times 100\%$

$$= \dfrac{5,000 - 3,800}{5,000} \times 100\%$$

$$= \boxed{24} \%$$

In other words, sales could fall by up to 24% compared to budget before we would start to make a loss.

Activity 5: Target profit level

Sales volume to achieve target profit $\quad = \quad \dfrac{\text{Fixed costs} + \text{Required profit}}{\text{Unit contribution}}$

$$= \dfrac{£5,700 + £10,000}{£1.50}$$

$$= \boxed{10,467} \text{ units}$$

Activity 6: Sanctuary Catering

(a)(i) – (iii)

	Standard	Vegetarian
Fixed costs	£32,500	£179,500
Meal contribution	£0.40	£1.00
Breakeven sales (meals)	81,250	179,500
Forecast sales (meals)	100,000	200,000
Margin of safety (meals)	18,750	20,500
Margin of safety (%)	18.75%	10.25%

(b)

	Standard	Vegetarian	Total
Contribution per meal	£0.40	£1.00	
Labour hours per meal	0.025 hrs	0.03 hrs	
Contribution per labour hour	£16.00	£33.33	
Ranking priority	2	1	
Labour hours allocated to type of meal	2,000*/0.025 hrs per meal 80,000 meals	200,000 meals @ 0.03 hrs each: use up 6,000 hrs	8,000 hrs
Total contribution earned	£32,000	£200,000	£232,000
Less: fixed costs			£212,000
Profit			£20,000

*8,000 available labour hours less 6,000 used in vegetarian meals = 2,000 labour hours left for standard meals

Activity 7: Limited factor decisions

	T	J
Contribution per unit	£6.00	£5.00
Hours taken	3	2
Contribution per labour hour	£2.00	£2.50
∴ Ranking	2	1

Optimal production plan:

	Units	Hours used		Contribution £
J	8,000	16,000		40,000
T	8,000	24,000	β	48,000
Total		40,000		88,000

Activity 1: Payback period – Kirby plc

Simple payback = 3 years and 8 months $\left(\dfrac{100}{150} \times 12\right)$ — Accept/~~Reject project~~

Kirby plc should **accept** the project on the basis of payback period because the payback is less than the required five years.

Year	Simple payback cash flow £	Cumulative cash flow £
0	(550,000)	(550,000)
1	150,000	(400,000)
2	150,000	(250,000)
3	150,000	(100,000) ← Payback between 3 and 4 years
4	150,000	50,000
5	175,000	225,000

Activity 2: NPV – Kirby plc

Kirby plc should **accept** the project as the NPV is positive.

Year	Cash flow £	DF @ 10%	PV £
0	(550,000)	1	(550,000.00)
1	150,000	0.9091	136,365.00
2	150,000	0.8264	123,960.00
3	150,000	0.7513	112,695.00
4	150,000	0.6830	102,450.00
5	175,000	0.6209	108,657.50
			NPV = £34,127.50

Activity 3: NPV and payback period

	0	1	2	3
	£000	£000	£000	£000
Capital expense	(720)			
Indirect labour cost saving		340	348	448
Operating cost saving		264	272	270
Net cash flow	(720)	604	620	718
PV factors 14%	1	0.8772	0.7695	0.6750
Discounted	(720)	530	477	485
NPV	772			

NPV = £772,000

The payback period is ___1.19___ years (to 2 decimal places)

Workings

Payback period: -720 + 604 = -116

Payback period = 1 + (116/620) = 1.19 years

Activity 4: IRR

$$IRR = a + \left[\frac{NPVa}{NPVa - NPVb} \times (b - a) \right]$$

IRR = 10 + [(1679/1679 + 49) × (20 – 10)] = 19.72%

Test your learning: answers

CHAPTER 1 Introduction to management accounting

1 ☑ A unit of product or service in relation to which costs are ascertained

This is the definition of a cost unit.

The hour of operation and the unit of electricity are both examples of cost units for which costs have been ascertained.

A measure of work output in a standard hour is an example of a particular cost unit which may be used for control purposes. It is not a definition of the term 'cost unit'.

2 ☑ A production or service location, function, activity or item of equipment for which costs are accumulated

This is the correct definition of a cost centre.

A unit of product or service in relation to which costs are ascertained is the definition of a cost unit.

An amount of expenditure attributable to an activity describes the cost of an activity or cost centre.

A centre for which an individual budget is drawn up describes a budget centre (which will not be in your assessment). Although a budget centre may also be a cost centre at times, this is not always the case.

3 ☑ Invoice processed

☑ Supplier account

It would be appropriate to use the cost per invoice processed and the cost per supplier account for control purposes.

Postage cost is an expense of the department and therefore is not a suitable cost unit.

4 ☑ Integrity

Integrity is the quality of being honest.

5 ☑ Investment centre

A manager of an investment centre has control over the costs, revenues and assets of the division.

A manager of a profit centre has control over costs and revenues but not assets.

A manager of a cost centre has control over the costs but not the revenues or the assets.

BPP
LEARNING MEDIA

1

	Capital	Revenue
A new telephone system. This will be used within the business for several accounting periods. All the associated costs of installation can be capitalised.	✓	
Depreciation of vehicles. Depreciation can be thought of as the way in which part of a capital cost is converted to a revenue expense.		✓
Salesperson's car. A company car is used by the salesperson to obtain benefits for the business in the form of sales.	✓	
Road fund licence for delivery van. Although the van is a capital item, the road fund licence is a revenue expense of running the van.		✓
Telephone bill. The bill for rental and calls on the telephone system is a revenue expense.		✓
Computer software costing £10,000. Another example of something that is used by the business to bring benefits. The software might be used for the main business activity, such as in design of buildings by an architect, or in the processing of information necessary to administer the business.	✓	
Repairs to the Managing Director's company car after an accident. This will not improve the earnings capacity of the car; it just restores it to what it was before.		✓

2

		Cost behaviour	
		Does fit the graph shape	Does NOT fit the graph shape
(a)	Plastic used in the manufacture of moulded plastic furniture. A bulk-buying discount is given at point A on the graph.		✓
(b)	Straight-line depreciation of a freehold factory. A new factory is bought at point A.	✓	

		Cost behaviour	
		Does fit the graph shape	**Does NOT fit the graph shape**
(c)	Rent of a warehouse. A further warehouse is rented at point A.	✓	
(d)	Electricity costs that have a standing charge and a cost per unit of power used. At point A the level of production reaches the point where a night shift is required, which uses electricity at a cheaper rate.		✓

Explanation

(a) This is a variable cost. The bulk purchase discount would give a one-off kink in the graph at point A. The graph would appear as shown below.

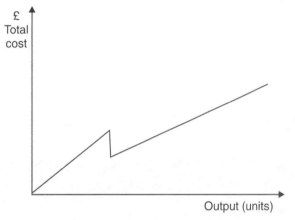

(b) and (c) are both stepped costs and will fit the graph shape.

(d) This is a semi-variable cost. At point A, where the cheaper rate of electricity kicks in, the graph will flatten as each unit of product will cost slightly less in electricity. This is illustrated in the graph below.

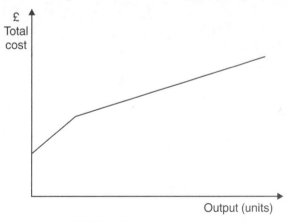

3   Total cost at 12,000 units   £ 28,500

Workings

Output	Units	Total cost £
Highest	13,500	31,500
Lowest	6,500	17,500
High–low	7,000	14,000

$$\text{Variable cost per unit} = \frac{\text{High cost - Low cost}}{\text{High output - Low output}}$$
$$= \frac{£14,000}{7,000}$$
$$= £2$$

At 6,500 units

	£
Total cost	17,500
Less variable cost (6,500 × £2)	13,000
= fixed cost	4,500

Using the fixed cost of £4,500, and the variable cost of £2 per unit, we can now estimate the total cost at 12,000 units:

	£
Fixed cost	4,500
Add variable cost (12,000 × £2)	24,000
Total cost	28,500

4

Cost card: Filing cabinet	£
Direct materials (3.80 + 1.80 + 0.90)	6.50
Direct labour	6.70
Prime cost	13.20
Production overheads (0.30 + 0.20)	0.50
Production cost	13.70
Non-production overheads	
– selling and distribution	3.00
Total cost	16.70

5   ☑   Be constant per unit of output

Variable costs are conventionally deemed to increase or decrease in direct proportion to changes in output. Therefore the correct answer is 'be constant per unit of output'. 'Vary per unit of output as production volume changes' and 'vary, in total, from period to period when production is constant' imply a changing unit rate, which does not comply with this convention. 'Be constant in total when production volume changes' relates to a fixed cost.

6   ☑   Electricity bills made up of a standing charge and a variable charge

The depicted cost has a basic fixed element which is payable even at zero activity. A variable element is then added at a constant rate as activity increases. Therefore the correct answer is 'Electricity bills made up of a standing charge and a variable charge'.

Graphs for the other options would look like this.

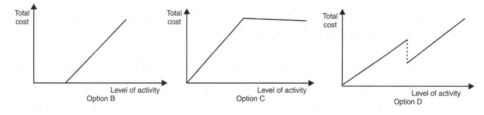

7   ☑   Graph 2

The cost described consists of a fixed amount up to a certain level of activity. This will be represented by a straight, horizontal line. At a certain point a variable element is added and the cost line will slope upwards at a constant rate. Graph 2 demonstrates this pattern, therefore the correct answer is Graph 2.

If you selected Graph 4, you had the right idea for the second part of the graph. However, Graph 4 depicts zero cost up to a certain level, which is not correct.

8 ☑ Graph 1

The cost described will increase in steps, remaining fixed at each step until another supervisor is required. Graph 1 depicts a step cost.

9 ☑ Graph 3

The cost described begins as a linear variable cost, increasing at a constant rate in line with activity. At a certain point the cost becomes fixed regardless of the level of activity. Graph 3 demonstrates this behaviour pattern.

10 ☑ A semi-variable cost

The salary is part fixed (£650 per month) and part variable (5 pence per unit). Therefore it is a semi-variable cost.

If you chose a variable cost or a fixed cost you were considering only part of the cost.

The option 'a stepped cost' involves a cost which remains constant up to a certain level and then increases to a new, higher, constant fixed cost.

11 ☑ The total of direct costs

Prime cost is the total of direct materials, direct labour and direct expenses.

All costs incurred in manufacturing a product describes total production cost. The material cost of a product is only a part of prime cost. The cost of operating a department is an overhead or indirect cost.

12 ☑ Cost of transporting raw materials from the supplier's premises

Cost of transporting raw materials from the supplier's premises is a part of the cost of direct materials.

Wages of factory workers engaged in machine maintenance and cost of indirect production materials are production overheads. Depreciation of lorries used for deliveries to customers is a selling and distribution expense.

13 ☑ The cost of special designs, drawing or layouts

☑ The hire of tools or equipment for a particular job

Special designs and the hire of tools for a particular job can be traced to a specific cost unit. Therefore they are direct expenses.

Salesperson's wages is a selling and distribution overhead and rent, rates and insurance of a factory describes production overheads.

CHAPTER 3 Materials costs and inventory valuation

1 (a) **FIFO**

	Inventory record card							
	Purchases			*Requisitions*			*Balance*	
Date	Quantity kg	Cost £	Total cost £	Quantity kg	Cost £	Total cost £	Quantity kg	Total cost £
3 Jan							100	880
16 Jan	400	9.00	3,600				500	4,480
27 Jan				100	8.80	880		
				150	9.00	1,350		
				250		2,230	250	2,250
5 Feb				180	9.00	1,620	70	630
9 Feb	400	9.30	3,720				470	4,350
17 Feb				70	9.00	630		
				350	9.30	3,255		
				420		3,885	50	465
25 Feb	500	9.35	4,675				550	5,140

Cost of material issues = £2,230 + £1,620 + £3,885
= £7,735

Value of closing inventory   = £5,140

(b) **LIFO**

	Inventory record card							
	Purchases			*Requisitions*			*Balance*	
Date	Quantity kg	Cost £	Total cost £	Quantity kg	Cost £	Total cost £	Quantity kg	Total cost £
3 Jan							100	880
16 Jan	400	9.00	3,600				500	4,480
27 Jan				250	9.00	2,250	250	2,230
5 Feb				150	9.00	1,350		
				30	8.80	264		
				180		1,614	70	616
9 Feb	400	9.30	3,720				470	4,336
17 Feb				400	9.30	3,720		
				20	8.80	176		
				420		3,896	50	440
25 Feb	500	9.35	4,675				550	5,115

$$\text{Cost of material issues} = \pounds2{,}250 + \pounds1{,}614 + \pounds3{,}896$$
$$= \pounds7{,}760$$

Value of closing inventory $= \pounds5{,}115$

(c) **AVCO**

Inventory record card								
	Purchases			Requisitions			Balance	
Date	Quantity kg	Cost £	Total cost £	Quantity kg	Cost £	Total cost £	Quantity kg	Total cost £
3 Jan							100	880.00
16 Jan	400	9.00	3,600				500	4,480.00
27 Jan				250	8.96	2,240	250	2,240.00
5 Feb				180	8.96	1,612.80	70	627.20
9 Feb	400	9.30	3,720				470	4,347.20
17 Feb				420	9.25	3,885	50	462.20
25 Feb	500	9.35	4,675				550	5,137.20

$$\text{Cost of material issues} = \pounds2{,}240.00 + \pounds1{,}612.80 + \pounds3{,}885.00$$
$$= \pounds7{,}737.80$$

Value of closing inventory $= \pounds5{,}137.20$

2

Materials control account

		£			£
1 Mar	Opening balance	12,400	31 Mar	WIP	160,400
31 Mar	Bank/payables	167,200	31 Mar	Production o/h control	8,300
			31 Mar	Closing balance	10,900
		179,600			179,600

Work in progress control account

		£			£
31 Mar	Materials control	160,400			

Production overhead control account

		£			£
31 Mar	Materials control	8,300			

3 $$EOQ = \sqrt{\frac{2C_oD}{C_H}}$$
   $$= \sqrt{\frac{2 \times £50 \times (15 \times 52)}{£19.65}}$$
   $$= \sqrt{3,969}$$
   $$= 63 \text{ rolls}$$

4 Reorder level = (maximum usage × maximum lead time) + buffer inventory
   = (200 litres per day × 8 days) + 0
   = 1,600 litres

5 Using the FIFO method, the total value of the issues on 30 April is

£	2,765

Date	Receipts Units	Issues Units	Balance	£
1 April			275 @ £3.20	880
8 April	600		600 @ £3.00	1,800
15 April	400		400 @ £3.40	1,360
				4,040
30 April		900		£
		275 @ £3.20	=	880
		600 @ £3.00	=	1,800
		25 @ £3.40	=	85
				2,765

6 Using the weighted average price method of inventory valuation, the total value of the components remaining in inventory on 23 March was £ 20,790

   Average price of inventory on 23 March:

Units		£
2,400	× £6.00	14,400
4,000	× £6.20	24,800
2,000	× £6.86	13,720
8,400		52,920

Average price per component = £52,920/8,400 = £6.30

Value of inventory on 23 March = (8,400 − 5,100) × £6.30

= £ | 20,790

7 Using the FIFO method of inventory valuation, the total value of the components issued on 23 March was £ | 37,140 | (to the nearest £)

The FIFO method uses the price of the oldest batches first:

		£
2,400	× £6.00	14,400
2,700	× £6.20	16,740
5,100		31,140

CHAPTER 4 Labour costs and expenses

1

	J. Sparrow	K. Finch	M. Swallow	B. Cuckoo
Total hours	39.5	37.5	38.75	37.5
Basic pay (35 × £7)	£245.00	£245.00	£245.00	£245.00
Time and a half	(1.5 × £10.50)	(2.5 × £10.50)	(1.75 × £10.50)	(0.5 × £10.50)
	= £15.75	= £26.25	= £18.38	= £5.25
Double time	(3 × £14.00)		(2 × £14.00)	(2 × £14.00)
	= £42.00		= £28.00	= £28.00
Total gross pay	£302.75	£271.25	£291.38	£278.25

2 Direct labour cost = 40 hrs × £10 per hr = £400

Indirect labour cost = 5 hrs × £4 per hr = £20

Alternatively:

Direct cost £

Basic pay (35 hrs × £10 per hr) 350

Overtime: at basic rate (5 hrs × £10 per hr) 50

400

Indirect cost

Overtime: premium (5 hrs × £4 per hr) 20

3 The hours recorded in the timesheet can be used to calculate M. Rooney's pay for the week.

Employee's weekly timesheet for week ending 5 April

Employee: M. Rooney			Profit centre: Widget carving			
Employee number: A450			Basic pay per hour: £10.00			
	Hours spent on production	Hours worked on indirect work	Notes	Basic pay £	Overtime premium £	Total pay £
Monday	6	2	10am–12am Machine calibration	80	10	90
Tuesday	2	4	9am–1pm HR awareness course	60	–	60
Wednesday	9			80	10	90
Thursday	6			60	–	60
Friday	6	1	3pm–4pm Customer care training	70	5	75
Saturday	6			60	20	80
Sunday	3			30	30	60
Total	37			440	75	515

4

☑	DEBIT	Work in progress control account	£70,800
	DEBIT	Overhead control account	£2,000
	CREDIT	Wages control account	£72,800

The overtime was not worked on any specific job and is therefore an indirect wages cost to be 'collected' in the overhead control account. The direct wages of £70,800 are debited to the work in progress control account and the total wages cost is credited to the wages control account.

5 | £ | 297.00 |

	£
First 400 units: 400 × 50p	200.00
Next 100 units: 100 × 70p	70.00
Last 30 units: 30 × 90p	27.00
Gross pay	297.00

CHAPTER 5 Allocation and apportionment

1   ☑ Spread common costs over cost centres

Overhead apportionment involves sharing overhead costs as fairly as possible over a number of cost centres. Apportionment is used when it is not possible to allocate the whole cost to a single cost centre.

2   (a) **Basis of apportionment**

	Total £	Machine shop £	Assembly £	Painting £	Services £
Factory rent, rates and insurance (floor area) 5:2:3:2	9,000	3,750	1,500	2,250	1,500
Depreciation of machinery (value of machinery) 12:4:3:1	4,000	2,400	800	600	200
Supervisor's salary (number of employees) 8:9:5:2	8,000*	2,667	3,000	1,667	667
Heat and light (floor area) 5:2:3:2	2,000*	833	333	500	333
Apportionment to all departments	23,000	9,650	5,633	5,017	2,700

* there is a slight rounding difference here

(b) **Reapportionment**

	Total £	Machine shop £	Assembly £	Painting £	Services £
Reapportionment of services (40:30:30)	–	1,080	810	810	(2,700)
Total after reapportionment	23,000	10,730	6,443	5,827	Nil

3 (a) **Basis of apportionment**

	Total	V	W	S1	S2
	£	£	£	£	£
Indirect materials	310,000	160,000	120,000	10,000	20,000
Indirect labour	1,125,000	400,000	650,000	40,000	35,000
Buildings depreciation and insurance (volume occupied) 60:30:8:2	100,000	60,000	30,000	8,000	2,000
Cleaning (volume occupied) 60:30:8:2	25,000	15,000	7,500	2,000	500
Machinery depreciation and insurance (value of machinery) 380:600:0:20	1,500,000	570,000	900,000	–	30,000
Supervision of production (supervisor hours) 15:20:0:0	70,000	30,000	40,000		
Power (% of power usage) 25:45:20:10	250,000	62,500	112,500	50,000	25,000
Heat and light (volume occupied) 60:30:8:2	20,000	12,000	6,000	1,600	400
Total after allocation and apportionment	3,400,000	1,309,500	1,866,000	111,600	112,900

(b) **Reapportionment**

	Total	V	W	S1	S2
	£	£	£	£	£
(step-down method) S2 first 40:50:10		45,160	56,450	11,290	(112,900)
				122,890	
S1 next 40:60		49,156	73,734	(122,890)	
Total after reapportionment	3,400,000	1,403,816	1,996,184	nil	nil

CHAPTER 6 Absorption costing

1   A   Overhead absorption rates are determined in advance for each period, usually based on budgeted data. Therefore statement (i) is correct and statement (iii) is incorrect. Overhead absorption rates are used in the final stage of overhead analysis, to absorb overheads into product costs. Therefore statement (ii) is correct. Statement (iv) is not correct because overheads are controlled using budgets and other management information. Therefore the correct answer is A.

2   A   Description B could lead to under-absorbed overheads if actual overheads far exceeded both budgeted overheads and the overhead absorbed. Description C could lead to under-absorbed overheads if budgeted overhead absorbed does not increase in line with actual overhead incurred. Description D could also lead to under-absorption if actual overhead does not decrease in line with absorbed overheads.

3   A   Budgeted overhead absorption rate $= \dfrac{£258,750}{11,250}$

$\qquad\qquad\qquad = £23$ per machine hour

	£
Overhead absorbed = £23 × 10,980 hours	252,540
Overhead incurred	254,692
Under-absorbed overhead	2,152

If you selected option B or C you calculated the difference between the budgeted and actual overheads and interpreted the result as an under- or over-absorption.

If you selected option D your calculations were correct but you misinterpreted the result as over-absorbed.

4 B   Overhead absorption rate $= \dfrac{\text{budgeted overheads}}{\text{budgeted labour hours}} = \dfrac{£148,750}{8,500}$

$= £17.50 \text{ per hr}$

If you selected option A you divided the actual overheads by the budgeted labour hours. Option C is based on the actual overheads and actual labour hours. If you selected option D you divided the budgeted overheads by the actual hours.

5 D

	£
Overhead absorbed = £17.50 × 7,928 =	138,740
Overhead incurred=	146,200
Under-absorbed overhead=	7,460

If you selected options A or B you calculated the difference between the budgeted and actual overheads and interpreted it as an under- or over-absorption. If you selected option C you performed the calculations correctly but misinterpreted the result as an over-absorption.

CHAPTER 7 Job, batch and service costing

1   £   16,346.88

	£
Materials	12,500.00
Direct labour – fitting 23 hours @ £8.60	197.80
– decorating 5 hours @ £6.50	32.50
Overheads 28 hours @ £12.40	347.20
Total costs	13,077.50
Profit 25% × 13,077.50	3,269.38
Cost to the customer	16,346.88

2 | 74.5 | pence

	£
Ingredients	840.00
Labour 7 hours @ £6.50	45.50
Overheads 7 hours @ £1.20	8.40
	893.90

Cost per pie = $\dfrac{£893.90}{1,200}$
= 74.5 pence

3   ☑ (i) and (iii) only

Cost per tonne–kilometre (i) is appropriate for cost control purposes because it combines the distance travelled and the load carried, both of which affect cost.

The fixed cost per kilometre (ii) is not particularly useful for control purposes because it varies with the number of kilometres travelled.

The maintenance cost of each vehicle per kilometre (iii) can be useful for control purposes because it focuses on a particular aspect of the cost of operating each vehicle.

The correct answer is therefore (i) and (iii) only.

4   ☑ An engineering company

All of the activities identified would use service costing, except the engineering company which will be providing products not services.

CHAPTER 8 Process costing - losses

1   ☑ At the same rate as good production

2   Debit | Scrap | account
    Credit | Process | account

3   **Step 1**   Calculate the number of normal loss units:
50,000 kg × 5% = 2,500 kg

Step 2   Calculate the expected output from the process:
50,000 kg – 2,500 kg = 47,500 kg

Step 3   Total the process costs:
£350,000 + £125,000 + £57,000 = £532,000

Step 4   Calculate the cost per unit of expected output:
= £11.20 per kg

Process account

	kg	£		kg	£
Materials	50,000	350,000	Normal loss	2,500	–
Labour		125,000	Abnormal loss	1,500	16,800
Overheads		57,000	Output	46,000	515,200
	50,000	532,000		50,000	532,000

4 **Step 1** Calculate the number of normal loss units:
6,000 ltr × 10% = 600 ltr

Step 2 Calculate the expected output from the process:
6,000 ltr – 600 ltr = 5,400 ltr

Step 3 Total the process costs:
£14,300 + £7,200 + £11,980 = £33,480

Step 4 Calculate the cost per unit of expected output:
$\frac{£33,480}{5,400 \text{ ltr}} = £6.20$ per litre

Process account

	ltr	£		ltr	£
Materials	6,000	14,300	Normal loss	600	–
Labour		7,200			
Overheads		11,980			
Abnormal gain	200	1,240	Output	5,600	34,720
	6,200	34,720		6,200	34,720

5 **Step 1** Calculate the number of normal loss units:
40,000 kg × 8% = 3,200 kg

Step 2 Calculate the expected output from the process:
40,000 kg – 3,200 kg = 36,800 kg

Step 3 Total the process costs and deduct the scrap proceeds for the normal loss:
(£158,200 + £63,500 + £31,740) – (3,200 × £1) = £250,240

Step 4 Calculate the cost per unit of expected output:
$\frac{£250,240}{36,800 \text{ kg}} = £6.80$ per kg

Process account

	kg	£		kg	£
Materials	40,000	158,200	Normal loss	3,200	3,200
Labour		63,500	Abnormal loss	1,800	12,240
Overheads		31,740	Output	35,000	238,000
	40,000	253,440		40,000	253,440

CHAPTER 9 Process costing – work in progress (WIP)

1 ☑ A notional whole unit representing incomplete work

2

		Materials		Labour/overheads	
	Units	**Proportion complete**	**Equivalent units**	**Proportion complete**	**Equivalent units**
Completed units	2,000	100%	2,000	100%	2,000
Closing work in progress	400	60%	240	50%	200
Total equivalent units			2,240		2,200
Cost per equivalent unit		£8,960/2,240 = £4.00 per EU		£4,290/2,200 = £1.95 per EU	

Valuation	£
Completed units	
Materials (2,000 × £4.00)	8,000
Labour/overheads (2,000 × £1.95)	3,900
Total	11,900
Closing work in progress	
Materials (240 × £4.00)	960
Labour/overheads (200 × £1.95)	390
	1,350

Process account

	£		£
Materials	8,960	Completed units	11,900
Labour/overhead	4,290	Closing work in progress	1,350
	13,250		13,250

CHAPTER 10 Budgeting: Fixed and flexed budgets

1

(a)

	Budget 4,000 units £	Actual 3,600 units £	Variance
Sales	96,000	90,000	6,000 Adv
Materials	18,000	15,120	2,880 Fav
Labour	27,200	25,200	2,000 Fav
Production overhead	5,700	5,900	200 Adv
Gross profit	45,100	43,780	1,320 Adv
General expenses	35,200	32,880	2,320 Fav
Operating profit	9,900	10,900	1,000 Fav

(b)

	Flexed budget 3,600 units £	Actual 3,600 units £	Variance
Sales 3,600 × £24.00	86,400	90,000	3,600 Fav
Materials 3,600 × £4.50	16,200	15,120	1,080 Fav
Labour 3,600 × £6.80	24,480	25,200	720 Adv
Production overhead	5,700	5,900	200 Adv
Gross profit	40,020	43,780	3,760 Fav
General expenses	35,200	32,880	2,320 Fav
Operating profit	4,820	10,900	6,080 Fav

	Flexed budget	Actual	Variance	Favourable F or Adverse A
Volume sold	72,000	72,000		
	£000	£000	£000	
Sales revenue	1,440	1,800	360	F
Less costs:				
Direct materials	252	265	13	A
Direct labour	288	240	48	F
Overheads	350	630	280	A
Operating profit	550	665	115	F

CHAPTER 11 Variance analysis

1

	Budget 200 units £	Budget per unit £	Flexed budget 230 units £	Actual 230 units £	Variance £ (A)/(F)
Sales	71,400	357	82,110	69,000	13,110 (A)
Variable costs					
Labour	31,600	158	36,340	27,000	9,340 (F)
Material	12,600	63	14,490	24,000	9,510 (A)
Fixed costs	18,900		18,900	10,000	8,900 (F)
Profit	8,300		12,380	8,000	4,380 (A)

CHAPTER 12 Cost bookkeeping

1 Debit | Materials control account |
   Credit | Payables control account |

2

Production overheads account

	£		£
Overheads incurred	3,690	Overheads absorbed	3,402
		Under-absorbed overheads	288
	3,690		3,690

3

Materials control account

	£		£
Opening balance	550	WIP control	4,670
Payables control	5,300	Administration overhead	760
		Closing balance	420
	5,850		5,850

Wages control account

	£		£
Bank (2,520 + 640)	3,160	WIP control	2,520
		Production overhead control	640
	3,160		3,160

Production overhead control account

	£		£
Wages control	640	WIP control 360 hours @ £7.80	2,808
Bank	2,700	Under-absorbed overhead	532
	3,340		3,340

Work in progress control account

	£		£
Opening balance	680	Finished goods	10,000
Materials control	4,670		
Wages control	2,520		
Production o/h control	2,808	Closing balance	678
	10,678		10,678

Finished goods control account

	£		£
Opening balance	1,040	Cost of sales (bal fig)	9,030
WIP	10,000	Closing inventory	2,010
	11,040		11,040

Receivables control account

	£		£
Opening balance	3,700	Bank	11,000
Sales	12,000	Closing balance	4,700
	15,700		15,700

Payables control account

	£		£
Bank	5,140	Opening balance	2,100
Closing balance	2,260	Materials control	5,300
	7,400		7,400

Cash at bank account

	£		£
Opening balance	2,090	Wages control	3,160
Receivables control	11,000	Payables control	5,140
		Production overhead control	2,700
		Administration overhead control	1,580
		Closing balance	510
	13,090		13,090

Administration overheads account

	£		£
Materials control	760	Statement of profit or loss	2,340
Bank	1,580		
	2,340		2,340

Sales account

	£		£
		Receivables control	12,000

CHAPTER 13 Marginal costing

1 (a) Absorption costing – unit cost

	£
Direct materials	12.50
Direct labour assembly (4 × £8.40)	33.60
Finishing	6.60
Assembly overheads (£336,000/(60,000 × 4) × 4)	5.60
Finishing overheads (£84,000/60,000)	1.40
	59.70

(b) Marginal costing – unit cost

	£
Direct materials	12.50
Direct labour assembly (4 × £8.40)	33.60
Finishing	6.60
Assembly overheads $\dfrac{£336,000 \times 60\%}{240,000} \times 4$	3.36
Finishing overheads $\dfrac{£84,000 \times 75\%}{60,000}$	1.05
	57.11

CHAPTER 14 Short-term decision making

1 Breakeven point $= \dfrac{£360,000}{£57 - £45}$

$= \boxed{30,000}$ units

Margin of safety $= \dfrac{38,000 - 30,000}{38,000} \times 100$

$= \boxed{21\%}$

2 Target profit sales $= \dfrac{£910,000 + £500,000}{£24 - £17}$

$= \boxed{201,429}$ units

3 Profit/volume ratio $= \dfrac{£(40 - 32)}{£40} \times 100$

$= 20\%$

Target profit sales revenue $= \dfrac{£100,000 + £200,000}{0.20}$

$= \boxed{£ \quad 1,500,000}$

Alternatively (100,000 + 200,000)/8 = 37,500 units

37,500 units × £40 = £1,500,000

CHAPTER 15   Long-term decision making

1   The payback period is [2] years and [9] months.

Time	Cash flows £	Cumulative cash flows £
31 Dec X6	30,000	30,000
31 Dec X7	40,000	70,000
31 Dec X8	40,000	110,000
31 Dec X9	20,000	130,000

The initial cost of the investment is fully covered after three years; however, as the cash inflows occur evenly throughout the year, this can be calculated more accurately.

2 years + £30,000/£40,000 × 12 months = 2 years and 9 months

2   (a)   £3,100 × 0.7972   =   £ | 2,471.32

(b)   £15,000 × 1.0000   =   £ | 15,000.00

(c)   £1,000 × 1.6901   =   £ | 1,690.10

(d)   £4,400 × 0.8734   =   £ | 3,842.96

3   £ | 3,701

Year	Cash flows £	Discount factor @ 7%	Present value £
0	(340,000)	1.0000	(340,000)
1	80,000	0.9346	74,768
2	70,000	0.8734	61,138
3	90,000	0.8163	73,467
4	120,000	0.7629	91,548
5	60,000	0.7130	42,780
Net present value			3,701

4   (a)

Year	Cash flows £	Discount factor @ 11%	Present value £
0	(90,000)	1.0000	(90,000)
1	23,000	0.9009	20,721
2	31,000	0.8116	25,160
3	40,000	0.7312	29,248
4	18,000	0.6587	11,857
Net present values			(3,014)

(b)   As the investment in the new plant and machinery has a negative net present value at the cost of capital of 11% then the investment should not take place.

	✓
Management should accept the project because the net present value is negative	
Management should not accept the project because the net present value is negative	✓
Management should accept the project because the payback period is less than 4 years	
Management should not accept the project because the payback is less than 4 years	

6   ☑   9.85%

$$IRR = a + \left[\frac{NPVa}{NPVa - NPVb} \times (b - a) \right]$$

$$IRR = 9 + \frac{22}{22 - -4} \times (10 - 9)$$

$$IRR = 9 + \frac{22}{22 + 4} \times 1$$

$$\therefore IRR = 9 + \frac{22}{26}$$

$$\therefore IRR = 9.85\%$$

Synoptic assessment preparation

Certain *Management Accounting: Costing* assessment objectives will be tested in the *AAT Advanced Diploma in Accounting* synoptic assessment. Therefore, at this stage in your studies, it is useful to consider the style of tasks you may see in the synoptic assessment.

However, it is recommended that the *AAT Advanced Diploma in Accounting* synoptic assessment is only taken when all other units have been completed.

Questions

1

Today's date is 30 June 20X6.

From the cost records you can see that on 1 June, HMF & Co had 9,000 kg of raw material inventory. The cost recorded was £31,500. In June the following movements took place:

8 June: 4,500 kg purchased for £9,000

15 June: 6,700 kg issued to production

HMF & Co want to know how the remaining inventory of 6,800 kg would be valued using different methods of cost accounting.

(a) Using the FIFO method, value the inventory held on 30 June.

£

(b) Using the AVCO method, value the inventory held on 30 June.

£

(c) Prepare a report for the partners explaining the possible consequences of a failure of control over ordering and receipt of materials.

To: Alice Gill and Rishi Jones

From: Jai Smith

Date: 31/07/X6

Subject: XXX

As at 30 June 20X6, HMF & Co's closing inventory valuation was £42,900. The partners expect to make sales of £4,230,000 in 20X7, and they expect the inventory valuation to rise by 15% by the year end. The gross margin is expected to be 40%, after deducting direct materials and direct labour.

(d) **How much does HMF & Co expect to spend on direct materials and labour in 20X7? Show your workings.**

2

Today's date is 30 April 20X5.

From the cost records you can see that on 1 April, DEL & Co had 9,000 kg of raw material inventory. The cost recorded was £31,500. In April the following movements took place:

8 April: 4,500 kg purchased for £9,000

15 April: 6,700 kg issued to production

DEL & Co want to know how the issue of 6,700 kg and the remaining inventory of 6,800 kg would be valued using the LIFO method of cost accounting.

(a)   Using the LIFO method, value the inventory held on 30 April.

£ [   ]

(b)   Using the LIFO method, value the issue made on 15 April.

£ [   ]

As at 30 April 20X5, DEL & Co's closing inventory valuation was £67,100. The partners expect to make sales of £5,600,000 in 20X6, and they expect the inventory valuation to rise by 20% by the year end. The gross margin is expected to be 43%, after deducting direct materials and direct labour.

(c)   How much does DEL & Co expect to spend on direct materials and labour in 20X6? Show your workings.

[   ]

(d) DEL & Co has produced a spreadsheet for the last quarter showing the variances. The original budget was based on selling and producing 70,000 units. However, only 65,000 units were actually produced and sold. There was a significant cost cutting initiative and DEL & Co managed to re-negotiate better factory rent prices than expected. Material prices were also reduced by changing to a different supplier although more material wastage occurred, meaning that labour time per unit increased.

◢	A	B	C	D	E
1					
2					
3	DEL & Co: quarter ended 30 April 20X5				
4		Original	Flexed	Actual	Variances
5		budget	budget	results	
6		£	£	£	£
7	Revenue	1,400,000	1,300,000	1,332,500	32,500
8	Direct materials	259,000	240,500	247,000 -	6,500
9	Direct labour	308,000	286,000	299,000 -	13,000
10	Variable production overheads	189,000	175,500	169,000	6,500
11	Fixed overheads	220,000	220,000	180,000	40,000
12	Operating profit	424,000	378,000	437,500	59,500

Send a report to the partners, Jackie and John, explaining the operating profit variance, the most significant favourable variance and the most significant adverse variance. Explain one possible cause for each of the two variances identified above.

From: Ben Singh

To: Jackie and John

Subject: Variances

Solutions

1

(a) Using the FIFO method, value the inventory held on 30 June.

£ | 17,050

Working

FIFO closing balance = ((9,000 kg – 6,700 kg) × £3.50) + £9,000 = £17,050

(b) Using the AVCO method, value the inventory held on 30 June.

£ | 20,400

Working

AVCO valuation per kg = (£31,500 + £9,000) / (9,000 kg + 4,500 kg) = £3

Closing balance valuation = 6,800 kg × £3 = £20,400

(c) Prepare a report for the partners explaining the possible consequences of a failure of control over ordering and receipt of materials.

To: Alice Gill and Rishi Jones

From: Jai Smith

Date: 31/07/X6

Subject: Consequences of failure of control

If material ordering and receipts are not carefully monitored, several problems could arise.

(a) Incorrect materials being delivered

It is important that receipts of materials are checked against what was ordered to ensure that the business has the correct material available when it is needed.

(b) Incorrect prices being paid

Material receipts and orders need to be checked in order to ensure that the business does not get overcharged.

(c) Deliveries other than at specified times

Materials receipts can require staff to stop production in order to deal with the receipt. It is important that deliveries are only received at a specified time in order to keep disruptions to a minimum.

(d) Insufficient control over quality

It is better to check the material's quality when it is received rather than waiting until it is used in production. Materials can be returned to the supplier and replacements sought before production starts.

(e) Stockouts and overstocking

Having too much inventory can lead to obsolescence. Running out of inventory can halt production.

(f) Invoice amounts differing from quantities actually received or prices agreed

A check is necessary to ensure that there are no errors with quantities and prices.

I hope this is useful to you. Please contact me if you have any questions.

Kind regards

Jai

(d) **How much does HMF & Co expect to spend on direct materials and labour in 20X7? Show your workings.**

Gross profit = 40% x sales = £1,692,000

Cost of sales = sales – gross profit = £2,538,000

Cost of sales = opening inventory + materials + labour – closing inventory = £2,538,000

Therefore materials + labour = £2,538,000 – opening inventory + closing inventory

Closing inventory = £42,900 x 1.15 = £49,335

Materials + labour = £2,538,000 - £42,900 + £49,335 = £2,544,435

2

(a) **Using the LIFO method, value the inventory held on 30 April.**

£ | 23,800

Working

(9,000 – 6,700 + 4,500) × £3.50 = £23,800

(b) **Using the LIFO method, value the issue made on 15 April.**

£ | 16,700

Working

(4,500 × £2.00) + (2,200 × £3.50) = £16,700

(c)

Gross profit = 43% x sales = £2,408,000

Cost of sales = sales – gross profit = £3,192,000

Cost of sales = opening inventory + materials + labour – closing inventory = £3,192,000

Therefore materials + labour = £3,192,000 – opening inventory + closing inventory

Closing inventory = £67,100 x 1.20 = £80,520

Materials + labour = £3,192,000 - £67,100 + £80,520 = £3,205,420

(d)

From: Ben Singh

To: Jackie and John

Subject: Variances

Hi Jackie and John,

As promised please find the explanations below:

The operating profit variance from the flexed budget was £59,500 favourable. This arose because the budgeted profit when flexed to the actual volume of 65,000 units was £378,000, whereas we achieved an actual profit of £437,500.

The single most significant favourable variance was fixed overheads, which was £40,000 favourable. This may have arisen because of the reduced factory rent that we paid.

The single most significant adverse variance was direct labour, which was £13,000 adverse. This is likely to have been because of the change in material supplier which led to lower quality material and more wastage. Labour therefore spent longer on each unit than expected.

I hope this is useful to you. Please contact me if you have any questions.

Kind regards

Ben

Glossary of terms

It is useful to be familiar with interchangeable terminology including IFRS and UK GAAP (generally accepted accounting principles).

Below is a short list of the most important terms you are likely to use or come across, together with their international and UK equivalents.

UK term	International term
Profit and loss account	**Statement of profit or loss (or statement of profit or loss and other comprehensive income)**
Turnover or Sales	Revenue or Sales revenue
Operating profit	Profit from operations
Reducing balance depreciation	Diminishing balance depreciation
Depreciation / depreciation expense(s)	Depreciation charge(s)
Balance sheet	**Statement of financial position**
Fixed assets	Non-current assets
Net book value	Carrying amount
Tangible assets	Property, plant and equipment
Stocks	Inventories
Trade debtors or Debtors	Trade receivables
Prepayments	Other receivables
Debtors and prepayments	Trade and other receivables
Cash at bank and in hand	Cash and cash equivalents
Long-term liabilities	Non-current liabilities
Trade creditors or creditors	Trade payables
Accruals	Other payables
Creditors and accruals	Trade and other payables
Capital and reserves	Equity (limited companies)
Profit and loss balance	Retained earnings
Cash flow statement	**Statement of cash flows**

Accountants often have a tendency to use several phrases to describe the same thing! Some of these are listed below:

Different terms for the same thing
Nominal ledger, main ledger or general ledger
Subsidiary ledgers, memorandum ledgers
Subsidiary (sales) ledger, sales ledger
Subsidiary (purchases) ledger, purchases ledger

Bibliography

Association of Accounting Technicians (2014) *AAT Code of Professional Ethics.* [Online]. Available from: www.aat.org.uk/sites/default/files/assets/AAT_Code_of_Professional_Ethics.pdf [Accessed 18 April 2017].

International Accounting Standards Board. (2003) IAS 2 Inventories. In *International Financial Reporting Standards* (2003). Available from: http://eifrs.ifrs.org [Accessed 18 April 2017]

Index

W

Wages control account, 74, 217, 233
Weighted average, 174

Work in progress (WIP), 169, 170
Work in progress control account, 41, 58, 217, 233

REVIEW FORM

How have you used this Course Book?
(Tick one box only)

☐ Self study

☐ On a course_____

☐ Other _____

Why did you decide to purchase this Course Book? *(Tick one box only)*

☐ Have used BPP materials in the past

☐ Recommendation by friend/colleague

☐ Recommendation by a college lecturer

☐ Saw advertising

☐ Other _____

During the past six months do you recall seeing/receiving either of the following?
(Tick as many boxes as are relevant)

☐ Our advertisement in Accounting Technician

☐ Our Publishing Catalogue

Which (if any) aspects of our advertising do you think are useful?
(Tick as many boxes as are relevant)

☐ Prices and publication dates of new editions

☐ Information on Course Book content

☐ Details of our free online offering

☐ None of the above

Your ratings, comments and suggestions would be appreciated on the following areas of this Course Book.

	Very useful	Useful	Not useful
Chapter overviews	☐	☐	☐
Introductory section	☐	☐	☐
Quality of explanations	☐	☐	☐
Illustrations	☐	☐	☐
Chapter activities	☐	☐	☐
Test your learning	☐	☐	☐
Keywords	☐	☐	☐

	Excellent	Good	Adequate	Poor
Overall opinion of this Course Book	☐	☐	☐	☐

Do you intend to continue using BPP Products? ☐ Yes ☐ No

Please note any further comments and suggestions/errors on the reverse of this page. The BPP author of this edition can be emailed at: lmfeedback@bpp.com.

Alternatively, the Head of Programme of this edition can be emailed at: nisarahmed@bpp.com

REVIEW FORM (continued)

TELL US WHAT YOU THINK

Please note any further comments and suggestions/errors below